SURVEY
OF JEWISH AFFAIRS
1989

SURVEY OF JEWISH AFFAIRS 1989

Edited by
William Frankel

Assistant Editor
Antony Lerman

Published for the Institute of Jewish Affairs
by Basil Blackwell

Copyright © Institute of Jewish Affairs Ltd.

First published 1989

Basil Blackwell Ltd
108 Cowley Road, Oxford, OX4 1JF, UK

Basil Blackwell, Inc.
3 Cambridge Center
Cambridge, Massachusetts 02142, USA

British Library Cataloguing in Publication Data
A CIP catalogue record for this book is available from the British Library.

Library of Congress Catalogue Card Number: 84–645587
ISSN 0957–5952
ISBN 0–631–17205–X

Typeset in 10 on 12pt Times
by Footnote Graphics, Warminster, Wiltshire
Printed in Great Britain by
T. J. Press Ltd, Padstow, Cornwall

Contents

Editor's Introduction

Nineteen-eighty-eight, the year reviewed in this volume, brought an extraordinary number of twists and turns in the Middle East, remarkable even by the normally volatile standards of the region. With greater perspective it may come to be seen as a memorable year, an historical watershed. But even in April 1989, when this Introduction was being written, it was already clear that the Palestinian uprising in the Gaza Strip and the West Bank, which became universally known by its Arabic designation, the *intifada*, had exerted a profound influence on the Arab–Israeli conflict, on Israeli attitudes and policies as well as on the still evolving relationship between Diaspora Jewry and the Jewish state. The political leadership of Israel, the nation's intelligentsia and the populace generally were all deeply affected by the *intifada*. Reactions varied between, and within, each group. But in every case the practical expressions of the hard thinking and heart-searching in which they all engaged, were still in the earliest stages of gestation.

Within Israel's habitually turbulent polity, the *intifada* introduced new elements of uncertainty, emphasizing the instability of its second Government of National Unity created after the stalemate of the 1988 general election. In that situation, the only other possible coalition would have been between the Likud and the religious parties which had strengthened their parliamentary representation.

But Mr Yitzhak Shamir, the Likud leader, shared at least one concern with the Labour Party and that was that the demands of the religious parties for the 'theocraticization' of the country were unacceptable. A continuation of the coalition including both major parties, albeit on different terms from its predecessor, was the least objectionable option despite disagreements on most major issues.

Chief of those remained the policy towards the territories occupied after the 1967 Six Day War. For twenty years, until the beginning of the *intifada*, Israeli political leadership had been able to avoid hard decisions. True, the whole of Sinai had been returned to Egypt as the price for peace. But relinquishing any part of the West Bank posed far more intractable problems. So long as Israel's neighbours and the PLO refused to recognize, negotiate or make peace with Israel, neither major party was under pressure to change the status quo and thus provoke intense political and religious controversy.

Labour, which was in power for the first decade after the Six Day War, had declared its readiness to trade territory for peace, but as time passed emphasis on that policy weakened. There were no Arab traders with whom to negotiate and the occupation was, in many ways, comfortable and secure. Out of office and later, when it was neutralized by its coalition partnership, Labour policy towards the peace process initiated by the Camp David accords appeared increasingly impractical; reduced to a personal campaign for an international conference by Mr Shimon Peres, the party leader.

By contrast, the position taken up by Mr Shamir was clear. He maintained a determined opposition to an international conference, which became the popular formula for those proposing movement in the stalled peace process, and refused any negotiation with the Palestine Liberation Organization (PLO). As David Capitanchik argues in this volume, it was the Labour Party which appeared to lose most because of the *intifada*. The violence provoked a reaction by Israeli public opinion against any concessions as a reward for disorder. Mr Shamir and his party were perceived as being more determined than Labour to use force to crush Palestinian violence. Moreover, Labour had lost its one clearly articulated idea—the so-called Jordanian option— when King Hussein severed administrative ties with the West Bank.

The *intifada* had begun as a spontaneous eruption of Palestinian resentment against the occupation. It proved unexpectedly durable and the hundreds of Palestinians, most of them young and ready to die for their cause, made it apparent, except to the most diehard, that repression, however forceful, would not bring it to an end, that the status quo was no longer tenable and that a political solution would have to be found.

Whilst the Israeli government, beset with its internal divisions and fearful of the security risk involved in territorial compromise, was not yet capable of formulating new policies, Mr Yasser Arafat, leader of the PLO, seized the initiative. He embarked on a successful diplomatic offensive designed to present his organization in a new and moderate guise. On 14 December 1988, for the first time, he explicitly accepted Israel's right to exist, ambiguously renounced terrorism and, while not abandoning the 'dreams' of the Palestinian National Covenant, publicly declared his adoption of a 'two-state' solution.

In a final flourish to his distinguished tenure of office as Secretary of State for the United States, Mr George Shultz recognized the Arafat statement as satisfying the condition precedent for a dialogue between his government and the PLO. To the Israeli government and large segments of the Israeli and Jewish public, the PLO could still not be trusted; deeds were demanded, not words, and in particular, an end to the *intifada*. But with so much gained from the uprising, which was still bringing daily propaganda victories in the form of reports and pictures of Israeli repression, the PLO would not (and possibly could not) comply. While the tables appeared to be turned, with the PLO calling for compromise and Israel rejecting its overtures, there was some real movement. The reality was that a kind of negotiation between the parties to the conflict had begun at the end of 1988 with the opening of the dialogue between the PLO and the USA, the latter acting in a sense as the channel for Israel.

With a new administration in Washington talking to the PLO, Israel appeared increasingly isolated internationally. Within Israeli society, already polarized between 'national' and 'liberal' camps, 'religious' and 'secular', questions relating to the nature of the Jewish state came acutely to the fore, as increasing numbers of reservists and conscripts agonized over what they had been asked to do in Gaza and the West Bank. It became clear that the Israeli army was ill-equipped for its role in riot control and the government did take steps to try to reduce fatalities. But the death toll continued to mount and by the end of 1988, despite widely recognized changes in the Palestinian position, a political solution still seemed far off.

For many Jews living outside Israel, the handling of the *intifada* and the Israeli government's response to apparent PLO moderation created a sharp dilemma. As far as could be ascertained, the majority of them remained overwhelmingly supportive of the Jewish state. But 1988 saw significant reservations expressed by leaders of major Jewish organizations, particularly in America, about aspects of Israeli policies, significant as a portent of change in Israel-Diaspora relations. As Jerome Chanes and Charles Fenyvesi explain, in separate articles, the voices of the American Jewish community are many and various, and in the past they could be counted on to stand firmly behind the policies of the Israeli government, whatever its complexion. If this is indeed changing, it is bound to have its reverberations on America's Middle East policy.

Not that the internal discussion about the *intifada* affected Jewish voting patterns in the 1988 US presidential election. Once again, Jews voted 2 to 1 for the Democratic candidate, defying predictions that their advanced material status would induce them to vote Republican in their economic interest. The continued romance between American Jews and the Democrats could not, however, be taken for granted. In 1988 young Jews were more likely to vote Republican than the older generation, suggesting that, while liberal instincts are fading very slowly, that is nonetheless the tendency. Voting proclivities might also be influenced by the influx of two major groups of new Jewish Americans—Soviet Jews and Israelis—described and analysed in the USA section of this *Survey* by Sylvia Rothchild and Moshe Shokeid. It remains to be seen how these groups will relate to the mainstream American Jewish community in the long term, but they are certainly not subject to the same influences as affected the Jewish immigrants of earlier generations.

The validity of Professor Nathan Glazer's comment that Israel is now the religion of the Jewish people is not diminished by the frequency of its quotation. In the Diaspora, organized Jewish life continued to revolve around support for Israel, political as well as economic. But in 1988 Jews in the Western world were struggling to come to terms with a changing Israel. They had less of a common language and emotional identification with the rising generation of Israelis than with the European Zionists who still controlled the major instruments of power. The old leadership was, inevitably, in the process of being replaced and the problems of this adjustment were compounded by Israel's new, brutalized image since the *intifada*.

The anxieties of Diaspora Jewry were not limited to those produced in Israel. There was continuing concern at the changing Jewish demographic pattern, the main feature of which, described by Sergio DellaPergola in the World Jewry section, is declining numbers through intermarriage and assimilation. A chart accompanying that article graphically illustrates the startling increase in intermarriage. The only segment of organized Jewry running counter to this pattern was that of extreme orthodoxy, which could show important gains both in the Diaspora and Israel.

The newly vigorous and assertive orthodox groupings dislike being referred to as fundamentalists and do indeed differ from Christian and Islamic fundamentalists in that the Oral law interprets the inerrant words of the Torah. But there is, nonetheless, a similarity between the zealots in the three faiths in their refusal to meet the challenges of contemporary life and thought by retreating to the fortress of the ancient texts. In the major Jewish communities, the movement towards orthodoxy and fundamentalism has been successful in recent years in establishing a confident role in what remain, essentially, secular societies. They offer an uncompromising and unambiguous form of Jewish identity increasingly able to combine ghettoization with the ability to benefit from the material advantages of modern life. In Israel, as the 1988 election demonstrated, Jewish fundamentalists mastered the political process, turning a secular creation to their advantage and throwing the liberal secular conscience into even greater turmoil.

For Jews in Islamic lands, the Jewish content of their lives, examined in this volume by Norman Stillman, remained a pale reflection of once flourishing and vibrant communities. Many of them were barely viable. Some suffered repression on the part of the authorities while others practised in relative freedom but had no future because there were so few young people. The long-term prospects for all these communities looked bleak. In the Soviet Union, by contrast, where repression eased and Jewish cultural life was being allowed to develop under *glasnost* and *perestroika*, the future, while not exactly bright, offered opportunities, as Zvi Gitelman argues in his contribution. Jews were able to take advantage of liberalization, but the same process unleashed popular forces of antisemitism which could gain ground if *perestroika* did not produce results quickly enough.

Because of its own economic stringencies, the World Jewish Congress has felt constrained to discontinue its sponsorship of the *Survey*, though it financed most of the contents of this volume. I gratefully acknowledge the generous support of the WJC since the inception of this series and pay tribute to the vision of Mr Jacques Torczyner, chairman of its Publications Committee, who initiated the project.

This is the first *Survey* to carry the distinguished imprint of its new publishers. We look forward to a long and happy collaboration with them and particularly with Mr Alyn Shipton, who was so receptive and co-operative in concluding the practical arrangements. Finally, I also acknowledge the assistance we have always received from Associated University Presses, publishers of the first five volumes. Their meticulous attention to the particular needs of a publication of this nature contributed much to its authority and success.

This, therefore, has been a year of change for the *Survey of Jewish Affairs*. I believe that its future has now been assured, so that it may continue its unique function as a year-by-year record of changing Jewish concerns in an ever more rapidly changing world.

London   WILLIAM FRANKEL
April 1989

Part A
ISRAEL

1

The *Intifada* and After

ERIC SILVER

The *intifada* was an explosion waiting for a match. It blew up on 9 December 1987 in Jabaliya, the biggest and most militant of the Gaza refugee camps. An Israeli patrol was trapped in a violent demonstration. The reserve soldiers shot their way out of trouble. One youth was killed and ten were wounded.

The rioters were protesting at the deaths of four Jabaliya residents the previous day when an Israeli driver lost control of his semi-trailer and ploughed into a convoy ferrying day labourers home from Israel. Word spread rapidly through Gaza and the West Bank that the driver was the brother of a Jewish businessman, Shlomo Takal, whose throat had been slit by a Muslim fanatic in the Gaza market two days earlier. The two incidents were unconnected, but many Palestinians believed—and still believe—that the road accident was an act of family revenge.

The Jabaliya clash provoked spontaneous riots in towns, villages and refugee camps throughout the occupied territories. In one form or another, with stones, petrol bombs, cement blocks, scrap metal and flaming tyres, they were to continue throughout 1988 and into 1989. By January 1989, the Israeli Defence Forces (IDF) announced that 352 Palestinians had been killed, more than 4,300 wounded and 5,600 arrested. Army sappers had demolished or sealed 200 Arab homes. Forty-five alleged ringleaders had been deported. Israel, for its part, lost 11 dead (4 soldiers and 7 civilians) in the territories, while about 300 soldiers and 40 civilians, mostly Jewish settlers, were wounded.[1] Palestinians put their own casualties much higher. The army figures were of those reported to the authorities by Arab hospitals.

By December 1988, the *intifada* ('resurgence') had transformed the

Eric Silver covered Israel for *The Guardian* and *The Observer* from 1972 to 1983 and has lived permanently in Jerusalem since 1987. He is the author of a biography of *Menachem Begin* (London: Weidenfeld & Nicolson; New York: Random House, 1984) and is currently writing a book about people who risked their lives to save Jews in Nazi Europe.

3

dialogue of occupation and the diplomacy of the Middle East. The young rioters, defiant to the point of martyrdom, had forced Israelis to recognize that staying in the West Bank and Gaza Strip was no longer an easy option. The Chief of Staff, Lieutenant-General Dan Shomron, and other commanders acknowledged that the insurrection could not be put down by military means alone.

No less significantly, it had forced the Palestinian leadership in Tunis to come to terms with the existence of a Jewish state, the Arab world to restore Palestine to the top of its agenda, King Hussein to renounce Jordan's claim on the West Bank, and the United States and the Western democracies to recognize the Palestine Liberation Organization (PLO). It was an extraordinary achievement for a backstreet army, rebelling as much against its own inept traditional leaders as against Israeli domination. The next volume of this *Survey* may record whether the *intifada* achieved more than that—a breakthrough towards negotiations and an eventual settlement, or descent towards a wider Arab–Israeli conflagration.

The spark which triggered the uprising that December day in the Jabaliya refugee camp was struck almost casually. The *intifada* was unplanned, though it became more and more co-ordinated. But just as the assassination of the Archduke Franz Ferdinand in Sarajevo was not the cause of the First World War, the Gaza traffic accident was not the cause of the *intifada*. The revolt sprang from 20 years of frustration and humiliation. The young Palestinians could see no way out of the cycle of harassment and petty resistance. The Jewish presence, with 118 settlements across the old green line border, was becoming more and more permanent. The older generation seemed supine, if not actually craven.

A new militancy was perceptible in the spring of 1987, eight months before the *intifada* broke out. Attacks on Israeli drivers and pedestrians became more violent, more daring. Youths throwing stones and petrol bombs stood their ground, even when their victims were armed. They were ready to risk life and limb. Two summit conferences towards the end of 1987 sharpened the young Palestinians' sense that they had nothing to lose, and that they had to take the initiative if they wanted to change their fate. No one, including the PLO, was going to solve the problem for them.

The first was an Arab summit in Amman, which relegated Palestine to second place behind the Iran–Iraq war in Arab priorities. West Bankers watched live coverage on Jordan television as King Hussein sent a second-rank minister to receive the PLO leader, Yasser Arafat, at the airport; as the king was given a green light to explore the possibilities of negotiating peace with Israel; and as Egypt, ostracized for signing a separate treaty with the Jewish state, was welcomed back into the Arab family. In the second summit, President Ronald Reagan and General Secretary Mikhail Gorbachev met without even mentioning Palestine in their final communique. The issue had gone stale for all but those who lived with the occupation. Israel had only to sit tight. It had nothing to fear from superpower pressure, even though the Prime Minister, Yitzhak Shamir, had blocked the efforts of his own Foreign Minister, Shimon Peres, to promote negotiations with Jordan under the umbrella of an international conference.

At about the same time, Israel's apparent vulnerability was revealed by a hang-glider raid across the Lebanese border. A member of Ahmed Jibril's Popular Front-General Command flew into Galilee and killed six soldiers before he in turn was shot dead. The impact was more psychological than strategic. A brave Palestinian could draw blood. But it was no accident that demonstrators were frequently heard chanting 'Six-one! Six-one!', like jubilant football fans, in the early weeks of the *intifada*.

Israel was caught off-guard by the uprising, as it had been by the hang-glider pilot. The security services so underestimated it that the Defence Minister, Yitzhak Rabin, stayed in the United States while Israel's ratings plummeted on the world's television screens, rather than rush home to take charge. The army, trained for a more conventional battlefield, had to improvize. Over the months, it tried live ammunition, rubber bullets, plastic bullets, beatings, deportations, detentions, demolitions, curfews, economic and administrative sanctions, sticks and carrots. Yet by the end of 1988, commanders admitted that all they could do was hold a line, maintaining enough control to give the government a chance to come up with a political solution. 'We have an *intifada*', an officer in the Israeli administration conceded. 'We have to get used to it. This situation is not abnormal any more.'

The *intifada* proved surprisingly resilient. The tactics changed from mass confrontation to ambushes and small-scale clashes, from boycotts to selective strikes. New grassroots leaders sprang up to replace those who had been arrested or deported. The technology of modern communications—radio, telefax, international trunk dialling, photocopying—was exploited to keep the pot boiling. The Palestinians did not need clandestine printing presses, hidden transmitters. According to a columnist in *Ha'aretz*, one *intifada* leaflet was run off on a coin-operated copier in the Supreme Court building.

By the middle of 1988, the Palestinians had passed a point of no return. They had sacrificed too much to stop. Rightly or wrongly, they felt they were winning. In Jerusalem middle-aged Arabs gloated over the fact that Israelis no longer shopped in the Old City. 'The Jews are afraid', they told you with the satisfaction of underdogs who suddenly discover they have sharp teeth. Dr Eyad Sarraj, the Arab director of mental health services in the Gaza Strip, said:

> The uprising has dramatically transformed the Palestinian self-image. They have regained their self-respect. They feel they have scored a significant victory over the Israelis. For the first time they feel equal, even more powerful. The national identity has been strengthened and sharpened. There is a new cohesion. A high level of aspiration is replacing hopelessness. People are now talking of an end of the occupation as a matter of fact.[2]

The *intifada* was a social as well as a national revolution, a revolt of the young
who had grown up under Israeli rule since 1967, a revolt of the normally
apolitical Palestinian housewife, a revolt of the village as well as of the
nationalist towns. Arab hospital doctors from Nablus told a conference
organized by Israeli professional colleagues that most of the *intifada* casualties they treated were under 19. Many of the boys worked in Israel. 'They
witnessed how well you treat your children', one of the doctors said, 'and how
they are free to say what they like and go where they like. They have been
spoiled by seeing it and are bitter that they can't enjoy the same.'[3]

Dr Ali Kleibo, a Bethlehem University anthropologist, said:

> People are using it to question the traditional institutions of Palestinian life,
> be it the educational system, the importance of community action (some-
> thing that has never happened before), the reorganization of the village
> into an educational, political and economic unit that goes beyond the
> hamula (extended family). The level of solidarity that you see now never
> existed before. We are totally involved in questioning relations that before
> seemed sacrosanct, that appeared to us as absolute. The system is being
> reshuffled—with the Israelis, with our village, with our family, the whole
> system. And we are the ones who are reshuffling it.[4]

With less of their partisan euphoria, Professor Yehoshafat Harkabi, a
Hebrew University authority on Palestinian nationalism and former Director
of Military Intelligence, summed it up from the other side of the barricade:
'The intifada is important in that the Palestinians showed a readiness to
suffer.'[5]

Dr Meron Benvenisti, a remorseless, often apocalyptic, Israeli analyst of
the Jewish–Arab drama, stressed the hard practicality of the *intifada*. He
wrote at the beginning of 1989:

> Yasser Arafat would like to believe that he is the Palestinian Ben-Gurion.
> But the Palestinian Ben-Gurion now lives in a refugee camp near Nablus.
> He's a 22-year-old youngster, perhaps now trying to organize a new 'shock
> force' after members of the previous units were arrested by the Israelis. He
> is a realist to the marrow, and he knows what Ben-Gurion also knew in his
> twenties: national independence is attained by stubbornly building eco-
> nomic, social, educational and military communal power, and not through
> declarations and speeches in exclusive international clubs.[6]

The uprising has had its darker side. Not every Palestinian merchant was
eager to cut his own economic throat, not every village *mukhtar* (headman)
voluntarily gave up the patronage that flowed from his Israeli connections,
not every Shin Bet informer suddenly fell silent. The young militants were
ruthless in cutting down such 'collaborators'. The revolution, like others
before it, imposed a rough justice.

According to the Israeli figures, 30 of the Palestinian fatalities up to
January 1989 were murdered by their own people. One victim, in the West

Bank village of Kabatiya, was stabbed repeatedly by a mob, then hung from an electricity pole. One third of the Palestinian attacks during the *intifada* were directed against mayors, *mukhtars* and other Arabs accused of co-operating with the Israelis. Many merchants had their shops burned down for opening during strikes.[7]

For all the new-found solidarity, the *intifada* also sharpened old rivalries which could yet jeopardize the Palestinian achievement. As the insurrection grew, Islamic revivalism, which claimed to have started it all, spread from its stronghold in the Gaza Strip to the West Bank and Jerusalem. Although the fundamentalists remained a minority, estimated to represent about 30 per cent of the population, they posed a serious challenge to the mainstream, secular Palestinian nationalism of the PLO.

Competition intensified after the PLO declarations in November and December endorsing a two-state solution, Arab alongside Jewish, to the problem of Palestine. To the fundamentalists, this was heresy. Sheikh Ahmed Yassin, their spiritual leader in Gaza, accused the PLO of 'kneeling before Israel'. Leaflet 37, issued by Hamas, the Islamic Resistance Movement, insisted on 'a Muslim Palestine from the sea to the river', the Mediterranean to the Jordan. It opposed all concessions, 'even of one speck of dust of the homeland's earth'. Hamas advocated a holy war 'in order to fly the flag of Allah over every centimetre of the land of Palestine'. Clause 11 of its manifesto stated:

> The Islamic Resistance Movement believes that all of the land of Palestine is sacred to Islam, through all the generations and forever, and it is forbidden to abandon it or part of it, or to yield it or part of it. No Arab state individually has this right, nor do all of the Arab states collectively, nor does any king or president individually, nor do all the kings and presidents collectively. No organization individually has this right, nor do all the organizations collectively, whether they are Palestinian or Arab.[8]

The battle fluctuated. Sometimes Hamas and the PLO called rival strikes and demonstrations on successive days, sometimes they combined in calling a single protest. What was clear by the end of the year was that Arafat would have as hard a fight with his fundamentalists as Israel would with the Gush Emunim settlement movement if they ever signed a compromise peace.

But that was still a distant cloud. Arafat commanded the diplomatic field. The *intifada* had coaxed him into the real world. It had given him an opportunity he was determined, at last, not to miss. To quote Benvenisti again:

> The Arabs in the territories did not allow the PLO to remain captive to its own illusions. They sent Yasser Arafat a clear message: the uprising must be translated into a realistic political programme, one rooted in reality.
> The illusion that Israel does not exist because the Palestinians are unable to accept its existence, or that it can be wished away, is a recipe for disaster.

To go on ignoring the true power relationship would have resulted in the loss of the little that can still be salvaged.

This was the juncture at which Yasser Arafat found his calling as a leader. Submitting to the constraints of reality, he sacrificed the maximalist formulations of the Palestinian revolution in favour of a political plan that recognized the facts of life—of which the cardinal component is acknowledgement of Israel's unassailable, permanent existence . . . In 1988, Yasser Arafat grasped that subjective will cannot overcome objective reality—and forced this realism on his movement.

Not all of Arafat's partners in the PLO could lightly repudiate 40 years of rejectionism, but most of them gave him a chance to prove he could deliver— a year or two, probably no more. The *intifada* strategists acknowledged a division of labour. If the Palestinian Ben-Gurion was building a society in the Nablus refugee camps, the Palestinian Weizmann was jetting from capital to capital out of a base in faraway Tunisia.

Although the Americans were prepared to talk to Arafat, if not yet to negotiate with him, even dovish Israelis needed to be convinced that the change was more than tactical. They monitored what PLO spokesmen said out of the side of their mouths to reassure an Arab audience, as well as what they said in English to the rest of the world. It was not always encouraging. PLO gunmen, though not Arafat's Fatah, continued cross-border raids and there was no let-up in the West Bank and Gaza rioting. Nonetheless, the Palestine National Council, meeting in Algiers on 15 November, endorsed the partition of Palestine. Professor Harkabi, one of the first to draw the world's attention to the Palestinian national covenant of 1968, which dismissed the Jewish state as 'entirely illegal, regardless of the passage of time', was satisfied that the Algiers declaration effectively abrogated the crucial Article 19.

The *intifada* tested Israel, morally as well as militarily, in a way that the 'armed struggle' had never done. With very few exceptions. the Palestinian rebels refrained from using firearms or explosives. They may not have possessed many, but they took a calculated decision to keep those they had out of sight. Unlike the terrorist chieftains in Tunis or Damascus, they were familiar with Israel's weak points, and they exploited them.

An Arab ruler—King Hussein, President Hafez Asad of Syria, President Chadli Benjedid of Algeria—would have had no trouble putting down the *intifada*. All three at one time or another had turned their big guns on dissidents threatening to undermine their regimes. Hundreds, sometimes thousands, were slaughtered in a matter of days—by Hussein in 'Black September' 1970, by Asad in Hama in 1982, by Benjedid in 1988. No more was heard of their *intifadas*.

There were Israelis, mostly retired generals now representing right-wing parties in the Knesset, who urged a similar ruthlessness on the Shamir government. But they remained a minority. For all the harshness of his less tactful pronouncements, the Defence Minister, Yitzhak Rabin, set limits to the Israeli response. So did the Chief of Staff and his regional commanders. Unlike their predecessors at the time of the invasion of Lebanon in 1982, their roots were in the liberal left of Israeli society. Their controlled reaction stemmed from a pragmatic as well as a moral inhibition. They knew that the country was fundamentally divided on the Palestinian question. After the bitter experience of Lebanon, they could not have relied on their citizen soldiers blindly to obey orders. They had to work within a national consensus.

The politicians, for their part, valued the goodwill of the United States and the West, the identification of Israel as part of the democratic family, in a way that never concerned Arab kings and presidents. Without that identification, Israel could not be sure of either American military and economic co-operation or of its increasingly important trade links with the European Community. As an open society with a vigorously independent press and a large foreign media corps, Israel could not conceal what happened in the West Bank and Gaza, even if the government had wanted to. Israel soon learned that even relatively restrained measures would drag its reputation through the mud, but it had reason to hope that the damage could be contained.

At the top level, the IDF of 1988 was a thinking army. Its commanders set the *intifada* in the context of Israel's relationship with its Palestinian neighbours and with the world at large. In an interview with Israel television's Arabic service, General Shomron ruled out a massive use of force. 'The *intifada* will end at some point', the Chief of Staff explained.

> The question is what legacy will it leave. I am saying that the residents of the territories will always be our neighbours. I therefore do not think that we have an interest in causing a great deal of suffering, even though we can do so the moment we make such a decision.
> I will go further. Israel is a law-abiding country. The law is not a technical concept. The law is a code of moral behaviour according to which a state decides how it wishes to regard itself and be viewed by the outside world. The world doesn't think that we are like Algeria, Syria or other Arab countries. They accept us as a progressive state, even though we employ force when necessary, because we act according to the law. I therefore find unacceptable, from every possible standpoint, the idea of employing a great deal of force for a short time in order to finish things off.[9]

Brigadier-General Zvi Poleg, who took over in the summer of 1988 as commander of IDF forces in the Gaza Strip, insisted that the *intifada* was not a war, even if the Palestinians perceived it as one. Soldiers could not behave as they would in combat. 'I'm not a diplomat,' he told the *Jerusalem Post*, 'I'm a military commander, but you must be able to see a number of aspects of the problem, and not just see it through the gunsights, because you're working with human beings. If a local person gets hurt, gets killed, you must first of all remember that he is a human being. He wasn't born in order for someone to kill him. He was born to live. So if there's no absolute need to shoot, don't'.[10]

The policy was clear, but its application was murky. Reporters covering the *intifada* were constantly struck by the gap between the rules as expounded by senior commanders and the practice they observed day after day in the field. Reserve and conscript soldiers home on leave testified to a large volume of unrecorded brutality. Claims that cases which made the headlines, the television news bulletins and the courts martial were aberrations soon lost credibility. Much, it seemed, depended on individual middle and lower rank officers, or on soldiers prepared to take an unpopular stand with their comrades. Where officers and men were convicted of unwarranted shooting or beating, the sentences tended to be light, months rather than years.

It was not necessarily a question of insincerity. The army's dilemma was real enough. The commanders had to set standards, but they also had to retain the confidence of their men, to appreciate the conditions under which they operated. They were not engaged in set-piece confrontations that could be controlled by well-drilled police work. A patrol ambushed in the Nablus casbah or an alley in a Gaza refugee camp could not always take out the rule book and debate how it should respond.

General Shomron acknowledged that there were 'grey areas'. He reminded the court trying four Givati Brigade infantrymen for manslaughter that a violent demonstration could not be dispersed without force. 'Let us be clear', the Chief of Staff insisted. 'These are not demonstrations over food subsidies, but violent disturbances that endanger the lives of our soldiers.' General Shomron confessed that the IDF had to improvise its responses. 'We are in a situation that is unknown', he testified. 'We have to deal with violence that is not a civil demonstration, but violence for political goals. It can happen that soldiers and commanders make a mistake with their behaviour. The IDF must do everything it can so that these incidents do not take place. The IDF has never before been faced with such a situation.'[11]

On such terms, the IDF's success or failure, in controlling the *intifada* and in living up to its own standards, could not be absolute. It achieved what it did only because there was a minimum consensus. The vast majority of soldiers obeyed orders and served in the occupied territories. By the end of 1988 only about 60 had refused and been court martialled, though other dissenters were diverted to tasks within the green line by officers who either respected their consciences or preferred to avoid trouble. Most soldiers, including many who identified themselves with the peace camp, saw a danger in Israel's allowing itself to be coerced into political concessions. On a superficial level, they resented the challenge. More profoundly, they sensed that they were fighting a campaign in a psychological war.

The Jewish state's security, if not its survival, depended on Arab generals' perceptions of its strength. What Israeli viewers saw night after night on their television screens was less the brutality that shocked the rest of the world than the taunting of their proud paratroopers by boys twirling slingshots and making obscene gestures. The impact was just as traumatic. The mighty IDF was made to look weak.

Soldiers served for a variety of overlapping reasons. Some wanted to maintain Israel's deterrent. Some were reluctant to let down their comrades. The *esprit de corps* of the platoon and the company is one of the secrets of the IDF's accomplishment. Some felt that by serving they could mitigate excesses. Others were eager to put the Arabs in their place.

The *intifada* influenced Israeli public opinion in conflicting directions. It persuaded many Israelis that something had to be done. The status quo of occupation became less attractive and less feasible. Reserve soldiers were required to serve up to 60 days a year to cope with the uprising. The army was worried about its effect on the defence budget and on the time available for conventional training exercises. West Bank settlers and their few guests ran a daily gauntlet of stones and Molotov cocktails. Israel's Arab minority identified itself increasingly as Palestinian rather than Israeli.

The *intifada* was estimated to have damaged the economy to the tune of $700 million (1.5–2 per cent of gross domestic product) in 1988. Labour costs rose by 2.5 per cent as employers had to replace Arab workers with Jews. Tourism, Israel's biggest net foreign exchange earner, fell by 14 per cent.[12] At the same time, however, the *intifada* heightened the Israeli's sense of vulnerability, as well as his distrust of Arabs in general and Palestinians in particular.

The underlying struggle of the October general election was between the yearning for peace and the imperatives of security. It ended in stalemate between the two major protagonists, Labour and Likud, but overall the voters played safe. Not quite enough of them were ready to take the risk of seeking a compromise peace. A petrol bomb attack on an Israeli bus, which killed a mother and her three children on the day before the election, reinforced defensive instincts.

The first response to the shock of the uprising was a swing to the right. A poll taken in December 1987, by Decima Israel, the local subsidiary of a Canadian political consultancy firm hired by Labour, found 49.5 per cent supporting parties of the left to 36.8 per cent supporting parties of the right. This was before the *intifada* had made its impact. In March 1988, the left's lead had been cut to 1.1 per cent (44.8 to 43.7). But from June the trend was back towards the left. Reflecting the national ambivalence, there was growing support both for getting rid of the occupied territories, preferably to Jordan, and for an 'iron fist' in putting down the rebellious Palestinians. In August Decima asked its sample which course was more dangerous for Israel, peace negotiations or the status quo. An overwhelming majority, 66 per cent, said the status quo was the more dangerous, while 28 per cent saw peace negotiations as more dangerous.

By the end of the year another poll, conducted by Dr Mina Zemach, logged 54 per cent of Israeli Jews ready to negotiate with the PLO, provided it recognized Israel and renounced terrorism.[13] A pre-*intifada* poll by Dr Zemach, in the autumn of 1987, had found only 37 per cent ready for such talks. Most rival polls confirmed this tendency.

A survey by the Hebrew University's Israel Institute of Applied Social Research in January 1989 pointed to a 'hawkish majority, but dovish trend'. Almost four out of every five Israelis opposed the establishment of a Palestinian state, but the institute's director, Professor Elihu Katz, discerned a gradual erosion of this opposition. The 'slow dovish trend' was again in evidence when the sample was asked whether it would concede territory in order to reach a peace settlement with the Arab states. A clear 65 per cent replied that they would give up at least some territory. The 45 per cent who would not give up anything in March 1987 dropped to 35 per cent in January 1989. Summarizing his findings, Katz concluded:

> Some 30 per cent of Israeli Jews (half of the left and 10–20 per cent of the right) are willing to grant the essential prerequisites for a Palestinian state: negotiations, substantial territorial concessions and recognition. If questions are worded to make evident that security and peace might be obtained in exchange for these concessions, the favourable proportion increases substantially, to 50 per cent or more.[14]

A poll, conducted for the *New York Times* early in 1989 by Hanoch Smith, came to strikingly similar conclusions. On the one hand, 82 per cent of Israeli Jews opposed immediate negotiations with the PLO, but 58 per cent said they would favour such talks if the PLO recognized Israel and ceased terrorist activities. A year earlier Smith's figure for those willing to talk if the PLO fulfilled these conditions was 53 per cent. The overwhelming majority remained sceptical. Arafat's declarations of November and December 1988 did not carry conviction. But according to Smith, 44 per cent thought a Palestinian state in the West Bank and Gaza was inevitable in the next 10 or 20 years, while as many as 62 per cent felt that talks with the PLO were inevitable in the next five years.[15]

After more than a year of *intifada* and three months of Arafat's peace offensive, Israelis seemed to be conditioning themselves to the probability of change. The Smith findings suggested that they were unlikely to join Gush Emunim in the trenches if and when an Israeli government took the plunge.

Notes

1. Foreign press briefing by the Deputy Chief of Staff, Major-General Ehud Barak.
2. Contribution to Hebrew University symposium.
3. Reported in *Jerusalem Post*, 6 April 1989.
4. Interview with author.
5. Foreign press symposium.
6. Article in *Jerusalem Post*, 22 February 1989.
7. Barak briefing and report in *Hadashot*, 4 April 1989.
8. Quoted in Sheffi Gabbai, 'Hamas and the uprising: the Mosque revolution', *Ma'ariv* weekend magazine, 16 December 1988; and Ori Nir, 'The uprising and Muslim extremists', *Ha'aretz*, 16 September 1988.

9. 27 October 1988 (edited text distributed by Israel Government Press Office).

10. *Jerusalem Post,* 8 September 1988.

11. Reported by Associated Press, 1 March 1989.

12. Bank Hapoalim Economic Report, issue no. 13, 31 January 1989; and *Jerusalem Post*, 7 March 1989.

13. *Yediot Ahronot*, 23 December 1988. The Decima poll was made available to the author on request.

14. *Jerusalem Post*, 10 February 1989.

15. *New York Times*, 2 April 1989.

2

The 1988 Israeli Elections

DAVID B. CAPITANCHIK

The inconclusive result of the elections to the 11th Knesset in 1984 led to the formation of a Government of National Unity headed by the Labour Alignment and the Likud. Two factors made a coalition between these ideological adversaries of the left and right necessary and, from their point of view, desirable. First, there was the result of the election itself which gave Labour only three seats more than the Likud, but one less than Labour had held in the previous Knesset. The Likud lost most, but neither part was able to form an acceptable coalition without the other. Second, there were the twin problems of tackling the country's huge annual rate of inflation (around 400 per cent) and extricating the army from the Lebanese quagmire into which it had been plunged following 'Operation Peace for Galilee' in 1982.

The coalition agreement between Labour, the Likud and a number of small parties, including the entire religious bloc, made the Labour leader Shimon Peres Prime Minister for the first two years of the 11th Knesset and the Likud's Yitzhak Shamir Foreign Minister. Under a rotation clause Mr Shamir and Mr Peres exchanged portfolios in October 1986, but with the economic and Lebanese crises out of the way there was little more upon which the coalition partners could agree.

The immobilism that followed the rotation would normally have led to an early dissolution of the Knesset and new elections before the four-year term was up. However, in part at least, the determination to honour the coalition agreement precluded an early election. Uncertainty, in all quarters, regarding the voting intentions of Israel's divided electorate, also played a part in

David B. Capitanchik is senior lecturer in politics at the University of Aberdeen, and an expert in Middle East and Israeli politics. He broadcasts frequently on these topics and is the author of numerous articles and studies on politics. This article is an edited version of two research papers on the Israeli elections published as *IJA Research Reports*, no. 7, 1988 and no. 1, 1989.

keeping the National Unity government alive until elections were held in November 1988.

The Israeli Political Scene in 1988

On the domestic front, 1988 saw the resurgence of some of the country's traditional economic problems, including severe labour disputes as well as financial crises in the company sector (Hevrat Ovdim) of the Histadrut and in the kibbutz movement. There was also considerable conflict between secular and religious elements in the population. The government itself was sharply divided over the peace process with the Arabs. Mr Peres, as Foreign Minister, strongly advocated an international conference under UN auspices with the superpowers present and the Palestinians represented in a joint delegation with the Jordanians. All this had been agreed between Mr Peres and King Hussein in April 1987. Mr Shamir rejected the so-called 'London Agreement' out of hand, demanding instead that the Arab states should negotiate peace treaties with Israel directly, with no intermediaries. As for the Palestinians, according to Mr Shamir they had been provided for in the autonomy proposals of the Camp David Accords that led to the signing of the Israel–Egypt Peace Treaty in March 1979.

Election year itself was dominated by the *intifada*—the uprising against the Israeli occupation by the Palestinian inhabitants of the West Bank and Gaza Strip which began on 9 December 1987. The parties and the public seemed to be preoccupied by little else other than the future of the territories and the problem of the Palestinians. Mr Peres's plan for an international conference received a severe setback at the end of July with King Hussein's decision to relinquish any further Jordanian involvement in or responsibility for the West Bank and its Palestinian inhabitants. Henceforth, so far as Jordan was concerned, the PLO was to be the sole representative of the Palestinian people.

Against the background of unremitting violence, strikes, sabotage and Israel's deteriorating international standing, debate focussed on the so-called 'demographic question'. Put very simply, this concerned the relative birth-rates of the Arab and Jewish populations living in the area between the mediterranean and the River Jordan now controlled by Israel. If Israel were to continue to hold on to the West Bank and Gaza, or decided to annex these territories, Jews would soon be in the minority and would then face two equally unacceptable alternatives: granting the Arabs full political and civil rights, thereby undermining the Jewish character of the state; or denying them those rights, thereby undermining Israel's democratic and liberal character.

The debate over the demographic question extended across the spectrum of Israeli political life. Prior to the outbreak of the *intifada* there was a tendency on the right to dispute the facts and argue that Arab population trends had been misinterpreted or exaggerated out of all proportion. For the centre-left, the issue of demography provided powerful backing for plans like those advocated by the late Yigal Allon which were intended as the basis of some peace settlement with the Arab states. The Allon Plan, which had been the main plank in the Labour Alignment's peace platform for at least a decade, would mean surrendering control of heavily populated Arab areas in the occupied territories and trading land for peace. Insofar as such plans were still realistic in the light of King Hussein's abandonment of the West bank, they remained Alignment policy.

On the right, the *intifada* appeared to have changed attitudes towards the demographic question. There was a shift away from disputing the facts in the direction of resolving any demographic dilemma and determining the future status of the territories by what became known as the 'transfer' option: encouraging all or part of their inhabitants to migrate to neighbouring Arab states and especially Jordan. Until recently, the historical connotations for Jews of the term 'transfer', and the obvious international ramifications of adopting such a policy, had meant that it was only voiced by the most extreme elements on the fringes of the far right and it lacked any respectability in the mainstream of Israeli political opinion.

However, during the course of the election campaign it was raised publicly by, among others, Rehavam Ze'evi, whose prestigious status as chairman of the Eretz Israel Museum in Tel-Aviv gave his pronouncements on this question the appearance of some dignity and validity. Ze'evi, a former General in the Israel Defence Forces (IDF), founded the Moledet Party whose platform consisted solely of the 'transfer' option. In late June 1988, Hebrew University researchers conducted a poll among the electorate to test awareness of the plan and its acceptability by the Israeli public by posing the problem indirectly. It was put to respondents that the Arab populations in the territories would eventually compromise the democratic nature and Jewish character of the state. Accordingly, they were asked how important these factors were and what should be done to ensure their continuity. Forty-nine per cent of all respondents stated that the 'transfer' of Arabs from the territories would maintain the Jewish and democratic nature of the state. Furthermore, while half of those polled believed that the maintenance of democracy was important, 97 per cent affirmed the importance of maintaining the Jewish character of Israeli society.

The division of opinion over this issue corresponded closely with Israel's internal demographic cleavages based on factors such as age and ethnic affiliation and it was linked firmly with party preference. Thus a 'hawkish' attitude towards the issue of 'transfer' defined supporters of the right as much as age and ethnicity. Those who held 'dovish' views regarding the territories and their future, on the other hand, were as markedly left-leaning and typically exhibited the demographic characteristics of supporters of Labour,

Mapam and the Citizens Rights Movement. They tended to be over 45 years of age and of European or American origin.

The Electorate

In each successive election between 1965 and 1984, the two major parties, Likud and Labour, albeit disproportionately, increased their share of the poll. In 1984, however, although the total number of votes cast was up by 135,955, Labour increased its vote by less than 16,000 and its share of the poll fell from 36.6 per cent to 34.9 per cent. As for the Likud, it received 57,639 votes less than in 1981 and its share of the poll dropped from 37.1 per cent to 31.9 per cent.

For the Labour Alignment, the disappointing results of the 1984 election were but a continuation of the trend which had become so dramatically apparent in the upheaval of 1977. Increasingly, Labour became the party of the older, more conservative and better-off voters of Ashkenazi descent, while the Likud appealed to the less well-to-do and, importantly, the young, especially those of Sephardi origin. In Israel, paradoxically, it was the middle class with something to lose that supported the left, while the right-wing parties based their support on the lower social strata.

There are a number of explanations for this phenomenon. First, the Labour movement was the 'establishment' for three decades after the founding of the state and for at least 20 years previously. During that time, as the single dominant party, it came to be identified as virtually synonymous with the state and its institutions. In particular, the Labour movement, through the General Confederation of Labour (Histadrut), also dominated the economy and the system of social welfare. Thus those who regarded themselves as disadvantaged *vis-à-vis* the better-off elements in society, namely recent immigrants of African-Asian origin—most of whom were Sephardim—regarded the Alignment as the party of the establishment and, as such, responsible for their predicament.

As the traditional opposition party, on the other hand, the Likud was able to appeal to those who regarded themselves as 'outsiders' in Israeli society. It was able to offer opportunities for upward political mobility for new generations of Sephardi political activists in the development towns and newly established urban and rural settlements. Upwardly mobile and politically ambitious youngsters of Moroccan origin, for example, first sought careers in the Labour Alignment, but there earlier generations of Sephardi immigrants from Iraq and Yemen already occupied top leadership positions. They turned instead to the Herut component of the Likud where they came to be regarded among the majority of Sephardi voters, especially in the Moroccan community, as more authentic and legitimate leaders than the senior Sephardis in top Labour positions.

It has been suggested that the Likud's apparent failure to exploit its manifest popularity among the now majority Sephardi community in the 1984 election was to some extent due to it being a victim of its own success. Whereas being seen increasingly as the natural party of government brought it new voters in greater numbers, in government it was obliged to be more conciliatory towards its opponents and potential coalition partners and more ready for compromise. This led to the emergence of parties further to the right with more extreme positions who were able to take votes away from the Likud.

Indeed, the main manifestation of right-wing tendencies in the 1980s has been seen in support for parties on the periphery of the political spectrum, namely Tehiya, Tsomet and Kach. However, the results of the 1984 election suggested that it was only Kach that was capable of inflicting any real damage on the Likud in 1988. Where it was strongest, Kach took votes from the Likud, while the Likud's vote was virtually unaffected in the strongholds of Tsomet and Tehiya. In the event however, Kach was prevented from standing in the 1988 elections under an amendment to Israel's electoral law which specifically rules out racist parties.

The Parties

Twenty-eight parties, 11 of them new, submitted lists for the scrutiny of the Central Elections Committee by the midnight deadline on 27 September 1988. These included eight religious parties, among them breakaway groups from Agudat Israel, Shas and the National Religious Party. There had been calls for the disqualification of four of the lists: Kach, Moledet, Agudat Israel and the Progressive List for Peace. The reform movement demanded the Aguda's exclusion on the grounds that through Aguda, orthodox Jewry is openly advocating discrimination against it. Labour and the Citizens Rights Movement demanded the disqualification of Kach and Moledet, while the Likud and Tehiya wanted the Progressive List for Peace to be disqualified. In the event only Kach was refused permission to stand.

Likud
Historically the Likud had been an alliance of parties generally to the right of centre but it had been a principal element in the ruling coalition only since 1977. The two main components of the Likud are Herut and the National Liberal Party which have been allied since 1961, but which maintained their separate identities and party organizations until a few weeks before the November 1988 elections when they finally merged.

The Religious Camp
Nowhere has the overall shift to the right in Israeli political life and the associated problems arising from generational change been reflected more

accurately than among the religious parties. In the 1984 election the ethnic divide, the main cleavage in Israeli electoral politics, affected the religious community to much the same extent as it did the political community in general. The crisis in the religious camp and the divisions and fragmentation that resulted were reflected best in the fate of the National Religious Party (NRP).

National Religious Party (NRP)   The NRP participated in every coalition government to 1988, traditionally winning about 10 per cent of the popular vote in successive elections down to and including that of 1977. Indeed, in that election it increased its share of the vote in spite of having been Labour's first choice for coalition partner. The NRP was unaffected by Labour's electoral unpopularity in that year.

Subsequently, the NRP entered the Likud-dominated coalitions only to emerge as the biggest loser in the elections of 1981 when its vote fell from 9.2 per cent (in 1977) to 4.9 per cent and its share of seats in the Knesset was halved from 12 to 6. In 1984, the religious camp as a whole held on to the same number of seats (13) as it won in the previous election, but the NRP's share fell again from 6 to 4.

The NRP went through a severe internal crisis, involving serious inter-generational tensions as well as ideological conflict. There was a significant shift to the right among younger elements who opposed territorial compromise as a solution to the Arab–Israeli conflict and who had been active in support of the West Bank settlers' movement—Gush Emunim ('Bloc of the Faithful').

Paradoxically, prior to 1988 none of this had arrested the party's electoral decline, as religious voters who traditionally supported the party's policies, but who otherwise felt no obligation to it, voted instead for the Likud. Thus in 1981, when the NRP committed itself in advance to joining a Likud-led coalition, the priority for religious voters seemed to be to keep the Labour Alignment out. Since Labour was the main threat to continued Likud rule, they readily abandoned the NRP and voted for the Likud instead.

The NRP also suffered from the 'ethnic factor'. In 1981, a former NRP stalwart of Moroccan origin, Aharon Abuhatzeira, who served as Minister for Religious Affairs in the first Begin government, broke away to form TAMI (Movement for a Traditional Israel). Purporting to represent low-income voters of Sephardi origin, TAMI won three seats in 1981. In 1984, when there was considerably more competition for the religious Sephardi vote, TAMI was reduced to a single seat, but its supporters did not return to the NRP. In May 1988, debilitated by a lack of electoral appeal and internal conflict, the NRP leadership passed to a member of the orthodox Sephardi community, Professor Avner Shaki, and thereby came under Sephardi dominance.

The Ultra-Orthodox Parties   In previous elections Israel's ultra-orthodox community was represented at the political level by the Agudat Israel Party.

Between 1949 and 1977, the Aguda never participated in government. It was enticed into the first Likud administration by Mr Begin who promised to do his best to ensure the implementation of the party's goals. In government, however, the Aguda was committed to following the instructions of its extra-parliamentary ruling body, the Council of Tora Sages, and therefore it declined to accept any senior ministerial portfolios, nor did it accept collective cabinet responsibility. Instead, in return for its support for the coalition it demanded various religious concessions which threatened to upset Israel's traditional religious status quo. These included legislation against conversion to Judaism performed by non-orthodox rabbis; tight restrictions on post-mortems; prohibition of archaeological digs at religious sites unless sanc-tioned by the orthodox religious authorities; prohibition of abortions; and exemption of all women from military service.

Even Mr Begin was unable to deliver most of the concessions demanded by the Aguda. For one thing, meeting its demands on religious conversion would have antagonized important elements among Diaspora Jewry, especially in the United States. Instead, the Aguda came to appreciate the material benefits of being in government. Aid to religious seminaries and orthodox schooling and the preservation of the value of family welfare benefits were among the many advantages it might have had to forgo if it returned to the opposition benches.

In 1984, a new party, the Sephardi Tora Observance Party (Shas) divided the ultra-orthodox camp and took votes also from the TAMI Party. The Aguda's share of the poll fell from 3.7 per cent in 1981 to 1.7 per cent and it lost two of its four Knesset seats. Shas, on the other hand, won 3.1 per cent of the poll, enough to give it four seats in the 11th Knesset. In the religious camp, the shift to the right among the Sephardi community was spearheaded by the rabbinical leadership, who used the prestigious and strategically placed seminaries in the Diaspora to raise funds which were channelled into political organization in addition to religious teaching. Foremost among the leaders was the former Sephardi Chief Rabbi of Israel, Ovadia Yosef, who had been behind the challenge of Shas to the Ashkenazi Aguda.

The orthodox religious parties were foremost in a national trend to the right in order to attract new followers and satisfy old adherents. However, it is important to distinguish between those religious parties which, along with the Likud, purported to represent all Israelis irrespective of class and income and the ultra-orthodox parties like the Aguda who seek to cut themselves off from identification with the Jewish state which they see as irreversibly secular. Thus where the right-wing parties, including the religious among them, present themselves as staunch nationalists, many of the ultra-orthodox elements are essentially anti-Zionist—Zionism being defined as a secular attribute of the modern state. In 1988, the ultra-orthodox parties, Agudat Israel and Shas, split and four parties competed for the ultra-orthodox vote. The main division between the Ashkenazi Aguda and the Sephardi Shas remained, but internal disputes between the followers of different rabbis and rabbinical courts divided both parties.

Labour Alignment

The parties which made up the Alignment were identified with the socialist-Zionist pioneer movement that built the first settlements and created the basic institutions of the new society. However, Israel's changing political demography, the traumas of the Yom Kippur War and corruption in high places all contributed to a decline of the Alignment's electoral appeal and, eventually, to loss of power for the first time in 29 years in the Knesset elections of 1977.

In 1988, the name 'Labour Alignment' no longer described the party's make-up. For the first time in six general elections, it did not include Mapam, which refused to join the National Unity government in 1984 and chose in this election to run alone in competition with the Alignment.

The gradual shift in the dominant values of Israeli society to those of conservatism and the right (religious, nationalistic, anti-collectivist) were reinforced by the *intifada*. Labour had been divided between its 'hawks' and 'doves', disoriented by King Hussein's renunciation of the West Bank and left wondering about the fate of the 'Jordanian Option', its principal proposal for the resolution of the Palestinian problem.

The party went through considerable turmoil over the summer months. There had been some disquiet over the leadership of Shimon Peres, who had already led it in three successive defeats. Peres seemed to have captivated international and Diaspora opinion, but remained unimpressive and even suspect to the Israeli electorate.

Furthermore, for the fourth election in a row, Labour faced the same dilemma: what should be the main thrust of its electioneering—capturing the right or holding on to its old left-wing base which was vulnerable to the appeal of the parties of the left? How was the party to present its economic ideas within a new socio-economic environment in which profits, as a sign of institutional viability, were more important than the claims of historically important groups like the kibbutzim? In Israel, as in all developed economies, viability, efficiency and the capacity to generate profit have superseded the old ideological view of working class rights.

Labour's New Faces   In the 1988 election, Labour made extensive efforts to present a new image to the electorate. This was to be seen in those who finally attained 'realistic' places among the top 45 candidates on the party's list (the candidates placed below the 45th place 'realistically' stood little or no chance of being elected). For example, there had been the very public process of 'democratization' within the party with the task of ranking candidates for the election list given to the Central Committee, thus widening the oligarchy of decision-makers. The practical outcome of this process was that individuals found it necessary to seek the backing of various groups and interests within the party. The most notable victim of the new procedure was Abba Eban who was unable to cobble together support for his candidature. The unique characteristics which, in the Israeli context, had served him well in the past, now proved to be serious handicaps. He no longer represented a desirable role model to the younger generation of power brokers. Eban's defeat symbolized, above all else, the passing of the old Ashkenazi guard.

Thus among the top 45 places on the party's list, 30 per cent were of Sephardi background and 25 per cent were in their 30s and 40s. Seventeen members of the previous Knesset were dropped and only the first six places on the list were reserved for the familiar 'veteran' leaders.

In its effort to restore its fortunes, Labour became a 'supermarket of ideas', typical, some would say, of the large modern mass parties of the Western liberal democracies.

Small Parties

The Arab Vote   Israel has 320,000 Arab voters who together make up some 18 per cent of the electorate. Potentially, therefore, there could be a bloc of at least 15 Arab seats in the Knesset, easily making it the third largest political grouping after the Likud and the Alignment.

However, the Arab vote has been fragmented by primary loyalties. Moreover, Arab communities have been the recipients of the patronage of the mainstream Jewish parties, especially the Alignment which, in addition to the Communists and the Progressive List for Peace, had included a few Arab candidates among the 'realistic' places on its list. In 1984, for example, the Arab vote gave Labour five seats and the Communists six.

The infrastructure necessary for a viable Arab party had been difficult to establish but, especially among young Arabs, group consciousness had been raised by the *intifada* and the Israeli authorities' response. In the 1988 election, therefore, there was an Arab party, headed by Abd El-Wahab Daroushe, who was elected as a Labour Member of the Knesset in 1984, but who resigned the party whip in protest against the policies of Labour's Yitzhak Rabin, the Minister of Defence.

The Arab Democratic Party stood for equal rights for Arabs, a two-state solution to the Arab-Israeli conflict and an international peace conference with the full participation of the PLO. In 1965, an attempt to form an independent Arab party was thwarted by the Supreme Court; in 1988, Mr Daroushe claimed that his membership of the Knesset gave him the legal right to form a political party. And indeed, the Central Elections Committee did not challenge the nomination of the Arab Democratic Party list.

In the 1984 election, for the first time since the establishment of the state, there was a clear majority in the Arab sector against 'Zionist' parties and for parties regarded as 'Arab'. These were Hadash, which consisted primarily of the Israeli Communist Party and a few small allied groups, and the Arab-led Progressive List for Peace, combining radical Jewish and Arab groups. Hadash and the Progressive List between them won 53 per cent of the Arab vote giving them four and two seats respectively in the 11th Knesset.

The Jewish Left The 1988 election saw Mapam (United Workers Party) standing as an independent party for the first time in 23 years. In 1984, Mapam had refused to enter the National Unity government and had finally left the Alignment. Accordingly, there was some doubt as to whether it would win enough votes to cross the 1 per cent threshold and thereby fail to be represented in the Knesset for the first time since 1949.

Mapam's election platform called for direct negotiations between Israel and the individual Arab states including the Palestine Liberation Organization if it agreed to recognize Israel and accept UN Resolutions 242 and 338; it opposed Labour's Jordanian option; and it focussed its appeal on blue-collar and employee sectors of the population.

The Citizens Rights Movement (CRM) and Centre-Shinui came to represent between them Israel's liberal establishment. The CRM could be said to represent a genuine strand of secular opinion in Israeli society. The kind and degree of secular liberalism it reflects, such as women's rights and opposition to compulsory religious observance, made it very much a minority movement. But in its leader, Shulamith Aloni, it had one of the more attractive personalities in Israeli political life.

In the 1984 election, Shinui and the CRM won three seats each, taking votes from new voters, but primarily from the Labour Alignment.

The Radical Right In the 1988 election the radical right was represented by Tehiya, Tsomet and Moledet.

Tehiya was formed in 1979 to oppose what some considered the 'excessive' concessions made to Egypt in the Camp David Accords. Advocating the imposition of Israeli sovereignty over the West Bank and the Gaza Strip, it was headed by Professor Yuval Ne'eman, a nuclear physicist and former chief of the Israeli Atomic Energy Authority, and Mrs Geula Cohen, a veteran of the Herut Movement. Tehiya benefitted from the Likud's more 'moderate' image among Israel's right-wing extremist elements and in 1984, it became the third largest party in the Knesset with 4 per cent of the popular vote and five seats.

Tsomet was headed by the former Chief of Staff of the IDF, Lt Gen Rafael (Raful) Eitan. General Eitan had been a close colleague and supporter of the Industry Minister, Ariel Sharon. He collaborated enthusiastically with Sharon who was Defence Minister at the time of the 1982 Lebanon invasion and Eitan was, in fact, the chief architect and leader of the military campaign. He formed Tsomet on leaving the army, but entered into an alliance with Tehiya in the 1984 election campaign.

Moledet is led by Rehavam Ze'evi (popularly known as 'Gandhi', a nickname he earned during his time in the IDF). As mentioned above, Ze'evi is chairman of the Eretz Israel Museum in Tel-Aviv and he used the prestige this position gave him to popularize his idea for the 'transfer' of the Arab population from the occupied territories.

The Results

The outcome of the election was in many ways more frustrating and did more to undermine confidence in the country's political system than any previous election result. As in 1984, neither of the two major parties won a clear victory. This time, however, the balance of power lay not with the smaller parties whose demands could be readily accommodated in the process of coalition-building, but with orthodox and ultra-orthodox religious factions, far removed from the mainstream of the country's political life and principal concerns.

Four years of a national unity government, which, in reality, was critically divided, saw little progress in resolving major foreign, domestic and economic problems. Foremost among these were the *intifada*, and the future of the peace process. There seemed little doubt that the uprising was the major factor weighing on the minds of the voters.

In the event, the results of the election were widely regarded as reflecting a major shift to the right in Israeli electoral choice. Although the Likud and the small right-wing parties won between them two seats fewer than the Labour Alignment and the parties of the left, it was believed that the religious factions, which had succeeded in regaining their traditional level of support, would be more likely to favour a government led by the Likud than one headed by Labour.

As a result, it was the outgoing Likud Prime Minister, Yitzhak Shamir, who was asked by President Herzog to form the new administration. However, he encountered prolonged difficulties owing to the extreme demands of the ultra-orthodox parties. Paradoxically, the issues at stake had little to do with the peace process, the *intifada*, or even the overall state of the economy. Instead, negotiations were dominated by demands for legislation to enforce stricter religious observance, special financial concessions for religious foundations and the 'Who is a Jew?' issue, which threatened to undermine relations between the state of Israel and Diaspora Jews.

After seven weeks of bargaining and horse-trading, Mr Shamir abandoned his efforts to form a narrow-based coalition with the religious parties and the splinter groups on the right, in favour a new broadly-based 'unity' government with Labour. The election which had been intended to break the stalemate in Israeli political life had had the opposite result—one which promised yet another period of immobilism with little prospect of agreement on how to tackle the country's urgent and most pressing problems.

TABLE 1   RESULTS OF THE 1988 KNESSET ELECTIONS[a]

List	Seats		Votes		% of total vote	
Likud	40	(41)[b]	709,305	(661,302)	31.07	(31.9)
Alignment	39	(44)	685,363	(724,074)	30.02	(34.9)
Shas	6	(4)	107,709	(63,605)	4.72	(3.1)
Agudat Israel	5	(2)	102,714	(36,079)	4.50	(1.7)
Citizens Rights	5	(3)	97,513	(49,698)	4.27	(2.4)
NRP	5	(4)	89,720	(73,530)	3.93	(3.5)
Hadash	4	(4)	84,032	(69,815)	3.68	(3.4)
Tehiya	3	(5)	70,730	(83,037)	3.10	(4.0)
Mapam[c]	3	(0)	56,345		2.47	
Tsomet[d]	2	(0)	45,489		1.99	
Moledet	2	(0)	44,174		1.93	
Centre-Shinui	2	(3)	39,538	(54,747)	1.73	(2.6)
Degel Hatorah	2	(0)	34,279		1.50	
Progressive List	1	(2)	33,695	(38,012)	1.48	(1.8)
Arab Democratic Party	1	(0)	27,012		1.18	
Others			55,505	(58,978)	2.43[e]	(2.8)

[a] Final official results issued by the Central Elections Committee for the 12th Knesset.
[b] The figures in parentheses are those of the 1984 elections.
[c] In 1984 Mapam was part of the Alignment.
[d] In 1984 Tsomet ran together with Tehiya.
[e] Twelve parties failed to cross the 1 per cent threshold and their votes are discounted in sharing out the Knesset seats.

The participation rate in Israeli elections remains high in comparison with other Western liberal democracies. Indeed, actual turnout is always considerably higher than the voting figures suggest since the electoral register comprises all holders of valid identity cards, regardless of where they live, on the day the election is held. Thus, of the possible electorate residing in Israel on polling day, some 90 per cent or more are likely to have voted, although officially 79.66 per cent actually did so. In 1984, the turnout was 78.8 per cent and in 1981 78.5 per cent.

Of the 28 parties initially registered for the 1988 elections, one, Kach headed by Rabbi Meir Kahane, was disqualified by the Central Elections Committee, and 12 failed to reach the 1 per cent minimum vote needed to qualify for a share of the Knesset seats. As in 1984, the number of parties in the 12th Knesset was 15. Three lists—Degel Hatorah, Moledet and the Arab Democratic Party—were represented for the first time.

The Major Parties
There was a clear shift away from the two major parties and a corresponding increase in support for the minority parties of the left and right. Between them, Tehiya, Moledet and Tsomet held 7 seats in the 12th Knesset, most of which, in other circumstances, might have been held by the Likud. Likud also lost to religious parties whose orthodox and ultra-orthodox voters, like the

supporters of the more extreme right-wing lists, preferred the fundamentalism of Shas, the Aguda and Degel Hatorah to the more accommodating
approach of the major blocs.

The Alignment seemed to have retained the support of the middle class and
the middle-aged, but there were few signs that it was able to increase its
appeal among the younger voters of Asian-African origin. In the development towns, where popular local leaders were given realistic places in the
Alignment's election list, there was little indication of any significant recovery
in the party's fortunes. The support given to the CRM and Mapam across the
country was clear evidence of the more ideologically committed defecting in
increasing numbers to the Zionist parties on the moderate left. What
underlay this shift remained unclear. In part it was due to voters feeling
uneasy that the major parties were compromising their principles in order to
gain power. 'National unity' was favoured by many among the electorate
especially at a time when the country's internal and external affairs were in
turmoil. However, the resultant 'immobilism' frustrated and disillusioned the
voters for whom positions of principle were more important than party
identification.

In Israel, with its electoral system of virtually pure proportional representation, particular interests can be more effectively pursued by small independent political parties than through factions within the framework of the larger
groupings.

The Small Parties

Israel's system of proportional representation guarantees that the widest
possible spread of opinion is represented in the Knesset. It is a hangover from
the days of the Yishuv when it was thought essential for all interests to be
included in the political framework so as to avoid harmful divisions in the
small Jewish community. After the establishment of the state, when Mapai
(Labour) was the single dominant party, pure proportional representation did
not prevent the formation of stable governments.

However, the situation changed after the upheaval of 1977 and since that
time the Likud competed with the Alignment for the favours of the small
parties. With the two major parties emerging from recent elections virtually
neck-and-neck, the small parties demanded the highest possible price for
their support. Indeed, since 1984, neither the Alignment nor the Likud was
able to pay this price in order to form a government on its own and they were
obliged to resort to so-called 'unity government' or 'broad coalitions'. The 13
small parties that won seats in the 12th Knesset divide into two broad
categories: secular and religious. Two of the secular parties, Hadash and the
PLP with 5 seats between them, are not regarded as suitable coalition
partners by either of the two major blocs. Of the remaining 11, 7 are secular
parties and 4 religious.

The Secular Parties

In Israel, traditionally, the left had been divided between Zionist and non-Zionist parties: between those who supported the idea of a Jewish state based upon socialist principles, and those for whom nationalism was incompatible with socialism. The latter comprised Jewish communists, far-left socialists and Arab nationalists; the former consisted of traditional socialist-Zionists and secular liberal Jews and Arabs concerned about civil liberties, women's rights, the defence of secular values against religious coercion and so on.

In the 1988 election, whilst the socialist-Zionist Mapam Party abandoned the Labour Alignment and campaigned alone, it is doubtful whether its three seats in the Knesset represented any advance on the support the party had when it was part of the Alignment. The same must be said for the Citizens Rights Movement which increased its representation in the Knesset from three to five. It seemed no coincidence that the Alignment had five seats fewer than it held in the 11th Knesset. Those who believe that participating in a broad coalition with the Likud obliged the Alignment to water down, if not abandon altogether, a whole range of liberal policies and principles defected to the smaller parties. There they hoped that either they would be able to insist on these principles being upheld as the price of participating in an Alignment-led coalition, or they would be free to voice them in the Knesset from the opposition benches.

On the right, as on the left, support for the small extreme parties was only marginally up on 1984. Tehiya ended up with three seats instead of the five it had when it ran together with Tsomet, but the latter held on to the other two, while Moledet's 'transfer' platform won it two seats. In sum, Likud and the extremist secular parties to its right gained together only one seat more than in 1984 when the Kach Party was permitted to stand. This would indicate that the more religious among Kach's supporters voted this time for one of the ultra-orthodox lists.

The Religious Parties

Israel's religious parties have traditionally claimed 13–15 per cent of the votes cast in Knesset elections, giving them between 15 and 18 seats. From the election of 1973 to that of 1984, however, religious voters tended to support the Likud and increasingly the main political cleavage in the religious community ranged along the so-called 'ethnic' divide between Sephardi and Ashkenazi Jews.

The most surprising and significant aspect of the results of the elections to the 12th Knesset was the relative success of the ultra-orthodox parties, both Sephardi and Ashkenazi. Between them, the Shas, Agudat Israel and the Degel Hatorah lists won 13 seats. The significance of this achievement does not lie in the overall strengthening of the religious camp, but rather in its takeover by the ultra-orthodox. Indeed, most of the 52 days it took to form a government following the 1 November elections were dominated by the controversy aroused by the demands of the ultra-orthodox as their price for participating in a narrowly based Likud- or Alignment-led coalition. Their most controversial demand was the amendment of the Law of Return to require that all those who convert to Judaism from another faith do so under the precepts of traditional Jewish law (Halakha).

The insistence on amending the Law of Return was voiced most strongly by the Agudat Israel Party, which virtually trebled its vote in this election compared with 1984. Historically an anti-Zionist party, the Aguda was founded in 1912 by ultra-orthodox German Jews. In 1984, its Knesset representation, usually four seats, was cut to two by the breakaway of the ethnic-based Shas Party. In 1988, however, Aguda found itself the beneficiary of the support of the Lubavitch Rebbe Menachem Mendel Schneerson, who lives in New York. Schneerson ordered his supporters in the Habad Movement in Israel to work for the Aguda. The combination of the resources of the dynamic and efficient Habad and the charisma of Schneerson seemed to have been major factors in contributing to the ultra-orthodox success.

Schneerson had been pressing for the amendment of Israel's Law of Return for 30 years. His followers said that this is because of his concern to preserve the essential Jewish character of the state. However, it was widely believed that Schneerson's motives had little to do with Israel, but rather with the Jewish world outside and especially in the United States. Lubavitch was locked in a conflict with the reform and conservative movements over the allegiance of young American Jews. In fact, it saw itself as engaged in a struggle for the soul of world Jewry in its entirety. It says a great deal for the centrality of Israel even among the normally anti-Zionist ultra-orthodox Jews of the Diaspora, that the struggle for their spiritual dominance should take place in the context of a general election in the modern state of Israel. By undermining conservative and reform rabbis and their converts in Israel, Schneerson hoped they would be delegitimized throughout the Jewish world.

The Habad movement differed from other ultra-orthodox sects who did not recognize the state of Israel. Its members served in the IDF and they participated in the religious stream of the state education system. Israel's top leaders often conferred with Schneerson at his home in New York.

Ovadia Yosef, the spiritual mentor of the Shas Party, does live in Israel and is a former Sephardi Chief Rabbi. Yosef's main rival was Rabbi Eliezer Shach, formerly the head of the Agudat Israel Council of Torah Sages, who gave the impetus and spiritual stature to the breakaway Shas Party four years ago. Shach still had a great deal of moral influence in Shas, although as an Ashkenazi he was debarred from membership of the Shas Council of Torah Sages, a wholly Sephardi body. However, he was strongly opposed to what he called the 'false messianism' of the settlers' movement Gush Emunim and the right-wing alliance of the NRP and the Aguda who supported the idea of a Greater Israel.

It was precisely because of his fears of spilling Jewish blood in order to hold on to the territories and because he believed that continuing current policies in the West Bank and Gaza must lead inevitably to conflict with the United States, that Shach supported the idea of a Labour-led coalition, even one that included 'anti-religious elements' like the CRM, Mapam and Shinui.

All the religious parties were outraged by the agreement between the Alignment and the Likud which led to the formation of the new 'unity' government. In what they regarded as a base act of treason by the Prime Minister designate, the concessions they extracted from the Likud in return for their support for a narrow coalition were snatched away the moment Mr Shamir was able to coax the Alignment into a broad government under his leadership. If anything was certain about the coming four years, it was that there would be no amendment to the Law of Return nor any further disruption of the traditional status quo regarding religious observance. Betrayed, offended and in the eyes of many Israelis deservedly cut down to size, the religious camp had either to go into opposition or join the government to obtain what was left of the religious camp's traditional spoils. It should have surprised no one that they chose the latter alternative.

The Arab Vote

In the 1984 election, there were clear indications that Israeli Arab voters were deserting the Zionist parties. In November 1988, the results in the Arab sector showed a further marked shift towards the parties with an Arab or Arab-Jewish identity. In 1984, 48.75 per cent voted for the Zionist parties and 51.3 per cent chose the Arab-Jewish lists. In 1988 59.3 per cent voted for the Jewish-Arab and Arab parties, while the Zionist parties' share of the Arab vote fell to 40.7 per cent. Among the Bedouin the change was even more dramatic: only 45.5 per cent voted for the Zionist parties compared with 90 per cent in 1984.

The Alignment was the main casualty of this change; its share of the Arab vote fell from 25 per cent in 1984 to 16.25 per cent. This was in spite of the fact that in the 1988 election the Alignment had exchanged Mapam for Ezer Weitzman's Yahad Party and had high hopes of gaining the 10,000 or so Arab votes polled by Yahad in 1984.

Nineteen-eighty-eight saw the emergence, for the first time, of a purely Muslim-Arab list, led by Abd el-Wahab Daroushe. In the past, parties like Hadash and the PLP, the majority of whose supporters were Arabs, were careful to stress their joint Jewish-Arab character by including Jews as well as Arabs in their lists of candidates for elections to the Knesset. Matti Peled, for example, appeared in the PLP list and Meir Wilner and Charlie Biton in the Hadash line-up. Indeed, Hadash had a Jewish leader. There were, however, no Jews among the list of candidates put forward by the Arab Democratic

Party in November 1988. One interpretation of this apparent shift in the preferences of Israel's Arab voters was that it heralded a long-term move towards an extreme Palestinian nationalist tendency. Indeed, it was widely believed in Israel that Israeli Arabs fully supported the *intifada* of their fellow Palestinians in the territories in complete disregard of their own immediate social and economic interests.

What is important to remember is that in November 1988, after eleven months of the *intifada*, 40 per cent of Israel's Arabs still voted for Zionist parties. Moreover, although some ignored PLO calls not to boycott the election and stayed away from the polls lest they be seen as identifying politically with the Israeli state, the Arab turnout was still 4 per cent up on 1984.

Israel's Arabs, however, are by no means homogeneous, neither in their political affiliations nor in their attitudes. The Jewish-Arab and Arab parties won six seats between them in the 12th Knesset. Their voting potential might have given them as many as 15 had they all supported one party. Hostility between the various factions, however, made it impossible for them even to enter into surplus vote agreements among themselves.

Politically the Arab community was divided along generational lines. The young, educated Arabs who made up the bulk of the Arab electorate, shared the ideological convictions of those parties, namely Hadash, the PLP and the Arab Democratic List, who supported Palestinian nationalism: the Zionist parties could not provide a focus for their identity. The older, more traditional generation, however, had been and remained more pragmatic, preferring to come to terms with their position as an Arab minority in a Jewish state and seeking the best possible life for themselves and their families. There was also a very large number, some would say the majority, who had no fixed allegiances.

Nor should the revolutionary change in the political allegiance of the Bedouin be regarded as an indication of extremism, although it was certainly a sign of growing bitterness over the failure of successive governments to resolve their grievances over such issues as land ownership. These problems had to be handled more sympathetically if there was not to be a further weakening of Bedouin loyalty to Israel and a strengthening of their Arab-Muslim identity.

The traditional voting patterns of the Druze remained unchanged in the 1988 election. Some 80 per cent of their votes went to Zionist parties and, as in the past, the Alignment with 28 per cent was the principal beneficiary while 20 per cent voted for the Likud.

Everybody acknowledged that Hadash and the PLP would not have demanded the establishment of a Palestinian state in the occupied territories as a price for their participation in a coalition. What Hadash and the PLP would have insisted on, it was argued, would have been greater equality for Israel's Arabs, better employment opportunities for educated Arabs, the development of the Arab village, and so on, objectives which the manifestos of both Labour and the Likud specifically reiterated.

Comments and observations

Israeli elections are free, fair and thoroughly democratic. Their conduct, while not entirely above reproach, is on a par with the best democracies in the world. In the 1988 election there was little violence and the incidence of malpractice was too small to prompt any questioning of the results.

Nevertheless, the results of the elections to the 12th Knesset confirmed the opinion of those who have long believed that stable government by parties representing the mainstream of opinion cannot be realized under the present system of proportional representation. A government that emerges after weeks of protracted and expensive bargaining with small unrepresentative factions has little connection with the will of the majority as expressed at the polls.

The new government was designed to serve two purposes: to release the major parties from the stranglehold of the more outrageous demands of the religious factions and to keep the Labour Alignment away from the opposition benches. Indeed, under the coalition agreement, if either of two major parties decided to leave the government, neither would attempt to form a narrow-based administration, but rather they would call immediately for new elections. Both Labour and the Likud seemed determined not to find themselves out of government without a hand on the levers of power.

Thus, those who supported Mr Peres in the hard pressed kibbutz and moshav movements and in the company sector (Hevrat Ovdim) of the Histadrut, were determined that come what may, their man had to have direct access to economic decision-making. Similarly, although they felt utterly betrayed and deceived by Mr Shamir when he abandoned his negotiations with them to form the new government, the religious parties did not hesitate to join in for whatever spoils they could obtain, even though these fell far short of their original demands.

After the November elections, many Israelis felt that it was time for Israel to have a strong opposition. Indeed, it was argued, given the strength of Labour and its left-wing allies and the potential support of the far left Jewish-Arab lists, life could be made extremely difficult for a Likud-led narrow based coalition. However, powerful elements within the Alignment and leading figures like Mr Peres and Mr Rabin, could not accept the idea of politics without real power. For them, as for their arch opponent Yitzhak Shamir, the imperative was to hold on.

In the wake of the 1988 election, holding on meant for Prime Minister Shamir heading a government in which the Labour Alignment had the power to veto the most extreme demands of his supporters. His fear was, his critics said, that Likud ideology could result in a conflict with the new Bush administration in Washington that might end in the Americans forcing a Shamir-led government to recognize and negotiate with the PLO. Shamir had ignored all calls from his supporters to annex any more of the occupied territories, in part because he feared the US reaction, but mainly because he did not wish to have to determine the status of the Palestinian population.

Electoral trends continued to move against the Labour Alignment. Without the resurgence in the fortunes of the religious camp, the shift towards the Likud might have been more evident. The Israeli Labour Party—the Labour Alignment—had lost its fourth successive election under the leadership of Shimon Peres. Since 1984, it had attempted to reform its inner party democracy and there had been a democratization of the process of drawing up the party's electoral list. That list included new faces, many of them young, local leaders of Asian-African origin from development towns. However, it had all been to little avail.

Meanwhile, the underlying strength of the Likud among the younger Sephardi voters, especially in the development towns, enabled it to increase its vote in absolute terms, although there was a marginal drop in the party's share of the poll. It was of considerable significance that the Likud's vote held up in the face of the combined onslaught of the religious parties and the extreme right-wing. Indeed, the Likud emerged from the 1988 elections on equal terms with the Alignment in what used to be some of that party's main strongholds.

Thus the elections to the 12th Knesset showed that whilst, for the time being, the Alignment remains one of Israel's two dominant parties, it still needs to find the means to appeal to the electorate in general, and especially to the nation's youth, if it is to reverse the long-term trend in favour of the Likud.

3

Arab Images of Jews and Israel

RONALD L. NETTLER

The Jews and Israel have appeared rather prominently in Arabic writings in our time, particularly, as one might imagine, since the inception of Zionism in Palestine and, even more so, since the establishment of the Jewish state in 1948. Formulated in various ways and from different perspectives, often in separate writings, and sometimes as a part of writings devoted to broader subjects, these discussions reflect a deep modern Arab and Islamic concern with the Jews. The roots of this concern lie, of course, in the new phenomenon of Jewish nationalism and statehood within the Muslim domain (*Dar al-Islam*), during the turbulent twentieth century—a century which seems to Arabs to have brought more harm than good, more historical dislocation than constructive adjustment. Since a significant part of the nagging pain of modernity which the Arabs have felt so acutely has been associated in their minds with the Jews and Israel, the literary expression of this complaint has been profuse.

Well before 1948, during the decades of Zionism's pre-state development, Arabic writings expressed the emerging Arab feelings of ambivalence, dismay, confusion and, eventually, anger at what was ultimately perceived as a massive threat. Such writings appeared both outside Palestine and within, in a variety of publications representing different views and opinions. And after a time, most evinced a clear hostility, shorn of any ambivalence or uncertainty.

With Zionism's transformation into a Jewish nation-state, the bitterness, suspicion and hostility were heightened. And, even more important, the forms of literary expression began to evolve into what would subsequently become a new and highly elaborated Arabic literary genre on the Jews and

Ronald L. Nettler is fellow in Muslim-Jewish relations in the modern period at the Oxford Centre for Postgraduate Hebrew Studies. His publications include studies and articles on contemporary Islamic religious doctrine on the Jews and Israel, and he is the author of *Past Trials and Present Tribulations: A Muslim Fundamentalist View of the Jews* (1987).

Israel. As a literary genre which expressed shock and resentment over a quite unpalatable historical development, it was bound to evince attitudes and outlooks, often quite monolithic, which were not merely negative and hostile, but also virulent, and, to some extent, even obsessive. This literature may be divided into three types, which continue until today as the main modes of expression in this genre (though obviously with somewhat changing orientations over the years). They are the following: secular nationalist; Islamic; Islamic fundamentalist. These categories of thought were in fact general twentieth century Arab orientations, each of which produced its own distinctive type of approach to the Jews and Israel.

We must always remember that these are 'ideal types' and, as such, in reality they sometimes overlap or even combine. But they do represent the main motifs in Arabic writings on the Jews and Israel. Let us look now at each in turn, as background to a survey of the main points in the writings which appeared during 1988.

Secular Nationalist

Secular nationalist writings were the product of ideological movements, state regimes and non-state movements, such as the Palestine Liberation Organization (PLO), which identified themselves as representing their peoples and ruling according to principles and ideas of Arab peoplehood and nation-state identities. Pan-nationalist orientations were strongly reflected in certain writings, as was socialism. The main outlook in most instances here represented a sharp divergence in formulation from most of the Islamic worldviews which were emerging at this time, though in fact they often, directly or indirectly, utilized Islamic concepts and terminology.

The early secular Arab nationalist writings on the Jews and Israel took their point of departure from the view of Israel as a *national threat* to individual Arab states, to the Palestinians and to the large pan-Arab nation. The main components of this trend were the notions of Zionism as a creation of Western imperialism; Israel as a territorial-national dagger in the heart of the Arab world; the Jews as an international threat (ideas borrowed from the *Protocols of the Elders of Zion*); and the Arab goal in the conflict being the total elimination of Israel. Insofar as Islamic motifs were incorporated in these writings, their use was derivative and secondary, as a way of ensuring that the general Muslim populace would find something here with which they could identify. And as was typical of all three types of writings, almost never was a distinction made between Jews and Israelis or Zionists.

Later, particularly in the post-Six Day War period, more emphasis was put on the Palestinian problem as the 'focus' of conflict, and both the early pan-Arab and nation-state emphases, though certainly not eliminated, often became secondary, even in writings whose ultimate origins were to be found in state nationalisms and pan-Arab doctrine. And in the Palestinian literature itself, this new emphasis was sharpened to a razor edge. In all of this new Palestinian focus, however, the essence of the earlier secular nationalist approach remained, only now with a specific Palestinian slant. Indeed, the oft-repeated Palestinian slogan of that time, the 'secular, democratic state', which would replace Israel and was the ultimate Palestinian goal, was perhaps the logical Palestinian culmination of the earlier secular nationalist thought.

Islamic

Like secular Arab nationalist thought, the general Islamic notions concerning the Jews and Israel saw Zionism and its expression in the Israeli state as illegitimate and deleterious to the best interests of the Arab Middle East. And like secular thought, Islamic thought likewise made little or no distinction between Jews and Zionists, Judaism and Zionism. On the contrary, the operative category here was that of the Jews. But the orientation was Islamic.

The Islamic orientation rested upon the wider Muslim concern over Islam's modern eclipse at the hands of the Christian West, and saw the Jewish challenge as a sort of microcosm of the larger predicament. Here the contemporary Jewish threat of Zionism and Israel was portrayed as a modern chapter of the ancient story of Jewish opposition to Islam and its prophet in seventh century Medina. Indeed, given Islam's propensity to see history as the writing of Allah's hand, the question raised here for Muslims was theological as well as political and historical; or more accurately, any political or historical crisis for Islam is necessarily seen as a theological problem, given the virtual absence of a distinction between these two realms in mainstream Islamic thought. And in the case of the Jews and their Zionism, the problem was especially acute. For the highly venerated early Islamic theoretical sources portrayed the Jews as having gone from being potential supporters of Muhammad's mission to being his worst enemies, allied with his pagan Arab opponents. Thus did the ancient Muslims feel constrained to oppose and defeat the Jews, and subsequently to put them under Muslim rule, where they remained until the modern catastrophe. The universal Islamic position on the Jews and Israel was that Israel must be dismantled (or destroyed) and the Jews returned to their proper place as subjects of Islam. The modern Islamic writings which express these views rely mainly on ancient Islamic sources and only secondarily on modern Western thought such as the *Protocols*.

Islamic Fundamentalist

For the Muslim fundamentalists, not only is all of the above true, but due to their extreme fundamentalist concern with the internal Islamic purity of

Muslim societies and their felt need for Muslims to refurbish themselves as preparation for a successful struggle with their external enemies, there has been an even more extreme tendency in their thinking about the Jews and Israel. For example, they often see perceived harmful Western influences within Muslim countries as part of the larger Jewish Zionist campaign against Islam. Thus have the fundamentalists tended to attribute influences of secularism, socialism, liberalism and other (in their eyes) harmful alien trends within their own countries to internal manifestations of Jewish Zionist influence; and thus also have they tended to see their own secular nationalist rulers and brethren as representing 'enemy Western interests' which are at least in part Jewish.

As the year 1988 approached, certain trends had emerged within the whole body of Arabic writings on the Jews and Israel. The large majority of secular nationalist writings increasingly evinced a portrayal of Israel as a state with which peace was possible and desirable; and this view most often had a Palestinian emphasis. It was mainly in the radical and somewhat marginal movements, such as that of Abu Nidal, that the erstwhile secular nationalist rejectionism remained strong. On the Islamic side, the fundamentalist writings took pride of place over general Islamic literature, as fundamentalists came increasingly to dominate Islamic developments, as they continued to influence the whole of the Middle East. These recent trends, then, appeared to be somewhat contradictory: on the secular side a seeming moderation within a narrowing focus on Palestine had occurred; while on the Islamic side the most extreme ideas had become dominant and these referred to the global Middle East situation, as well as to Palestine. It is within the framework of these two trends that I discuss the writings of 1988.

1988: The Year of the Intifada

Arabic writings on the Jews and Israel from the year 1988 revealed an intensification of these trends. This happened within the context of a certain central emphasis which followed political developments: the Palestinian issue in light of the *intifada*, the Israeli elections, the Palestine National Council meeting in Algiers and Yasser Arafat's new statements.

Indeed, so true was this, that for Arabic writings, 1988 may be chronologized according to the main events of the *intifada*; though with such an evolving political process as the *intifada*, identifying the 'main events' is at best a subjective exercise. For our purposes 'events' are in any case literary potrayals rather than actual political events on the ground; but of course these portrayals reflect and are directly related to immediate concrete events, as well as reflecting deeper political processes.

Two writings in particular, one from each of the two main trends in 1988, the secular nationalist and the Islamic fundamentalist, were wholly representative of their respective trends. Given the very high degree of repetitiveness in Arabic writings on Israel, each of these pieces may, I believe, even be seen as a 'microcosm' of the trend which it represents. The economy of this approach enables us to achieve a clear view of the forest, without, as it were, having the perspective obscured by the parading of a plethora of similar trees.

Secular Nationalist Writings

The secular nationalist writings of 1988, whether the journalistic output of a nationalist orientated nation state such as Egypt or the various Palestinian nationalist writings, evinced a specific concern with the Gaza-West Bank issue and the *intifada*. The image of the Jews and Israel was almost exclusively portrayed in this context. In general, the portrayals reflected a view of Israel as being unwilling (and perhaps constitutionally unable) to do what was required to achieve the full settlement so desired by the Palestinians. But at the same time, Israel was seen as a state with which, given the proper conditions, Arab parties did want to establish peaceful relations. The reasons why such relations had not as yet happened, in this view, had to do with the nature and behaviour of Israel, rather than with anything the Arab side may have done. Indeed, Israel's failure was seen as deriving from a virtually inherent flaw in its national character. Resistance to common sense, to reason, and even to evident self-interest, was seen to be the very stuff of the Israeli Jewish mentality. The only way to deal with it was through the application of extreme pressure, political and physical, in order to force Israel to its senses. And this was for Israel's own good, as well as that of everyone else involved.

There is in this attitude what would appear to be a profound internal contradiction: an Arab willingness to make peace, on certain conditions, coupled with an abiding antipathy towards and distrust of the potential partner in peace, Israel. Such a 'contradiction' may perhaps be found in every party approaching proposed negotiations for peace with an erstwhile enemy. On the Arab side in the late 1980s the discrepancy is very striking and the contradiction throughgoing. This was manifested in the language used by the writings, which, implicitly or explicitly, raised basic doubts about Israel's interest, ability and desire to seek to conclude a true peace arrangement. Indeed, the sought-for peace was portrayed as something which Israel, intrinsically antagonistic towards peace, would have to be forced into, in a sort of surrender to *force majeur*. The portrayal of Israel was that of a state and a people whose unfortunate predisposition had to be thwarted by the Arabs, so that they would be coerced into the arrangements so needed by all parties. Israel's nature was such that total surrender and capitulation were the only 'peace' it could ever participate in; and this would need constant maintenance and surveillance by the Arabs in order to make it stick. This 'contradiction' would then seem to be a natural accompaniment to the profound change from the erstwhile view of Israel as a state to be eliminated to the recent more conciliatory approach, while the original conception of Israel's unpleasant nature by and large remained.

I have chosen as an example of secular nationalist writing a piece, 'From the occupied lands', from the most important Egyptian newspaper, *al-Ahram* (23 November 1988). In this editorial article, Israel's image is mainly that of an occupying army fighting a brutal war of suppression against the Palestinian people's struggle to regain its rights and its land. After an Israeli occupation of two decades in the West Bank and Gaza, eleven months of this new form of Palestinian resistance in the *intifada* has now raised the probability of Palestinian Arab success to a near certainty. Indeed, says *al-Ahram*, 'Whatever the new government in Israel, it will not be able to stop the Palestinian *intifada* or to influence the political results realized by the *intifada*...' Nor, the article continues, 'will the employment of massive force as Yitzhak Shamir has threatened ... have a negative effect [on the Palestinians]...' For such Israeli techniques, says *al-Ahram*, will only strengthen Palestinian resolve towards a final victory. Israel, in this view, though remaining brutally suppressive towards any manifestation of Palestinian desire for self-determination, has now and forever lost the ability to make such suppression successful. The Palestinians, with the force of history and right on their side, and with unprecedented self-confidence, have embarked upon a one-way path towards ultimate victory.

Like most secular Arab nationalist thought, *al-Ahram* is here certain the Palestinians will ultimately achieve the goal of their struggle. This interesting view bespeaks a long-standing, general Arab idea that in spite of Israel's intrinsic objectionable nature and characteristics, which make it a mortal danger to the Arab world, it is in fact a 'paper tiger'. Its power and efficacy, derived from its brutal nature, have seemed so daunting to the Arabs only because of Arab disunity, misconceived methods of addressing the issue and lack of self-confidence. Israel's 'power', then, has been efficacious mainly as a result of misguided Arab policy, internal Arab disarray and misplaced extremism. Confronted by proper Arab policy and conduct, Israel's internal contradictions and weaknesses would grow very deep indeed, bringing confusion, attrition of physical power, demoralization and, ultimately, capitulation to Arab terms of settlement; the latter, from an Arab perspective, constitutes a 'coming to reason' in the search for a solution. Zionism itself, in this conception, as the guiding spirit of Jewish statehood, is the source of these internal Israeli problems. A proper peace strategy on the part of the Arabs, cognisant of Zionism's structural flaws and itself motivated by a desire for a realistic solution, would in this view secure the necessary results.

For *al-Ahram*, the Palestinian *intifada* and the support of Arab states for the uprising, constitute a profound turn towards a proper policy based on a deep understanding of the Israeli Jewish nature as well as of international politics. The goal of this policy is Israel's evacuation of the occupied West Bank and Gaza and the creation there of an independent state ruled by the PLO. Devoid of the erstwhile Arab cry for the dismantling (or destruction) of Jewish statehood, this policy can find obvious favour with Western governments whose support is crucial, while in its moderation it will inevitably exacerbate certain internal Israeli Jewish contradictions. This in turn would help to soften Israeli public opinion and would make it virtually impossible, for internal as well as external reasons, for Israel to turn its full power against the Palestinians of the *intifada*. Thus, says *al-Ahram*, 'The political foundation of the *intifada* ... is that it will continue inexorably until the goal has been realized: the removal of the occupation forces and the achievement of [Palestinian] independence.' Israel itself knows the process is inexorable and 'will continue for years'. 'Objective observers have seen clearly that Israel will not be able to employ unlimited massive power against the Palestinians in the occupied land' because aside from stiffening the Palestinian resolve, this would also alienate the support of friendly Western states which Israel so badly needs. Nor will Israel be able to expel large numbers of Palestinians or 'to attack their refugee villages and towns with artillery or planes, for example ...' Not only would such extreme measures incur the wrath of Western nations but 'they would bring the *intifada*, in its full force, into the heart of Israel, becoming there a civil war in which Jews would kill Jews'.

These views, already pervasive throughout the main sectors of the Arab secular nationalist camp, became sharpened and more focussed in 1988, as a result of the *intifada*. After a long evolutionary process, beginning years, even decades, ago in certain Arab intellectual-political circles, and attaining its first experience of practical implementation in the Camp David agreements, the secular Arab nationalist idea of Israel and peace was expressed in a call for an historic compromise: the Arabs would relinquish their erstwhile policy of, and practical planning for, the elimination (by whatever means) of Jewish statehood, while Israel would relinquish the territories it took in the Six Day War, and in part of these territories Israel would allow the establishment of a Palestinian Arab state. This new state would constitute a partial compensation to the Palestinians for the lands they lost in 1948 (and later), while it would provide Israel with the recognition and readiness for peaceful coexistence from the Arabs and Palestinians, which it had sought so unsuccessfully for so long. And presumably the surrounding Arab states would thereby feel satisfied that justice had been done—provided their lands occupied in 1967 were also returned (the Golan Heights would remain to be negotiated). Egypt itself, in the Camp David agreements, had been the pioneer, providing the example for the Palestinians and others to follow. *Al-Ahram*, as Egypt's leading newspaper, thus exemplifies this line.

Loaded with negative images of Israel and Zionism and characterized by a proposed policy whose main method is playing upon and manipulating what are perceived as Israel's highly unflattering internal features, this view nevertheless evinces a clear and strong idea of peace with Israel. Absent are the well-known Arab demonization of Israel and the avowed goal of her removal. This new approach constitutes an historic ideological change brought to its fullest expression and most comprehensive Arab acceptance yet in the year of the *intifada*. And though some Arab parties were no doubt ambivalent in their acceptance of this policy and viewed it as a tactic towards Israel's ultimate elimination in stages, and though virulent antisemitic portrayals yet abounded in some of the literature, the very fact of the new formulation seemed itself at least to be of great intellectual significance; its real political significance will be clear only with the passage of time.

Muslim Fundamentalist Writings

No such change was to be found in Muslim fundamentalist thinking. Here the old 'rejectionism' appeared in its hardest form yet. Voluminous and complex, Muslim fundamentalist writings on the Jews and Israel derive their deepest meaning from the comprehensive fundamentalist worldview which has been assiduously constructed in our century. Almost universally held by most Muslim fundamentalists, this worldview sees the modern period as involving an unprecedentedly disastrous decline for Islam and an equally unprecedented defeat of Islam by an alien civilization, the West. Islam's decline is conceived as having begun centuries ago, as a result of Muslim rulers and institutions themselves straying from 'true Islam', while the West in modern times has thereby been capable of walking with impunity over the somnolent Muslim body. But in fundamentalist terms the crisis is not just one civilization's domain of material power over another. Even more profoundly, it is essentially a problem of the weakening and attrition of the Islamic values and way of life, which themselves would provide the strength required for the Islamic *ummah* (nation) to defeat its enemies. The fundamentalist technical term used to refer to this comprehensive life which is true Islam, is *Aqidah*, the creed.

Aqidah as held and practised by the Muslims of the earliest generations is for the fundamentalists the necessary prerequisite for Islam's inner revitalization and the restoration of its (rightful) place of leadership in world history. All Muslims, individually and collectively, must return to this Islam. Those Muslims who will not, or cannot, and who persist in aping the ways and thoughts of Western secularist decadence are to be considered enemies of the faith, like the Western opponents of Islam themselves.

The Muslim fundamentalist idea of the Jews and Israel was constructed within the boundaries of this general fundamentalist worldview. Fundamentalism's conception of Israel as an illegitimate entity doomed to pass from the scene sooner or later, was informed by the basic principles of this worldview as well as by ancient Islamic attitudes towards the Jews and Judaism. The year

1988 saw issued a very important Palestinian fundamentalist document on the Jewish–Israel question. This document typified the trend of fundamentalist writings which emerged during the course of the *intifada*, within the West Bank and Gaza territories as well as without. And although all these writings came as response to the *intifada*, they also rest upon earlier fundamentalist writings and, of course, interpretations of Islam's ancient sources.

On 18 August 1988, the main Muslim fundamentalist organization in the West Bank, al-Hamas ('Zeal'), made its existence known to a wider public in Israel and abroad. It proclaimed itself through the issuing of its Covenant, entitled 'The Covenant of the Islamic Resistance Movement–Palestine (al-Hamas)'. Thirty-six pages long, this document systematically treats all aspects of Palestinian-Israeli relations, from the perspective of Islamic fundamentalist doctrine. A four-page letter from al-Hamas to the Palestine National Council meeting held in Algiers in November, entitled 'A Document for History . . . From the Islamic Resistance Movement, al-Hamas; presented to the Nineteenth Palestine National Council in Algiers', was later attached to the Covenant. This part was a compressed reaffirmation of the principles set forth in the main Covenant, carrying a specific plea to the PNC not to accept the idea of negotiating a two-state 'solution' to the Arab-Israeli conflict. Strongly implicit is the usual fundamentalist allegation that those so-called 'Muslims' prepared to compromise in negotiations for a two-state solution are themselves so corrupted by Western outlooks that they now constitute part of the enemy camp. They have, in fundamentalist terms, become part of the Western secular (and Jewish) menace lurking within the Muslim world. With PNC acceptance of negotiations al-Hamas would see this body thereby as having become an internal fifth column in the Arab world. In both documents, the image of the Jews and Israel stands out clearly and sharply.

This conception of the Arab-Israeli conflict includes no place for compromise and accommodation with the Jews and Israel. All of Palestine in this view is an inalienable territory of the larger Islamic realm. As part of this realm since Islam's conquest of it in the seventh century, Palestine constitutes a region in the sacred Islamic patrimony which renders it legally, in Islamic terms, *waqf* property. This means no part of it may ever be negotiated away to any non-Muslim party. Palestine is by divine fiat, as it were, an integral and inseparable area in the Abode of Islam (*Dar al-Islam*), belonging collectively to the universal Muslim nation (*ummah*). And it contains, in Jerusalem, Islamic holy sites, most important among them the al-Aqsa mosque. Thus, according to the letter to the PNC, 'The land of Palestine—complete and undistorted in shape—is the property of the Palestinian people and the entire Muslim community . . . Any Zionist presence in the land, whether in all of it or part of it, whether from the occupation of 1948 or 1967, does not nullify this Palestinian-Muslim right of possession. This right is unconditional . . .'

In addition to this Islamic legal and theological principle of property ownership, the Covenant raises the issue of the identity and nature of the present 'squatters' in Palestine: the Jews and Israel. And this raises serious problems. For according to Islam's ancient teachings, the Jews represent a once-valid but now falsified and distorted religion, which has been completed and superseded by Islam. The proper place for the Jews—as well as for the Christians—is under Islamic rule, where Islam will treat all with tolerance and kindness. The most improper place for the Jews is in their own state, on territory seized from the Islamic patrimony. In Islamic terms, this constitutes a sharp affront to Allah and a violation of His law. Moreover, without the restraining power of Islam's rule, the alleged Jewish proclivity to harm others and foment civil disturbances inevitably comes to the fore and threatens serious disruptions, or even worse. Palestine's problems are one serious example of this danger, but the larger inversion of proper power relationships between Islam and the West in the modern world is, in this view, also (at least in part) attributable to the Jews. In any case, the Covenant tells us that as regards Palestine, 'under Islamic rule it becomes possible for the followers of all religions to live together in security and with a guarantee for themselves and their property. In Islam's absence there, conflict arises, oppression intensifies, evil spreads and disagreements and wars arise'. Islam must return to rule Palestine once again, or conflict will never cease. This entails the removal of Israel.

Given this view of the problem, what then does the Covenant envisage as a solution? It rejects all negotiated political solutions, as these would obviously require compromise and accommodation from the Arabs and Muslims. And for al-Hamas dreaded compromise refers not only to the West Bank, Gaza and Jerusalem, but also to any negotiations which would leave in Palestine a living Jewish state, whatever its territorial dimensions. The Covenant says: 'There is no solution to the Palestine problem except *Jihad*. As for political initiatives, proposals, and international conferences, it is all a waste of time and a great frivolity. The Palestinian people is too noble to have its future thus mockingly played with . . .' The letter to the PNC further elaborates:

> al-Hamas proclaims its rejection of all proposed political schemes for the solution of the Palestine problem. It reaffirms that all of these schemes—in their great variety and detail—flow in the strategic direction of the Zionist enemy in the most extreme measure; and the real application of these schemes to territory would be a defeat for the Muslim community and a calamitous loss for it. The Camp David agreements were surely a witness to this . . . al-Hamas proclaims its determination to continue the Jihad until the liberation of all of Palestine . . .

The Two Trends in Juxtaposition

With the growth of religious fundamentalism in the Arab Muslim Middle East and what appeared to be its pervasive influence, there had been a discernible diminution in the popular appeal of secular nationalism (in so far as such an appeal ever existed on a large scale). And this had appeared concomitantly with the growing acceptance on the part of secular nationalists, organizations as well as governments, of some sort of phased settlement with Israel towards a two-state solution. The portrayals of Israel and the Jews found in the writings of these two camps corresponded with their visions of future Arab-Israeli relations. If, as some have argued, the continuing successful spread of Islamic trends signifies a deep indigenous Middle Eastern process of a modern reconsecration of the ancient civilization, then the Islamic views of Israel and the conflict may persist for a long while and may manifest a great staying power. In the words of one recent commentator: 'We may be entering an era in which the motivating factor against Israel will not be Arab nationalism, nor Arab unity, but an increasingly religious climate which could foment processes leading to war . . .'[1] If this should turn out to have been the case, then in retrospect the year 1988 will be seen to have been a most crucial time in the development of the process.

Notes

1. Alouph Hareven, 'Is another Arab war coalition possible?', *Jerusalem Quarterly*, no. 49, winter 1989, p. 113.

4

Jewish Fundamentalists in Israel and Secular Modernity

ELIEZER SCHWEID

A story current in Israeli debates on problems of relations between religious and secular, records a memorable meeting between Israel's first Prime Minister, David Ben Gurion, and the notorious rabbinic authority of the fundamentalist community in Bnei Brak, Rabbi Avraham Yishaya Karlitz, known after his book as the 'Hazon Ish' (The Vision of Man). It was during the very first years of the state when Ben Gurion was concerned with the problem of enlisting young women to the Israeli Defence Forces. He was interested in a wide national consensus so he paid a visit to the Hazon Ish at home, a rare gesture of respect and goodwill, with the hope of moving this influential halakhic authority towards an understanding of the Zionist view.

There are some variations of detail in the accounts of their conversation. One essential point is, however, quite clear. Ben Gurion failed to achieve his aim. He faced a firm demand to comply with what this fundamentalist rabbinic authority considered as the only faithful halakhic decision.

In his attempt to make his position palpably clear the Hazon Ish used—so it is related—a parable: 'When two carriages oppose each other in a narrow road, it is the vacant one which must turn aside, wait, and let the loaded carriage have its way!' Ben Gurion, deeply hurt, retorted: 'Are you considering us, the secular Zionists, vacant vessels? After all it is we who built the Land of Israel and established the Jewish state!'

Eliezer Schweid is John and Golda Cohen Professor of Jewish philosophy at the Hebrew University of Jerusalem. His many works include *Jewish Nationhood* (1972), *Israel at the Crossroads* (1973), *The Faith of Israel and its Culture* (1977), *A History of Modern Jewish Philosophy* (1978), *Judaism and Secular Culture* (1981), *The Cycle of the Jewish Year* (1984), *Between Zionism and Judaism* (1985) and *Introduction to Jewish Thought in the Twentieth Century* (forthcoming). This article is an edited version of a lecture delivered to the Institute of Jewish Affairs on 20 February 1989.

One may assume that this was no news for the Hazon Ish. One may even concede that he was aware of the fact that only through the instrumentality of the state could his fundamentalist community come back to active life, and even flourish after the total destruction of the major Jewish religious centres in Eastern Europe during the Holocaust.

Yet it seems that he was not too greatly impressed by Ben Gurion's argument. Even then the fundamentalist community in Israel was on the way to recovery from a long period of inferiority. Achievements in terms of secular culture and material civilization were taken for granted and did not evoke much respect. One had of course the benefit of use, but could it be considered a worthy load for a Jewish carriage? Where Jewishness and Judaism were concerned, only the strict traditional faith and only the strict halakhic norms were considered adequate contents in the eyes of the rabbi. Therefore, when he was questioned about a problem relating to faithfulness to the Jewish way of life, the Hazon Ish could not regard Ben Gurion's carriage in any other way. Whatever loads there may have been on that carriage, for him, they were not Jewish. So it was clearly and simply an empty vessel, which eventually might again be loaded with contents taken from the over-loaded carriage, moving heavily in the opposite direction.

Looking at the parable from the point of view of secular ideology, the Hazon Ish has reproduced, in the simile of a movement in two opposite directions, the classical secular image of orthodoxy in general and of fundamentalism in particular.

From a 'progressive' point of view all the trends within the orthodox Jewish fold were considered anachronistic. They lagged behind modernity *at their best*, because when speaking of fundamentalism it was seen not only as lagging behind the progress of modernity; it was a reaction, a movement backwards, a retreat to the darkness of the Middle Ages. To progressives, this meant that orthodoxy was doomed to oblivion; in two or three generations it should have disappeared for good.

Modernist ideologues, historians and sociologists were aware of the fact that orthodoxy, even in its fundamentalist version, was not a mere 'remnant' of the past. As all the other Jewish religious movements of the nineteenth century, it was also an effect of modernity. Paradoxically, even the rejection of everything new could be in itself a major innovation. The authentic old tradition was dynamic, open to necessary changes, attuned to flowing historical situations. One could therefore claim that there was an element of continuity in the progressive movement and a change in the 'petrification' of fundamentalism. However, it was generally accepted that fundamentalism moved backwards to the past. It was considered by modernist scholars and thinkers as a blind refusal, a retreat.

And it seemed that this classical stance towards fundamentalism could be substantiated quite convincingly when studied in the context of the nineteenth century or even the first decades of the twentieth century. Moreover it could be justified even by the self-image of the fundamentalist rabbinic leadership itself. They were painfully aware that they lagged behind the main historical process. They could not but recognize their inadequacy to respond successfully to economic, social and political conditions. They were determined in their refusal, but they could not avoid the costs of their refusal. The younger generation was deserting in large numbers, tempted out of the fundamentalist home. Whilst the secularist elite proved to be prosperous, active and creative, fundamentalism was very close to losing its battle against the historical dynamic. It took all the emotional energy of fanaticism, based on a fundamentalist belief in a supernatural messianic intervention, merely to survive.

There were then sufficient reasons for the self-assumed sense of victory in the secular camp. As to the future, they could see no cause for anxiety. When the Zionist enterprise would reach the phase of establishing a state, they could see no reason to doubt its secular, modern character. It would be either a liberal democracy or a socialist utopia. In both cases, religion, mainly represented by modernist versions, would remain a private affair.

Against this background one may surmise the feeling of disappointment in the hearts of many secular leaders when the hoped-for historical moment arrived, and they could not but admit that their calculations were somewhat inaccurate. Apparently, some important factors had escaped their attention. Not only did they have to face the necessity of making concessions for the sake of a quite considerable orthodox community, but far more than that, they also had to recognize the beginning of a reverse historical development. For strange as it may seem, precisely because of the instrumentality of the state, an enhanced process of revival began in the orthodox camp. Moreover, the fundamentalist groups began then their upward movement, aspiring to lead the entire orthodox community.

For the progressive left in Israel all this came as a completely unexpected development. Were they not so alienated from the use of theological language they would have called it a 'miracle'. Suddenly, they witnessed the strange revival of semi-East European *shtetlach* in Jerusalem, in Bnei Brak, then in other towns and cities of Israel.

But former ideological positions are not easily abandoned. The Israeli radical secularists still strongly believed that they confronted merely an historical setback. For in their eyes, orthodoxy in general and fundamentalism in particular were still 'petrified remnants of the Middle Ages', 'reactionary forces' or 'primitive retreats'.

Radical secularists opt for a political explanation for this revival. It may be the result of grave political mistakes, rooted in the historical conditions of absorbing immigration from many cultures, and of defects in Israel's constitution. With constitutional re-enactment the whole fanatic anachronism would duly vanish like a shadow in the sun. But such an explanation is no longer valid in the post-World War II context, and in the context of a post-modern Western culture, which has been developed in the state of Israel.

Orthodoxy, with its fundamentalist 'avant-garde', has succeeded in installing its communities into the fabric of a secularist economy, society and politics. For good or bad orthodoxy, with all its extremes, must be conceived as part and parcel of a post-modern Jewish peoplehood, especially as it has been developed in the biggest centres of the Jewish people, namely in Israel and the USA.

This is not to deny the cause for anxiety from a secular humanist point of view. Jewish orthodoxy, and fundamentalism even more so, has a variety of negative traits. It may corrupt some vital systems of Israeli society, its democratic laws and its Zionist morality. Israeli society should therefore find the means to protect itself against these dangers. But it seems that this will not be done successfully unless it is realized that the negative traits of fundamentalism are indicative not only of its segregated 'anachronistic' existence. Rather it reflects certain faults and weaknesses inherent in Israel's post-modern Jewish society in its entirety. So much so because orthodoxy, including its fundamentalist extremes, is now growing on the soil of secular modernity itself, either through the instrumentality of secular modernity, or as a direct and adequate response to certain aspects of secular modernity. In other words, orthodoxy, with its fundamentalist extremes, related to modernity both as recipients of its advantages, and as respondents to its faults and weaknesses, especially with regard to the problems of maintaining a full and unique Jewish identity. This being the case, one may perhaps discover, besides orthodoxy's weaknesses and fundamentalist abuses, even some possible positive contributions in terms of society, culture and spiritual values.

If we act not solely out of frustration and hostility, but rather in keeping with the values of democracy and pluralism, we should protect ourselves against the dangers of fanaticism, yet strive to include these living Jewish communities in our pluralist vision. The main response should be a positive effort to amend faults, confront dilemmas and solve cultural problems within our secular culture, the very faults, dilemmas and problems which motivate much of the growth, expansion and influence of post-modern fundamentalism.

The first question to be considered in this context is: what made it possible for the fundamentalist communities to install themselves in the fabric of Jewish Israeli society?

Economically, the fundamentalist communities have succeeded in gaining their social emancipation. They have been emancipated from relative poverty and reached the middle class. This has been achieved with the help of political means. But we should be aware of the complexity of such an argument. Political organization is also a function of economic resources; one cannot begin without finance. It should therefore be acknowledged that in the second half of our century the fundamentalist community also succeeded in adapting itself to the modern economic system, through a variety of wealth-generating professions. They were now, at last, able to achieve their economic and political emancipation without being coerced or tempted to neglect any of their religious absolutes in traditional Torah studies, observance of strict halakhic norms, family and congregational life-style.

Politically, however, the fundamentalist leadership in Israel did change attitudes, and manifestly so. From a policy of hermetic segregation they have developed a policy of political intervention. Forming political parties, they became involved fully in the political game, winning the economic, organizational and ideological profits of participation in governmental enterprises.

Being concerned only with representing the interests of their communities, they were able to use their relatively small power very effectively. Very soon they mastered the art of political manipulation, and it must be said that sometimes they were to prove themselves to be superior to their secularist teachers. The rising tide of bitterness in the secular camp after the victory of the fundamentalist parties in the 1988 elections was at least partially the result of that sort of 'double shame'. But be that as it may, the fact of political integration as equals cannot be denied. And again, it should be noted that this was achieved without having to pay any outwardly visible 'religious prize'.

What is behind this manifestly dramatic change? Here, we come to the basic questions. First, a generally accepted observation: paradoxically, segregated and ideologically non-pluralist minorities are the first beneficiaries of a truly tolerant and pluralist society. Existing as minorities that have neither chance nor aspiration to change society in which they live towards their own ideals, they adopt, at least at the start, a neutral approach. They are not responsible for the nation or for the state. They are responsible only for their communal autonomy. In their communal realm they can fully extend their unique life-style, and doing so they are not disturbed from the outside. Their language, dress and manners may seem a little strange but in a pluralist society this fact only stimulates a sense of curiosity. There exists a variety of strange modes of behaviour in our late twentieth century societies. The *haredi* type is not the strangest of them all.

Yet there is something more to be observed in this context, for in a really pluralist society there is not only tolerance towards different communities, but also an openness to let different minorities have an impact on the general public domain. Democratically speaking, they have the right to feel at home everywhere—in their city or in their state.

Admittedly, Israeli society is far from an ideally tolerant society, but because of its unique situation it has established by law a public domain which is wide open to the demands of religious orthodoxy. The fundamentalist community was able to exploit this to their advantage once their leadership realized how much could be achieved through organized political pressure.

The use of pluralist principles and toleration, without complying with their underlying ethical values, or the use of political power without a feeling or responsibility for the nation as a whole, may be described as cynical, even parasitical. Many secular leaders in Israel indeed tend to use these terms.

But the fundamentalist parties were only able to use their relatively small political power as efficiently as they did because they were taught and encouraged to do so by their bigger predecessors. After all, the small religious parties were not the inventors nor the initiators of that sort of political game. They entered an existing market in which a highly compartmentalized society was represented by many political parties, each one taking care first and foremost of its own narrow interests. Claiming to be nationally responsible, they testified to their real priorities when they proved ready to form coalitions on the basis of: 'You seek to fulfill your religious demands in the public domain and let us have our interests in secular areas'.

The religious parties were generally not more and not less cynical than other parties. They acted on common ground, and as a part of a system. To change this behaviour the system would have to be changed and this could not be achieved through a one-sided attack on the fundamentalist parties. The secularist parties would have to confront their political system and their political ethics. By doing so, they might reduce the manipulative power of the small parties and thus keep the fundamentalist minority in its proportionate place.

But the main factors are more profound. It has already been stated that Israeli society is highly compartmentalized. This fact is one of the most problematic characteristics of the post-modern secularist syndrome. It is a source of many faults and a hindrance to the development of a renewed Jewish culture. One other aspect of this characteristic is the notorious tendency towards narrow expertism, combined with a decline in the demand to belong to a whole, through creative participation in a wide and general concept of culture.

The tendency towards narrow expertise which is felt in almost every area— the economy, administration, technology, exact sciences, even the arts—has opened the way for narrow experts, who are efficient enough to contribute in their particular profession without being expected to absorb any amount of general culture as a social precondition for the use of their expertise. They can participate in a certain defined area of secular civilization while remaining clearly outside all its other domains, so that they may stay both in and out.

Many experts in finance, technology, administration, and also in the exact sciences and the arts, are now at the same time religious fundamentalists. The required expertise can be acquired in a relatively short course of study, thereafter it can be practised successfully without any necessity to neglect strict Halakha, to cut short traditional Torah studies, or to reflect critically on the assumptions of fundamentalist belief. In the post-modern secularist system, one can participate in one compartment for the sake of economic sustenance, then return to the main compartment for the sake of social and spiritual values.

This is in fact the ideal fulfilment of the fundamentalist stance, formulated against the challenge of the Enlightenment in the nineteenth century. A Jew should first secure his complete measure of religious education, then he may study whatever he needs for the sake of economic sustenance, but not as an end in itself, only as a means to an end. The distressing fact was that at the beginning of the Enlightenment the accepted social ideal of education hardly allowed for such solutions, while now it is easily achieved. Every member of the secular community can function in the one segment for which he is best equipped. He does not identify himself spiritually with his profession, for it does not require of him adherence to any philosophy or creed. Secular activity at its best is spiritually neutral and halakhically permissible, for it is merely instrumental. For the sake of meaning he moves to his inner sanctum of family, synagogue or school—there he finds his full expression as a believing Jew.

The fundamentalists of the early nineteenth century turned their backs on the Enlightenment, as well as its consequences—emancipation. Both the national and the humanist ideals of secular education were conceived then as a complete cultural alternative to traditional religious education. To be 'enlightened' meant then to comply with a certain humanist set of values, to internalize a certain humanist *Weltanschauung* through a comprehensive philosophy, and to accept a definite life-style comprising aesthetic values and cultural manners. Much importance has been attached to professional expertise, but this was only one component of an educational package which had to be accepted in its entirety. For in order to be accepted as a professional, the individual had first to be accepted into a certain cultural milieu, and this meant a change in outward appearance as well as in the inner core of personal values. The traditional religious response was total rejection.

But this is no longer the case in the post-modern secular culture. Our secular education has long neglected the humanist ideal of a full 'general' education, which distinguishes the elite and the middle class. There is no longer a clearly defined, standard package of higher culture. One needs, of course, a certain common basis of language and the essential information required for general orientation. But apart from this everyone is invited into the cultural supermarket to choose pragmatically according to his priorities, relating to knowledge and profession. Which means that now a member of the fundamentalist community may also have his choice. He is not compelled to confront a complete alternative to his religious education. He is not facing a spiritual challenge to his religious belief, and what is more, in this he is not any different from his secular colleagues in the same professions as they also do not attach much spiritual meaning to their knowledge. Why then should he reject the offer of a good profession?

And there is yet another development which facilitates a practical participation in modern civilization: the collapse of the variety of secular ideologies and philosophies which have informed the main secular movements in Israel.

These ideologies served as a unifying factor. Through an ideology one could identify with one's society, nation, history, as a complete whole. It signified orientation in the world, a final end, a meaning. Now there is nothing of the sort, at least on the popular level.

One generation ago, when a secularist Israeli was asked what his secularism consisted of, what he meant when he called himself a secularist, he would have produced a ready answer. He was a socialist, a Zionist, a combination of both, a communist, a liberal and so on. Nowadays secularist Israelis reply to the same question with a negative answer—they are not religious. But when a positive answer is requested, in most cases they will admit that they really do not know.

We have returned to our point of departure. It is now understandable why it is relatively easy for a fundamentalist to use the instrumentality of secular civilization, yet keep his outward position. We can also go beyond that to an understanding of his growing sense of superiority, the sense so directly articulated in the parable of the loaded versus the vacant carriages. The rabbi was so sure of his superiority because he knew exactly what he was representing in spiritual terms, in faith, in life-style, in ethical orientation. And he also knew that his secular rivals hardly knew what he represented, and that this is because their knowledge of their own culture, from its very sources, was wavering. The fundamentalists see their secular compatriots as rarely identifying themselves with their basic cultural values, rarely able to manifest those values for 'self-fulfilment'. They are easily tempted by sensuality, as their morality is relativist, permissive, loose. Besides, their life-style lacks true meaning, they have no roots. One should have mercy upon them, yet they may be dangerous too. So one should try to teach them, albeit cautiously, lest one be infected by their vicious ways. First one should separate oneself from their society, then, one may try to reach and preach.

This means that the fundamentalist leadership considers itself now not only as entitled to participate in secular material achievements; they have also something to offer in spiritual terms. They believe that they have the right answers for ethical and spiritual problems created by secularism, problems that secularism itself cannot solve.

Thus secularism became, in the eyes of the fundamentalists, the equivalent of spiritual dullness. Worse than that, secularism became identified with idolatry. From the fundamentalist point of view, the secularists admire the ideals of material success, sensual satisfaction, earthly power. At their best they keep the code of a utilitarian morality. Fundamentalists aver that secularism became a different reality from what had been expected by its false prophets. The hopes of social ethical progress, of spiritual elevation throughout humanism, have been tragically reversed. In our age we have witnessed the bestiality which may come out of godless humanity. But even in its best political form, secularism has created a deep crisis, and it does not possess the values and the moral authority needed for a solution. Authentic religion is the only viable answer.

It is the combination of being able both to participate in some of the material and political achievements of modernity, and to criticize it as if from the outside, that, for fundamentalists, constitutes the essential difference between yesterday and today. Only through this combination can a fundamentalist preacher claim sufficient knowledge of the truth about secular culture and present his answers as relevant to dilemmas raised from the depth of secular existence. It is not my intention to propose acceptance or rejection of these simplistic views about the 'essence' of secularism as a way of life. The relevant fact in the context of this discussion is that the fundamentalist preacher has succeeded in establishing a certain communication with those outside of his community; he has even succeeded in convincing some of his listeners to cross the border. There exists a certain reservoir of secular Israelis, not so large as to endanger the majority of the secular camp, but not so small as to be considered insignificant, which is ready to lend a sympathetic ear. The preaching of the fundamentalist has produced a positive 'feedback'. It has materialized in the form of the so-called 'movement of return', the *ba'aley te'shuva*, from secularism back to the fundamentalist creed.

It should be stressed that this movement has been initiated only by the fundamentalist community and not by other trends in orthodoxy. For the fundamentalists this sort of activity became significant, so they were prepared to invest a considerable amount of energy and finance to keep it going. As already stated, the relative success of this movement in recent years does not signify any real turn in Israeli society and cannot endanger the secular majority. Still, it has a certain significance both to the fundamentalist community and the secular one. For the fundamentalist community it is a reassessment. It reaffirms its claim to be relevant to its modern surroundings, not lagging behind modernity. The fundamentalist preacher interprets this re-affirmation as a proof of his superiority.

A positive response to the fundamentalist challenge is significant also for the secularist community. It brings home the recognition that something indeed has gone wrong. That the dilemmas described by the fundamentalist preachers are not mere inventions; they do exist and create a wide feeling of crisis. There is a crisis of identity, a problem of rootlessness, a lack of spiritual meaning and of loneliness. And there are those who are attracted by the solution proposed by the fundamentalists.

For the fundamentalist community these facts are sources of strength, persistence and pride. But it would be right for the secularists to see that their own crisis, produced by an over-compartmentalized and spiritually impoverished culture, is the ground on which fundamentalism grows. The secularists should be aware that they encourage the persistence and expansion of fundamentalism, mainly by failing to confront their own spiritual, ethical and cultural problems by applying their own values.

If this analysis is correct and fundamentalism is growing not only because it draws on resources of the past, but also because it is a response to the tensions of the present, then the fundamentalists cannot be unaffected by the basic process of modernity, namely change. The fundamentalist community only pretends to remain stable. In fact it has changed a great deal; it keeps on changing, absorbing, consciously and unconsciously, much from its secular surroundings.

There are already significant structural changes, first of all in the status of women in the family, and in the community—significant because women function in that community in a peculiar way, as agents of some elements of secular social values and secular culture. There are also manifest changes in terms of organization and leadership. This must effect further changes in terms of education, culture and social life-style.

Fundamentalism is now to be considered not as a remnant of a former age, but rather as a living component of the cultural syndrome of our age. It is sustained by modern resources and motivated by modern crises and dilemmas. Therefore, if we rightly feel endangered by its fanaticism, we must have a positive response to its challenge, trying to solve the tensions, problems and crises of our secular society out of its own moral and spiritual Jewish and humanistic resources.

If this were done, we may hope to create sufficient common ground for a pluralist *modus vivendi* in Israel, and the Zionist dream of a Jewish cultural renaissance may come true. If not, what is probably going to happen is what always happens when two half-empty half-loaded carriages are approaching each other in a narrow road, while each of the two typical Israeli drivers firmly believes that the carriage rushing towards him is empty, and his own is the only one loaded.

Part B
THE MIDDLE EAST

5

The Changing Concerns and Shifting Priorities of Arab Politics

P. J. VATIKIOTIS

To explain the changing concerns and shifting priorities of the Arab states in the Middle East one must point to the changes in the Arab political arena that have occurred in the last 15 to 20 years. Ten years ago Israel concluded and signed its first peace treaty with an Arab state, after 20 years of periodic warfare. The Israel-Egypt peace treaty of 1979 was a direct result of the Camp David Accords signed the previous year. Its immediate result was that Egypt, the weightiest Arab state, ended its state of belligerency and recognized the state of Israel. Israel returned Sinai to Egypt. An outstanding, unsettled territorial dispute, the Taba enclave, remained. Negotiations for its settlement were protracted; they ended with the ruling by the International Court in The Hague in favour of Egypt. The repercussions of this treaty on inter-Arab politics consisted of an immediate attempt to ostracize Egypt from the community of Arab states and a decision to stand fast against further negotiated peace settlements between other Arab states and Israel. Another consequence of the treaty was the reorientation of Egypt's external policy towards the West and the evolution of a close relationship with the USA. This reorientation in itself ended the earlier active and central role of the Soviet Union in the region.

It ought to be noted, however, that despite all the appendices to the treaty providing for the promotion of trade, commerce and tourism between Israel and Egypt, so far the effort—and traffic—has been strictly one-sided: from Israel. The Egyptians settled for what they called a cold or 'frozen peace'.[1]

P.J. Vatikiotis is professor of politics with reference to the Near and Middle East at the University of London. He is the author of, among other works, *The Egyptian Army in Politics* (1961), *Politics and the Military in Jordan* (1967), *The Modern History of Egypt* (1969), *Conflict in the Middle East* (1971), *Nasser and His Generation* (1978) and *Arab and Regional Politics in the Middle East* (1984).

And yet the treaty survived the Israeli invasion of Lebanon in 1982 and the *intifada*, the Palestinian uprising in the occupied territories of the West Bank and Gaza in 1987–88. Egypt herself withstood and weathered Arab opprobrium, ostracism and opposition.

A more significant aspect of the treaty was the end of a collective Arab policy towards Israel, the Palestine question and relations with the Western or Eastern superpowers. In fact, that kind of collective stand was eroded by the 1967 Six Day War and virtually disappeared with the demise of President Nasser of Egypt in 1970. After this there was no single radical Arab national leader who could impose any collective Arab policy. To this extent, individual Arab states experienced a change of concerns and a shift in their national priorities: they became more concerned with the maintenance and protection of their respective regimes, and acquired at least theoretically a measure of initiative and flexibility in the conduct of external policy.

The Impact of the Gulf War

Other events of the last decade contributed further to the changing concerns and shifting priorities of the Arab states. Most important of these was the protracted Iran–Iraq War in the Gulf. Initially a war arising from a territorial dispute between Iran and Iraq over the control of the Shatt el Arab at the top of the Gulf, it was nurtured by the more subtle and occasionally open support by the Iranians for the Shia community in Iraq against the Ba'th regime of President Saddam Hussein in Baghdad. The war also soon developed into a sectarian conflict between the Shia revolutionary regime of Khomeini in Tehran and the Sunni Ba'th regime of Saddam Hussein in Baghdad. Relevant to inter-Arab politics was the ethnic Arab versus Persian character the conflict soon acquired. Oil-rich Arab states, especially Saudi Arabia, came to the aid of Iraq with massive financing. The Iraqi regime had to accommodate itself with its erstwhile enemy, Saudi Arabia. Even more significant, the threat posed by Iran forced the Arab states to abandon their earlier hostility to Egypt and actively seek her support for the protection and defence of the smaller, weaker Arab Gulf states, as well as Iraq, in the war against Iran. In order to do this they had to re-admit Egypt back into Arab councils as a full member. And this was consecrated in the Amman Arab League summit in December 1987. It also implied Arab acceptance of Egypt's right to conclude a peace treaty with their common enemy, Israel. Inevitably, the moderation of Egypt's position and policy regarding Israel and the USA was gradually adopted by the other Arab states. In fact, with the heightened Iranian threat in the Gulf several of them actively sought the protection of the United States (for example, Kuwait) and the procurement of vast quantities of arms from it.

Such a shift affected the Arab states' approach to the Palestinian issue. In inclining towards at least less belligerent declarations about the conflict with

Israel and the admission that accommodation in the form of a peaceful settlement was possible, these states were signalling their concern with different priorities. Israel's invasion of Lebanon and the dislocation of the Palestine Liberation Organization's (PLO) structures and bases in that country were followed by Syrian manipulation of that organization, its fragmentation and internecine conflict. To that extent the PLO lost its earlier ability to influence inter-Arab politics or to extract special treatment from rich Arab state patrons. Thus in both the Amman and Algiers summits (in November 1987 and June 1988 respectively) relatively modest financial assistance was forthcoming. In short, the PLO lost the centrality in Arab state councils it had enjoyed in the recent past. The shift in the priorities of Arab states tended in itself to Palestinianize the Arab–Israeli conflict further; in practical terms to bring or pit the major adversaries—Israel and the Palestinians—more directly against one another with significant implications for the peaceful, or otherwise, resolution of the conflict.

In the long term, the fairly bleak economic prospects most Arab states face will perhaps have the greatest impact on their politics. It is not simply the decline in oil revenues which forced them into more circumspect domestic policies and more moderate external perceptions. The missed opportunities to restructure their economies and reorder their economic priorities during the halcyon days of the 1970s oil boom with its huge revenues, has condemned them, more or less, to economic stagnation. Politically dangerous have been the socially dislocating consequences of rampant consumerism in the economies saturated with cash—but cash very unevenly distributed. As the available cash dwindled, governments, in the absence of any serious structural economic reform, were unable to feed the growing mass of urban unemployed for whom immigration to the north was more difficult than a decade ago. Food riots and other disturbances have been a thin veil for a more serious extremist religious challenge to the political establishment, as the October 1988 events in Algiers demonstrated.

In practical terms the Gulf War was still simmering, while negotiations for a peace settlement dragged on. The jockeying for political position and advantage among both the belligerents and the immediate gallery of spectators/neighbours was in full swing: Saudi Arabia, for example, was trying to reassure Iran about its peaceful intentions, and its willingness to assist it with the task of reconstruction. Syria was already betraying its intention to embarrass Iraq over the Kurds in the hope of countering its own pro-Iranian stand throughout the Gulf War: a revival of the Damascus–Baghdad rivalry in inter-Arab councils.

Iraq's own immediate concerns after the ceasefire seemed to be the further brutal supression of the Kurdish autonomy movement, by chemical weapons if necessary, normalization of its relations with Egypt and Saudi Arabia, reassessment of its inter-Arab policy and maintenance of good relations with both Washington and Moscow in the hope of continuing to receive very substantial assistance from both East and West. An additional concern was reconstruction after a devastating nine-year war. Iraq had to revive its oil industry—infrastructure and ancillary structure—which provided its single largest export. This and the Kurdish minority issue constituted a tricky area of Iraqi diplomacy, especially as they involved domestic security, the relationship with neighbouring Turkey and Iraq's standing in the international community. The re-establishment of a pattern of relations with the Arab Gulf states was another major Iraqi preoccupation. The expansion of trade, primarily with the West, was crucial for the health of Iraqi state revenues.

The battle over oil intensified once the ceasefire took hold in the Gulf. Anxious to increase much needed revenue, Iraq and Iran will seek to maximize their oil exports which could force a drop in world prices, especially as other major Arab exporters—Saudi Arabia, Kuwait and the Gulf states—may have to lower their oil prices in order to compete and stay in the market. The Gulf War was a serious constraint on Iranian and Iraqi disruptive or revolutionary policies in the region. The export of Iranian-style Islamic revolution and Iranian oil was severely curtailed during the war, as were Saddam Hussein's aggressive attentions towards Kuwait and other Gulf states.

The economic consequences of the end of the Gulf War will very much influence the political fortunes of several of the Arab states. Moreover, the Arab states have entered a period in which familiar and unfamiliar economic forces rather than too familiar political ones pose the main threat to the survival of their regimes. The popularity and survival of their governments will, in these countries, depend more on what they do at home, that is, on their domestic policies.

Social and Economic Realities

Despite massive oil revenues of $1.5 trillion in a decade and massive investment in infrastructure, there has been no fundamental restructuring of the economy of any of the Arab oil states. They remain heavily dependent on the oil industry and on the industrialized world for their economic survival. The tremendous growth in their financial resources has only widened the economic gaps within their own respective societies and between them and other Arab states. This may be taken as an overall indication of the economic imbalance among the Arab states. When one looks more closely at a breakdown of basic economic and social data the imbalance acquires ominous proportions.

Forty-five per cent of the Arab world's 198 million population is under 15 years of age; 49 per cent of it illiterate. Only 28 per cent of the 195 million hectares of land or 14 million square kilometres is farmed or cultivated. In a relatively short period of 30 years the urban population in the Arab world increased from 27 to 46 per cent, and will reach 60 per cent in the year 2000, and all of it concentrated in a very few large cities: for example, 4 million, or one-third of Syria's population, live in the capital city Damascus, 11 million in Cairo. These masses end up in non-productive employment, further exacerbating the structural economic imbalance of these countries. Clearly not all who migrate to the city find work, thus adding to the economic and social tensions which erupt periodically into serious riots.

Despite the ideological commitments of a succession of new and more radical nationalist leaders and rulers in several of the Arab states, in some cases massive foreign aid has been added to astronomical income from oil revenues. Thus, despite a very high annual rate of economic growth in the 1970s in particular (over 8 per cent per annum), industry's contribution to gross domestic product (GDP) remained low, between 6 and 8 per cent. It remains below 10 per cent in the Arab states in the 1980s. Nor has there been any appreciable industrial diversification.

This suggests that the Arab states remain single-commodity cash export economies: oil in Arabia, the Gulf and Iraq, phosphates in Jordan, cotton in Egypt. Moreover, most of these industries are situated or concentrated around urban centres, so that there is even less development in rural areas, yet another source or cause of imbalance.

Despite its declining contribution to the economy, agriculture still employs 50 per cent of the workforce in the Arab states. Because of its rather low productivity, none of these countries enjoy 'food security'. In most staples productivity has fallen in the last decade making it essential to spend a great deal of money importing them. Food imports by Arab states have risen from $100 million in 1970 to $32 billion in 1988. Egypt alone imports 70 per cent of its food at an annual cost of about $5 billion. The Gulf states and Saudi Arabia depend entirely on imported food. All of this suggests that agricultural development has not kept pace with the growth of population (which will be 300 million in these states in the year 2000), and the food imports bill will reach $200 billion per annum in the year 2000.

Egypt, Syria and Jordan do not face a food problem only. The central issue related to further agricultural development is that of water resources, irrigation, power supply and land reclamation. This in turn is influenced or affected by certain political conditions, like relations with neighbouring states: Egypt with the Sudan (and Ethiopia), Syria with Turkey (and Iraq over dams on the river Euphrates); Jordan with Israel.

The economy of the Arab world also exhibits an imbalance in manpower resources. The booming oil economies in Arabia and the Gulf elicited an influx of massive migrant labour from the economically less rich Arab states, especially Egypt and Jordan. The remittances of this migrant labour force to their home countries swelled the revenues of those states. At the same time they represented a veritable drain of skilled and unskilled labour from those countries. However, with the recession in the oil industry a large proportion of this migrant labour force was dismissed. Jordan, which in the last 20 years has expanded greatly its educational facilities, now has a surplus of university graduates, engineers, physicians and teachers who, in the absence of adequate employment opportunities, must also emigrate. Egypt experienced this difficulty as early as the 1960s. The imbalance that manifests itself is one of an Arab East possessing wealth, at least theoretically, but not much else. For example, Saudi Arabia with a population of under 10 million has a national per capita GDP of $7,500, whereas Egypt with a population of 50 million has a per capita GDP of $1,100.

Nor did the booming oil industry promote greater Arab economic integration, let alone unity. On the contrary, it heightened political tensions between the Arab states and sharpened their differences: for example, Syria against Iraq, the Arab states against Egypt. Jordan remained greatly dependent on financial subsidies and aid from the rich oil states. In 1987 it received $450 million. At the Baghdad summit of 1978 the oil-rich states pledged aid to the so-called confrontation states—Syria and Jordan—and the PLO. Due to the recession in the oil industry, Kuwait suspended aid to them, and aid to Jordan has diminished by over $100 million a year. Syria looked to Iran for aid ($400 million in 1987) and thus sided with that country in the Gulf War. Following the inevitable rapprochement with Egypt in the face of the Iranian threat, Saudi Arabia and Kuwait have undertaken to help Egypt repay a $5 billion outstanding military debt to the US.

The fall in oil prices and the dollar therefore reduced the purchasing power of oil revenue and led to deficits in the balance of payments of the Arab states. The resulting austerity in Arabia and the Gulf states affected the labour-exporting states of Egypt and Jordan. In fact, Jordan's financial plight is serious and its economic prospects in the 1990s rather bleak.

In the meantime, expenditure on weapons and military procurement remains very high despite the decline in revenue. This has resulted in a swelling of the external debt of these states and huge budget deficits. Despite a $40 billion external debt for Egypt and $4.5 billion for Syria, there are, according to latest estimates, some 3,500 combat aircraft in Arab air forces. Egypt has spent over $7 billion on military hardware, and now has a $5.5 billion defence budget (1987), or nearly a fourth of its state budget; Jordan: $4 billion; Syria: nearly $9 billion, or 30 per cent of the state budget; Iraq: $25 billion; Kuwait: $1 billion.

Political Implications

Even though statistics for the Arab world should be treated with caution, these figures imply serious economic problems for the Arab states, the political implications of which may be incalculable. Thus the 1988 Algiers Arab League summit was quite circumspect and in fact brought to an end the ten-year programme of 1978. Following on from the Amman summit of

November 1987, it highlighted the new economic concerns of individual Arab states, and emphasized their political priorities of defending their respective regimes in the face of the Iranian threat in the Gulf, which they viewed as a challenge to Arab primacy in the Peninsula and the Gulf. To this extent, these summits also highlighted the keen interest, led by Jordan, to bring Egypt back into inter-Arab councils because of its political weight and potential military protection role. The summits also marked a new departure in the perception of the Arab conflict with Israel. Tending to shift the burden of the immediate responsibility for the resolution of that conflict on to the Palestinians themselves, the Arab states at the summit accelerated the Palestinianization of the Arab–Israeli conflict. This process is evident from the *intifada* on the West Bank and in Gaza, King Hussein's disengagement from the West Bank in July, the November Palestine National Council (PNC) meeting in Algiers and Mubarak's attempt, along with Hussein, to construct a new 'moderate constellation of Arab states' to promote a negotiated peace settlement with Israel.[2]

Whether the Arab states will be able to feed their populations by the end of the twentieth century is no longer a hypothetical question nor is it an exercise in futurology. It is now the nightmare of all politicians and Arab rulers in these states and lies at the heart of political survival. Food and water may yet replace weapons as these states' most expensively sought-after commodities. They will render irrelevant our more traditional stereotypes of political analysis for that part of the world, and render obsolete all their related shibboleths. Thus it will no longer be possible in the 1990s to wax lyrical about such themes as Arab unity and the prizes of economic development based on astronomical oil and gas revenues. We may even witness urgent rescue missions by the industrial world to bring food and water to some of these countries, and to help them create employment opportunities for their young populations, short of simply propelling them to go north. Barring a miracle by imaginative leadership, we may yet witness more instances of the type of domestic conflict seen in Algeria in 1988, and possibly conflict between the worse off and better off states over scarce resources.

For a moment the October 1973 War seemed to break the spell of self-doubt and deep frustration, by providing the Arabs with a military victory of sorts—the crossing of the Canal (*ubur*) by the Egyptians. However, once on the East bank they were soon proclaiming themselves not victorious Arab soldiers but the triumphant descendants of Muhammad Ali Pasha and his son Ibrahim Pasha, the founders of modern Egypt.

In the aftermath of the October War the oil weapon revived dreams of power and past glory, Arab supremacy over Israel and Muslim supremacy over the Christian World. Yet before the decade had ended the dream was shattered and the expectations undermined. There were the American inspired Camp David Accords followed by the conclusion of a peace treaty between Egypt and Israel; war between Iraq and Iran broke out in the Gulf, representing a new threat to the Arab states and the 'Arab nation'; the Soviet forces invaded Afghanistan in support of a Communist regime in Kabul and in a war against indigenous Islamic resistance forces; Israel destroyed by direct air bombing the first Arab nuclear facility at Osirak near Baghdad; Israeli settlement of the occupied West Bank was accelerated.

For the Arabs, the Lebanon War marked the end of a decade of high expectations: the oil boom, and the accompanying virulent campaign against the West, were soon marred by deep frustration and disillusionment. A decade of the Arab quest for the reassertion of identity, when Arab Islamic values were pitted against those of Western materialist civilization and technology, ended in yet another experience of self-doubt and deep frustration.

Israel invaded Lebanon in order to destroy the PLO infrastructure and expel it from Beirut, yet no Arab state seriously considered going to the aid of the beleaguered Palestinians. The dream of Arab resurgence began to fade, and the pattern of Arab impotence repeated itself. Whilst some Arabs felt relieved that they were not dragged into the Lebanon mess, they all resented Israel more than ever before; so much so in fact that this resentment came to be expressed often in antisemitic and anti-Jewish terms. The question asked was why were the Arabs so powerless? Was their impotence due to their particular societies and culture? Or was their passivity during the Lebanon episode an expression of deep divisions among the Arab states, that is, the result of more mundane, practical weaknesses? Egypt was offered a role in this crisis of Arab confidence, when Yasser Arafat begged Egypt to intervene with Israel to stop the massive shelling of PLO positions in Beirut. Egypt was being perceived in a new Arab capacity because of her relationship with Israel; so, despite increased resentment against Israel, in reality a relationship with the Jewish state was now both useful and helpful.

Egypt

Interestingly, though the press in Egypt was virulently anti-Jewish during this crisis, Egypt was acting diplomatically and politically as a moderating catalyst in Arab–Israeli relations, with a new perception of the Arab–Israeli conflict developing in Iraq and ultimately even in the PLO. To the extent that the Lebanese crisis exposed the Arab world's lack of concerted or co-ordinated effort, it therefore improved Egypt's position and image as a positive moderating influence on the Arab states and in inter-Arab politics. At the same time Jordan became the focus of United States efforts to deliver the Palestinians in an expanded Camp David style peace process, in tandem with a US inspired Lebanon–Israel agreement in May 1983. But this was successfully negated by Syria. Saudi Arabia too, in its role as guardian of the interests of Lebanese Muslims, acted to prevent any accommodation with Israel.

Palestinianization of the Arab–Israeli conflict finally led to the proclamation of an independent Palestinian state at the November 1988 meeting of the Palestine National Council in Algiers. Immediately after that Algeria and Egypt restored full diplomatic relations. To what extent this was linked to Egypt's recognition of the proclaimed Palestinian state is a matter for speculation. What is clear is that developments on the Palestinian front seemed to accelerate Egypt's return to the centre, if not the leadership, of Arab affairs. In any event, the kind of state proclaimed by the Palestinians is a vindication of an old Egyptian Arab policy dating back to 1959–64. At that time, motivated by a policy of destabilizing the Hashemite regime in Jordan, and competing with Iraq and Syria for Arab leadership, President Nasser promoted the idea of a Palestinian entity (*al-Kiyan al-Falastini*), created the PLO and inspired an Egyptian proposal for a Palestinian state alongside Israel.[3] It proposed a state incorporating the East and West Banks and the Gaza Strip. Whilst it reflected Egypt's position regarding the future of the West Bank and Gaza, the scheme was opposed by Jordan as tantamount to the Palestinianization of Jordan. The objective too was to avoid a war with Israel, transfer the burden of responsibility to the Palestinians themselves and maintain Egyptian supremacy in Arab councils.

The Palestinians

In proclaiming their state, the Palestinians referred to the UN Partition Resolution 181 of 18 November 1947. They rejected the resolution then— what is it that makes them, and the Arab states, accept it now, 40 years later? The answer is in the economic, social and political changes I have already outlined, and this includes the new orientation and vital concerns of an Egypt at the centre of these developments, but maintaining its peace treaty with Israel.

For the Arab states, the economic factor is the main priority, and this is directly linked to security. If economic security factors demand at some point a peaceful settlement of their conflict with Israel, the Arab states will probably work towards achieving that end. In the meantime, the proclamation of a Palestinian state will constitute an object of inter-Arab disagreement and conflict, not unlike the 1959–64 period, when Egypt's initiative in founding the PLO brought it into conflict with Syria, Iraq and Jordan.

The difficulty the Arabs and the Palestinians have to overcome this time round if they desire to achieve a negotiated peace settlement between the PLO and Israel is the fact that the PLO was originally created in 1964 for the express purpose of liberating Palestine from Jewish control or occupation, that is, destroying the state of Israel. It would be highly unnatural for Israel to acquiesce in its own destruction or elimination. The crux of the matter is not terrorism or other related features of Palestinian resistance to Israel, nor is it the nature of the PLO. The principal obstacle remains the objective for which the organization was originally created by the Arab states.[4]

The more immediate aim of the recent intense diplomatic-political campaign by the Palestinians and the Arab states may not be so much the establishment of a Palestinian state on the West Bank and in Gaza as the extraction of United States recognition of the PLO and, by extension, the break up of the close United States–Israel relationship. They went some way towards achieving this on 15 November 1988, when the United States announced officially that it would be initiating direct talks with the PLO in Tunis. Tantamount to a recognition of the PLO by the United States, the announcement came in the wake of developments at the special UN General Assembly session on Palestine held in Geneva. The PLO chairman, Yasser Arafat, addressed the session on 13 November and then made a direct statement in a press conference recognizing the right of Israel to exist as a state and renouncing terrorism in all its forms. The US decision was also the result of intensive diplomacy behind the scenes by the Swedes and, significantly, the Egyptians. Egypt once again emerged as a powerful catalyst for further peace negotiations between the Arabs and Israel.

The American decision to hold direct talks with the PLO could be an epochal turning point in the 40-year Arab–Israeli conflict. Ostensibly, the Americans claim to be satisfied that Yasser Arafat has met their conditions for a dialogue: acceptance of UN Security Council Resolution 242, recognition of Israel's right to exist and the renunciation of terrorism in all its forms. Nevertheless, although it has the potential to transform the US–Israel relationship and to affect the delicate balance of forces in the Middle East, the dialogue between the PLO and the Americans is far from clear in its aims. Even as the dialogue began, the precise importance being attached to such factors as the PNC debates and resolutions, the *intifada* and the proclamation of a Palestinian state remained unclear. So too what might be expected of Israel and Jordan, and for that matter Syria. In the meantime, the PLO was left to deal with its own dissatisfied constituent parts.

The US–PLO dialogue may be a time-buying device intended to strengthen Arafat's moderation and neutralize his radical Palestinian detractors, as well as a preliminary or exploratory round of negotiations leading to direct talks between the PLO, Israel and Jordan. In the meantime, by recognizing the PLO the Americans have rid themselves of collective Arab pressure for the resolution of the conflict. The Americans may have soured their special relationship with Israel, but they have not endangered its security.

Notes

1. See 'Relations between Egypt and Israel, 1977–82', in P. J. Vatikiotis, *Arab and Regional Politics in the Middle East* (London 1984), pp. 226–39.

2. See P. J. Vatikiotis, 'Arab politics and security', *Global Affairs*, vol. 3, no. 4, pp. 99–113.

3. Ahmed Baha El Din, *Iqtirah Dawlat Filastin*, Beirut, January 1968, first published in the Cairo weekly, *al-Musawwar*, 13 October 1967.

4. See Moshe Shemesh, *The Palestinian Entity 1959–74. Arab Politics and the PLO* (London 1988).

6

Seeds of a Post-Khomeini Era: the First Decade of the Islamic Republic of Iran

BARRY RUBIN

The year 1988 brought dramatic changes for Iran and its Islamic government. During the previous decade, the country had already gone through a devastating revolution; a profound transformation of political and economic life; several waves of internal purges; a steep loss in revenue; an extended confrontation with the United States, its former closest ally; and eight years of bloody war causing hundreds of thousands of casualties plus massive devastation. In 1988, Iran was forced to end the Iran–Iraq War on terms it had always previously rejected and began the political transformation to a post-Khomeini era, which commenced with Khomeini's death in June 1989.

This article provides a portrait of contemporary Iran, the main events of 1987 and 1988, and key issues for the future.

Khomeini's Role

The Islamic Republic of Iran is ruled by a dictatorship with strong populist overtones. Ayatollah Ruhollah Khomeini, its unquestioned leader, united a heterogenous opposition to overthrow the Shah in 1979, directed the establishment of an Islamic government, destroyed rival claimants for power, confronted the United States in the hostage crisis and rallied the country in the face of Iraq's 1980 invasion.

Ironically, Khomeini's role fitted more closely with Iranian political traditions than with traditional Muslim thought. Iran's history has alternated between

Barry Rubin is a fellow at the Johns Hopkins University School of Advanced International Studies. He is author, among other works, of *Paved with Good Intentions: The American Experience and Iran* (1980), and he is co-editor of *The Israel-Arab Reader* (1984).

periods of high centralization under charismatic leadership and those of decentralization and decline in which the national government lost control of outlying provinces. This experience makes Iranians believe that a ruler accepted as legitimate must exercise dictatorial power and ruthlessly suppress opponents. There is little demand or capacity for liberal democracy. The Khomeini regime's record of torture is at least as bad as that of its predecessor and it has resorted to executions far more often than did the Shah's regime.

Yet charismatic dictatorship is an effective way of coping with the two great threats to Iran's political stability: highly factionalized domestic politics and severe vulnerability to the influence of foreign powers. Only a figure invested with tremendous legitimacy and authority can mediate disputes and enforce discipline among his highly individualistic countrymen. One member of parliament commented in regard to the need for a single leader, 'If there is a Leadership Council, Iran will be another Lebanon.' Another stated that the people could hardly shout at rallies, 'We are your soldiers, Oh Council of Leadership', the way they pledged allegiance to Khomeini. Khomeini institutionalized this role by creating his constitutionally mandated office of *velayet e-faqih*, making him the chief jurisprudent in determining whether government policy and performance were properly Islamic.

By obeying Khomeini, the current leaders of Islamic Iran climbed from obscurity to power. Not only did his charisma maintain the regime's base of support among the masses but he also functioned as a mediator to resolve disputes within the elite. As the revolution became consolidated, this latter role became increasingly important. He set the general political agenda; no one could openly dissent from his positions or criticize him. Even when he yielded day-to-day administration of the country and war to lieutenants, Khomeini remained the final authority. Iran could reach a ceasefire with Iraq only when Khomeini agreed. Competition within the elite reinforced this primacy since rivals would quickly brand any dissenter from Khomeini's line as a traitor to the revolution. This is what happened when enemies of President Abol Hassan Bani-Sadr convinced Khomeini to denounce him. Denied Khomeini's mandate, Bani-Sadr was transformed from the nation's chief executive to a friendless refugee virtually overnight.

Khomeini viewed disunity as a major threat to the revolution's survival and thus constrained the factional battle. At the same time, his lieutenants jockeyed to manipulate Khomeini into supporting them and their positions.

Khomeini's Ideology

The main tenets of Khomeini's creed, and hence of the revolution, include the following:

Iran must be governed by an Islamic leadership that puts Khomeini's ideology into practice.

The United States is the Great Satan and chief enemy of Iran and of all those who are properly Islamic. The secret Iran arms deal, though approved by Khomeini as an emergency measure, indicates that his lieutenants may be more opportunistic than their chief when they gain power.

The Soviet Union is another, albeit secondary, Satan with which Iran can sometimes co-operate though remaining wary of its atheistic communism and imperialist ambitions.

Iran must be nonaligned, 'neither east nor west', using Islam and the masses' support to neutralize the superpowers.

Other countries should follow Iran's lead in a worldwide revolution of the 'dispossessed' and of oppressed countries against great power influence. But this does not necessarily mean that Iran must directly liberate other countries. Followers may interpret Khomeini either as advocating 'Islamic fundamentalism in one country' or as demanding export of the revolution as a high-priority policy. Except in Lebanon, the regime has tended towards the former view, being cautious and unsuccessful in trying to spread the revolution.

Anyone who violates revolutionary unity is a dangerous enemy. All enemies, no matter what their political complexion, are linked together in conspiracies against Iran.

The Iran–Iraq war was a crusade of right against wrong and was supposed to continue until the overthrow of the Saddam Hussein regime in Baghdad and its replacement by an Islamic one.

Iran should exclude the influence of Western culture and stress Islamic culture, particularly in education and the role of women.

There are also significant areas—particularly concerning domestic issues— where Khomeini did not impose a view. For example, he left a margin for debate between advocates of economic statism and free-enterprise. Khomeini tended to favour the latter camp although, in 1987, he temporarily backed the former position as an emergency war measure.

Reinterpretations of Iran's National Interest

Khomeini's revolution redefined Iran's national interest, sometimes merely changing rhetoric, at other points developing a new response to challenges posed by its geopolitical situation. Both Khomeini's regime and the Shah believed in a strong central government and wanted Iran to be the preeminent regional power in the Persian Gulf.

On international alliances, however, they differed from their imperial predecessor. Iran's central national security issue has long been a simultaneous threat from two superior powers. In ancient times, invaders came from the east and west; during the last 150 years, great powers tried to exercise influence across the north/south frontiers. Iran had to contend with Russians to the north, seeking territory and political control, and the British—later, the Americans—from the south who were interested in the strategic Persian Gulf and oil.

Different Iranian governments advocated varying approaches to this problem. Since Tehran could not hope to compete militarily with these states, appeasement became an acceptable doctrine in Iran's political culture. Since military resistance was useless, the army was primarily a force for maintaining internal order. A weak Iran had few foreign ambitions. The regime tried to maintain good relations with both powers by making concessions while playing one off against the other.

Shah Mohammed Reza Pahlavi (1941–79) tried a new departure by developing a strong alliance with one power—the United States—to deter the other—the USSR. This strategy was a response to Soviet aggression in the 1940s, Iran's new oil wealth, instability in the Arab world and his own ambition. Iran was to be a regional power in its own right, exercising hegemony over the Persian Gulf. Tens of billions of dollars were spent to equip an army that could perform these tasks.

Khomeini jettisoned the Shah's alliance with America in favour of non-alignment. He argued that Iran could maintain the balance between the United States and USSR without allying with either. Khomeini interpreted alignment as subordination.

Thus, implicitly, Khomeini had a clear sense of the national interest. His top priority was to secure the Islamic revolution in Iran. A second emphasis was on maximizing Iran's influence in its region. Khomeini's anti-Americanism sprang from his belief that the United States posed a danger on both of these fronts. Only in third place came the will to extend the revolution. The main manifestation of Iran's interest in exporting Islamic revolution was in Lebanon, where it could strike at Israel and Western presence at little cost or danger to itself. Iran sponsored terrorist groups against Iraq, Kuwait, and other Gulf regimes, but carefully avoided, and was deterred from, widening the war to include other countries.

While Khomeini's views were often impractical and inaccurate, it would be wrong to see him as a fanatic with no grasp of reality. It should be remembered that his movement did overthrow the Shah, held American hostages without being crushed by the United States and repelled an Iraqi invasion without superpower assistance. Many of his lieutenants were shrewd politicians rather than ideologues. The xenophobic aspects of Khomeini's revolution were unattractive to outsiders but served a pragmatic function by imposing national unity and seeking to deter Iranian politicians from their traditional practice of seeking to take power by securing foreign money and support. While his ideology made Khomeini continue the hostage crisis and the war with Iraq longer than necessary, in the end, he gave way on both issues to a rational calculation of regime interest.

On regional policy, Khomeini sought to maximize Iran's influence in the Gulf, minimize the US presence and destroy Iraq's capacity to threaten Iran. Here, he miscalculated. Iran's aggressive and verbally militant policy made it impossible for the Gulf monarchies to appease Tehran, pushed them closer to the United States and isolated Iran.

Iranian Leadership Factions

There are three main factions in the Iranian leadership, differentiated by personal loyalties, opportunism and ambition, rather than ideological differences. In the past, they co-operated in eliminating other contenders for power. They will probably compete for power in the post-Khomeini era and, until a new single leader emerges, there may be a period of internal conflict that could involve the Iranian armed forces.

Beginning with the revolution's triumph in February 1979, the Islamic politicians clustered around Khomeini systematically began to eliminate all alternative political groups and ideologies. The Shah's supporters were purged, imprisoned, executed or forced into exile, then the relatively moderate cabinet of Mehdi Bazargan and Ibrahim Yazdi was removed from office in November 1979. In 1981, Bani-Sadr was forced to flee. Leftist groups that opposed the ruling clique, particularly the Mujahaddin e-Khalq, were smashed. In 1983, the pro-Moscow communist party (Tudeh) was broken up and its leaders were imprisoned.

Afterwards, only staunch Khomeini supporters were allowed to engage in politics, though they were allowed a degree of freedom to express differences among themselves in the press and parliament. Elections were sharply contested; parliament rejected some cabinet members and bills proposed by the government.

The ruling group's main factions have some common factors: first, they cannot be defined along radical/moderate or ideological lines but were rather clustered around individuals. Second, there were no clear differences among them on foreign policy or national security issues even when one examines the nuances of their leaders' statements. All of them hewed as closely as possible to Khomeini's views and were subject to rapid changes in their composition and positions. Third, none of them monopolized support in the army or Revolutionary Guards (Pasdaran) though all assiduously courted them. Fourth, despite Khomeini's attempts to impose a cultural revolution negating Iranians' traditional inferiority complex and appeasement policy toward foreigners, all three groups may seek covert foreign help in order to gain or retain power. Finally, however, against any threat from other groups the three factions stood together. The ability to unite when necessary was a major factor ensuring the regime's survival.

Faction Leaders

President Mohammed Ali Khamenehi enjoyed the backing of the cabinet and much of large elements in the state bureaucracy. Born in Azarbaijan, Khamenehi became a cleric and was an Islamic activist under the Shah's regime. Immediately after the revolution, Khomeini appointed him a member of his Revolutionary Council, Friday prayer leader in Tehran and his personal representative to the army. He was wounded in a May 1979 assassination attempt. Khamenehi was elected secretary-general of the Islamic Republican Party (a post he held until that party's dissolution in 1987), president in October 1981 and chief clerical guide after Khomeini's death.

Prime Minister Hussein Musavi supported a stronger state role in the economy and backed land reform and nationalization of trade. Khomeini was not enthusiastic about these ideas and the conservative Council of Guardians blocked them. In 1987, Khomeini, as an emergency war measure, gave some support to these measures. Musavi lost power and his job was abolished after Khomeini died.

Ali Akhbar Hashemi Rafsanjani was speaker of the Iranian parliament. A cleric and charter member of Khomeini's Revolutionary Council, Rafsanjani was an ally of Ayatollah Beheshti, architect of the regime's institutions, and President Mohammed Ali Rajai, both assassinated by opposition elements. Rafsanjani resigned as interior minister when he became parliamentary speaker. He also played a major role in removing Bani-Sadr.

In 1988, Rafsanjani seemed to emerge as the most powerful figure in Iran after Khomeini, and he became president in 1989. His position was bolstered by his good working relationship with Khomeini's son, Ahmad. Western observers viewed Rafsanjani as the most 'moderate' of the factional leaders. He was an advocate of private enterprise, the main figure behind secret US–Iran exchanges in 1985–86, and moved quickly on becoming commander-in-chief of Iran's military. When Tehran needed to court Moscow to avoid passage of a UN sanctions' resolution, for example, Rafsanjani was also lavish in praising the Soviets. He might best be described, like his fellows, as an opportunist.

Ayatollah Hussein Ali Montazeri was designated as Khomeini's successor in the post of *velayet e-faqih* in November 1985. Many Iranians regard him as unintelligent and other clerics have questioned his credentials for the job. Imprisoned and reportedly tortured under the Shah's regime, Montazeri was released in late 1978. Along with Rafsanjani, Montazeri was a leading author of Iran's constitution. Khomeini made him chief cleric in Qom but there were hints that he, too, was later disappointed with Montazeri's performance.

Among the factions, Montazeri's backers were the least organized and his personal ability seemed the weakest. When Montazeri was removed as successor to the post of *velayet e-faqih* by Khomeini in 1988, he lost tremendous power literally overnight. Hence, the Khamenehi and Rafsanjani groups succeeded in weakening him while Khomeini was still alive. The secret Iran–US negotiations of 1986 seem to have been initiated by Rafsanjani and later joined by Khamenehi as a way of increasing their influence in internal politics. Not only might they receive credit among the military for obtaining American arms, but some of the funds supposedly earmarked for weapons went to finance the individuals and factions involved. These events were accompanied by arrests of both radical and moderate followers of Montazeri.

The tendency in the West to portray Montazeri as a hardliner is questionable. During the 1979–81 hostage crisis he commented, 'The United States enslaved Iran for 25 years and the Iranians want to be finally released from this subjugation.' But he then added, it was 'impractical to sever relations between us and the United States'. Montazeri supported—despite opposition from rivals—a programme to encourage expatriates to return because Iran desperately needed their skills. He criticized the Hizballah (Party of God) thugs and pleased bazaar merchants with his call for less state intervention in the economy.

By designating Montazeri as successor, Khomeini sought to entrench the revolution after his death. Still, Chinese leader Mao Zedong also desperately tried to impose his ideology through successors at a time when his authority and charisma seemed total, but could not impose his will on those leading the country after his death. Khomeini faced a similar problem. But the Iranian regime, like China's, seemed more likely to survive precisely because it was able when necessary to alter many of its founder's policies.

The question remains whether anti-American and anti-Israel extremism will continue as tenets of the regime. To pose as loyal Khomeini followers and to stir public opinion, politicians may affirm these ideas during the succession struggle. Moderation is not inevitable. Still, a belief that outside states can control their country's political affairs is a double-edged sword which might impel Iran's leaders to seek such foreigners' favour. To stay in power, Khomeini's successors may have to make concessions to economic and strategic realities.

The men who must deal with the day-to-day realities of running Iran showed signs that they doubted the country could stand isolated against almost everyone else. Thus, in 1988, they engineered a rapprochement with Britain, France and Canada, though Iran used hostages as diplomatic leverage in the former two cases. Khomeini himself evinced disappointment at the lack of new Islamic revolutions and justified building good relations with countries as diverse as Pakistan, Turkey, North Korea and Vietnam. He did not punish those involved in the secret contacts with the United States but, rather, promoted Rafsanjani while silencing critics of those dealings. As the main three factions adopted a more 'pragmatic' stand, new radicals— most importantly Interior Minister Ali Akbar Mohtashemi—criticized them for abandoning radicalism. Yet even Khomeini was being forced to retreat from some of his most prized positions.

Concerning regional policy, Iran's leaders gradually concluded that the war with Iraq was unwinnable and that continuing it endangered the regime's very survival. Rafsanjani convinced Khomeini to accept a ceasefire in July 1988. Relaxation of controls or repression at home, however, was less likely since this would impinge more directly on the regime's prerogatives and power. Shifts in foreign policy were made precisely to avoid crises that might result in domestic political changes.

Opposition Movements

The forces currently in opposition to the Islamic regime—the emigres, the left and ethnic minorities—were unlikely to take power. The exiles were badly divided and many of their supporters had fled, been executed or purged. They based their strategy on the vain hope that the regime would soon collapse.

The left was also split into quarrelling groups and its constituency remained limited to certain urban and student sectors. Tudeh's links with the USSR and the Mujahaddin's decision to align itself with Iraq in the war were major handicaps in broadening their base of support. The two groups were decimated by repression without making any appreciable progress in shaking the government's power.

Minority groups could cause problems in the future but seem to be largely subdued. The Arabs of the south-west failed to rally to the Iraqi invaders; the Baluchis of the south-east and the nomadic tribes of west central Iran dislike central government interference but caused little trouble. The Turkish-speaking Azaris of the north-west rallied briefly behind the late Ayatollah Kazem Shariatmadari but never mounted a real insurgency.

Only the guerrillas of the Kurdish Democratic Party (KDP) and its smaller Marxist allies caused the regime real problems. Yet Iran's army occupied most of Kurdistan while fighting Iraq. In short, the Kurds or Azaris might only emerge as a threat if the central government broke down and they received major Soviet assistance.

One important group standing outside the ruling circle was the 'traditional-ist' clergy. Senior ayatollahs—like Ahmad Azari Qomi and Reza Musavi Golpaygani—never fully accepted Khomeini's revolutionary policies as appropriate Shiite Islamic practice and resented the power of political clerics with fewer theological and scholarly qualifications than themselves. They were staunch anti-communists and did not necessarily share the regime's antipathy to the West. One of these bitter men, Ayatollah Sadiq Ruhani, openly called the regime 'worse than the communists' at a November 1985 speech in a Qom mosque. Clerics associated with the holy city of Mashad were displeased by the predominance of Khomeini's former students in Qom. Though cowed by Khomeini, they might not be so easily controlled by his successors.

If they survive, Rafsanjani, Khamenehi, and their followers, should dominate the scene in the immediate post-Khomeini era. If they can find some formula for working together or if a strong man emerges without too much strife, the regime could survive in its present form. If their competition turns to bloodshed, Iran will face serious internal problems.

The Regime's Institutional Framework

Many observers underestimated the Islamic regime's staying power because they failed to understand its underpinnings. It stood not only on slogans and Khomeini's charisma but on policies and institutions designed to strengthen adherents and punish opponents by distributing money, monitoring dissent, controlling culture and education, and managing the media. Although these kinds of structures have an Islamic content, they are typical of Third World dictatorships.

The number of Islamic clerics passed 100,000 and continued to rise. Many of them function as local political agents of the government. The *imam jomehs* are clerics who serve as Khomeini's personal representatives and deliver the main sermon at massive Friday prayer gatherings. There are mass-membership Islamic Associations in villages and factories. Mosques became centres for military recruiting, the rationing system, ideological indoctrination and clearances for students wishing to attend a university. Mullahs hold many offices, including about half the legislators and one-quarter of the judges. By constitutional provision, clerics occupy half the positions on the Council of Guardians, which determines the constitutionality of parliament's decisions, and dominate the Assembly of Experts, which chose Montazeri as Khomeini's successor.

Neighbourhood Komitehs keep an eye on every household. A web of charitable foundations and welfare programmes support political loyalists. The Crusade for Reconstruction employs urban slum-dwellers to build roads, schools and houses. The Foundation of the Dispossessed controls many industries. The Ministry of Islamic Guidance censors and oversees the media.

For those who do not conform, the forces of repression are as strong as they were under the Shah. The old secret police, SAVAK, was renamed and streamlined as SAVAMA. Hizballah street gangs beat up critics, break up opposition rallies, and harass nonconforming women. Prisons are full, torture is plentiful, and executions are more frequent than in the pre-revolutionary era.

The armed forces were thoroughly and repeatedly purged. Senior officers were retired, imprisoned, shot, or fled the country. Their replacements owe their posts to the revolution and evinced loyalty to it. The government placed Islamic political commissars to supervise the army, whose units were systematically moved out of encampments near major cities. Khomeini was so impressed by the success of the Islamicization process that, in 1987, he promoted officers to the rank of general and admiral for the first time since the revolution.

The regime organized its own parallel army, the Revolutionary Guard (Pasdaran), and favoured it with money, weapons, its own cabinet-level ministry, control over antiaircraft defences, former army bases near Tehran and other cities, munitions factories and a large share of the drafters called up for the war. The Pasdaran was given responsibility for internal security and combatting opposition movements. Its own navy, consisting mostly of speed boats, carried out most of the attacks on tankers. The Pasdaran even trained pilots for its own planned air force. There was sporadic friction between the regular army and Pasdaran over predominance and in deciding the conduct of the war. Khomeini tried to soothe this rivalry. As the Pasdaran became more of a regular military force, a new militia, the Basij, was organized among young and older Iranians.

Thus, a well-entrenched Islamic regime entered 1987.

The Events of 1987–88

In its earlier days, the war had augmented the regime's domestic support. By about 1985, however, the fighting began to be counterproductive due to a variety of factors. It absorbed resources and prevented economic development. Iraqi attacks on installations, loading facilities and tankers reduced Iran's oil exports; lower petroleum prices further cut the nation's income. There was inflation, unemployment and a shortage of many goods.

Iran's leaders repeatedly promised that total victory was imminent but their people lost enthusiasm as the war seemed to be endless and unwinnable. There were fewer volunteers for the military and even a strict 1986 law and Revolutionary Guard patrols found it difficult to stop draft-dodging and raise fresh troops. In 1985, Iraqi bombing provoked riots in Tehran. Iraqi missile attacks, particularly intense during the first four months of 1988, as well as panic at possible chemical attacks on civilian centres, demoralized the home front.

The use of chemical weapons by Iraq also undermined Iranian discipline on the battlefield. In the human wave assaults that took place regularly between 1980 and early 1986, Iranian losses were extremely heavy. This tactic, relatively effective as long as Iraqi forces were on Iranian territory, was less useful as Iraqi troops dug in on their own side of the border with strong defences and stiffened resolve. Consequently, Iran's last all-out offensive was conducted in January 1986.

By this time, Iran had no viable strategy for winning the war. Tehran had hoped either that Iraq would collapse from within—due to an uprising by the sizeable Shiite community, a coup, or an economic crisis—or that Iranian forces would make a military breakthrough. In fact, the Shiite community remained quiet because of ferocious repression, the degree to which the Iraqi regime had integrated it and Arab nationalist sentiments which set Iraqi Shiites apart from their Persian co-religionists. Through Arab solidarity, intimidation and fear of the Iranians, both Saudi Arabia and Kuwait gave Baghdad billions of dollars which allowed its economic survival. Indeed, Iraq was able, using new pipelines, to export more oil than Iran.

All these factors provided an impressive array of reasons for ending the war. But throughout 1985–87, these 'objective facts' remained meaningless in the face of Khomeini's refusal to make peace. Only when Iran's supreme leader was persuaded to give way did the country's policy change.

One of the new elements in 1987 had been growing international pressures on Iran to end the war. On 20 July 1987, the UN Security Council unanimously passed Resolution 598 calling on both sides to accept a ceasefire, withdrawal of troops to internationally recognized borders and a negotiated settlement. The United States and others sought to pass a follow-up resolution that would impose sanctions, including an arms embargo, against Iran for refusing to comply.

But Iran out-manoeuvered this campaign by pronouncing itself ready to accept a ceasefire if the UN first found Iraq guilty of starting the war. Tehran courted the Soviet Union and helped convince it to block an Anglo-American effort to introduce a mandatory arms embargo against Iran at the 25 September 1987 UN Security Council meeting. China, which had been selling large amounts of arms to Iran, including Silkworm anti-ship missiles, also opposed sanctions.

Iran threatened to attack US convoys of reflagged Kuwaiti tankers. It did escalate attacks on Kuwait through terrorism and sabotage, firing Silkworm missiles at port and oil installations, mining Kuwaiti and Gulf waters. Iranian speedboats stepped up attacks on tankers of countries not participating in the convoys.

At the same time, however, the Iranians tried to avoid direct confrontations with US and European warships or the tankers they were convoying. But when, in September 1987, American forces found an Iranian ship dropping mines in the Gulf, they attacked, seized, and later scuttled it. Several Iranians were killed. On 8 October US helicopters sank three Iranian gunboats that fired on a patrolling American helicopter 15 miles south-west of Iran's Farsi island. Iran's response was contradictory. 'We do not wish to get into a conflict with the United States and we say so explicitly', said Rafsanjani, but he also threatened war on America.

Iran's relations with Britain and France also suffered in 1987. When an Iranian consular official was arrested for shoplifting in England, the senior British diplomat in Tehran was beaten and detained in May. London recalled its diplomats and, after an attack on a British tanker in September, closed the Iranian military purchasing mission in London. A French attempt to arrest an Iranian employee in Paris led to the two countries' besieging each other's embassies.

Iran also became involved in a heated conflict with Saudi Arabia. On 31 July 1987, Saudi police fired on demonstrating Iranian pilgrims. Between 400 and 600 people, mostly Iranians, were killed. A mob in Tehran sacked the Saudi embassy and Khomeini declared Saudi Arabia unfit to control the holy places. The Saudis broke diplomatic relations.

Ironically, two months after the Mecca incident, the Iranian government executed Mehdi Hashemi, a supporter of Montazeri and a staunch advocate of spreading the revolution abroad, including to Saudi Arabia. Hashemi had been arrested in November 1986 when he complained about the secret US–Iran arms deal, which his followers soon leaked to the press. Hashemi and his allies attacked Iranian leaders who sought a 'normal' rather than a revolutionary state. In contrast, the three main factions wanted an Islamic fundamentalist policy but one which would ensure the regime's survival. Khomeini supported the latter, ruling, groups.

Iran's 1988 elections generally continued this trend. In preparation for the balloting, Khomeini ordered the dissolution of the Islamic Republican Party, which had become an arena of struggle rather than unity among the leading factions. This was a defeat for Khamenehi who had led the organization.

In the voting itself, a new 'radical' group emerged, led by the youthful Interior Minister Ali Akbar Mohtashemi who, as Iran's ambassador to Syria, had supervised liaison with the terrorist groups in Lebanon. Yet the country's situation was worsening and there was little appetite for new adventurism. Iran's leaders were increasingly convinced that the war must be stopped. If the elderly, ailing Khomeini died while fighting still continued, his successors would find it difficult to violate their master's insistence on total victory.

Apparently, the final events changing Khomeini's mind were: Rafsanjani's pessimistic evaluation after becoming commander-in-chief of the military, Iraq's successful return to the offensive and the downing of an Iranian airliner by an American warship. There were two major Iraqi victories in 1988—the recapture of the Faw peninsula and an advance on the Basra front. Iranian forces broke and ran. On 3 July the *USS Vincennes* destroyed an Iranian commercial plane which it mistook for an attacking fighter. Rafsanjani seems to have told Khomeini that the Americans would continue massacring Iranians until the war ended.

While Rafsanjani convinced Khomeini to—in the latter's words—'drink the poison' of ending a war he now believed was endangering the Islamic regime, other leaders did not object. Trying to end its dangerous isolation, Tehran repaired relations with Britain and France. Khomeini announced a ceasefire to his 50 million subjects on 20 July 1988.

The Islamic Regime and the United States

The Iranian government perceived itself as being involved in three distinct conflicts with the United States. First, internal interference. Khomeini firmly, if erroneously, believed that the United States dominated Iran under the Shah. But US influence over Iran is not merely an issue of historical interest. Khomeini and his colleagues feared that the United States was constantly engaged in conspiracies to overthrow them and to regain control of the country. Khomeini responded by taking the offensive. We do not need the United States, he argued, and if the leaders unite and the people are mobilized behind the proper Islamic ideology, we can defy America. Some of his colleagues, however, were more sceptical. They continued to fear American power and, perhaps, secretly hoped that the United States would assist their ambitions.

Second, regional conflict. The United States was also considered the main factor blocking Tehran's objectives of regional primacy, spreading Islamic revolution or its own influence over Iraq, Saudi Arabia, Lebanon and others. It particularly reviled and wished to destroy Israel. Iran's leaders perceived the United States as protectors of these target countries.

Of course, the Islamic regime's own behaviour—anti-American threats and actions, holding US diplomats as hostages and encouraging terrorism—were the main cause of the bilateral conflict. Similarly, Iran's regional subversion and attacks on shipping forced the United States to aid the Gulf Arab monarchies, who moved closer to Washington for protection. The Iranian threat of revolution dissolved the long-standing enmity between the United States and Iraq.

US support and friendship for Israel was also an important element in the passionate hostility of Islamic Iran. But Tehran argued that it was first necessary to destroy US support for 'reactionary, traitorous' Arab regimes. Once these countries were revolutionized, Iran's leaders claimed, Israel's destruction would be relatively easy. Again, however, Iran's behaviour did not always correspond to its rhetoric and Tehran became involved in secret arms deals with Israel.

Third, global confrontation. Iran saw itself as a model for worldwide revolution. Khomeini's version of class struggle views the majority of humanity—the oppressed—embattled against evil forces headed by the United States. America was seen as the prime and ultimate enemy—the Great Satan.

Khomeini was extremely sensitive to Western, especially US, cultural and intellectual influences in Iran, including the affinity of the middle class to these ideas, and the American training of his military officers. In this sense, Western thought and customs (sometimes referred to in Iran as 'Westoxification') posed a far greater threat to the Islamic regime than did Marxism. Washington's influence in the Persian Gulf and Middle East was also stronger than that of Moscow. Thus, Khomeini could not eliminate the possibility that his successors would seek a rapprochement with the United States. By portraying America as so fearsome and omnipotent, he also laid a basis for a return to Iranian deference and appeasement.

Iran and the USSR

The Soviet Union was considered the number-two Satan and Tehran was particularly angry about its occupation of Afghanistan and aid to Iraq. A mitigating factor was that the USSR's regional allies, Libya and Syria, supported Iran against Iraq. The very historical fears of the USSR that made Iran eager to avoid offending its powerful neighbour, also bred mistrust and discouraged any dependence on Moscow.

Iran's turn away from the United States did not mean a tilt towards the USSR. A central objective of the revolution was to demonstrate that Iranian sovereignty and security could be protected without subservience to either superpower. Moreover, the Iranian leadership correctly calculated that the superpower balance prevented either country from directly attacking Iran or overthrowing its government even if they wanted to do so. In the 1979–81 hostage crisis, Moscow warned Washington against military intervention; the United States created a Rapid Deployment Force explicitly aimed at deterring any Soviet invasion of Iran.

Iran, Israel and the Jews

Israel, however, had far less leverage in Iran. The Islamic revolution seemed fanatically anti-Israel because it viewed anti-Zionism as an Islamic cause, sought to woo Arab Muslims, and held views of Jews which could only be called demonological. One of the new regime's first acts was to give the former Israeli embassy in Tehran to the Palestine Liberation Organization (PLO). After the Iran–Iraq War began, however, PLO leader Yasser Arafat had to give some support to Iraq and his links with Khomeini deteriorated.

Iranian leaders stated that there would be no relations 'in principle' with Israel. The Iranian media made the most bloodcurdling threats and published the most extreme distortions about that country. In Lebanon, Iran financed and trained Shiite Muslim fundamentalist groups which attacked Israeli forces in the country and, later, across the border.

Israel hoped that traditional contacts could be maintained, particularly given a congruence of interests, including common enmity with Iraq. Israel and Israeli citizens sold arms to Iran early in the war until, in 1982, Tehran seemed close to victory. In 1985 a US–Israel approach to Iran developed into an arms-for-hostages arrangement. In 1988, the possibility of an Iraqi victory and the spiralling arms race in the Gulf—particularly the introduction of medium-range missiles—made Israeli leaders welcome an end to the war.

There were about 80,000 Jews in Iran at the time of the revolution. By 1988, about 55,000 had left, mostly to the United States and Israel. Several Iranian Jewish leaders were arrested and about a dozen were executed between 1979 and 1983, accused of Zionist activities and corruption. There was no intensive persecution and the community was allowed to continue functioning, particularly in comparison to the Bahai who were severely persecuted. But the situation of the Jews had returned to something akin to the Middle Ages, when insecurity bred pervasive fear and intimidation.

Conclusions

The Islamic Republic institutionalized itself to stay in power. It purged the army and named new commanders loyal to the revolution. The Revolutionary Guard was built as a politically loyal, parallel army. A wide range of economic, juridical, local government, intelligence, politicized religious, welfare and other agencies permeated Iranian society. Opposition groups were broken up, their leaders imprisoned, exiled, or killed.

Despite many tribulations, the Islamic Republic survived its first decade. The price, however, was that Khomeini had to abandon much of his ideology. The acceptance of a ceasefire in the war, the reopening of contacts with the West, the inability to spread the revolution (and the low priority put on these efforts), the decline of popular enthusiasm and other factors contradicted Khomeini's fondest principles. The triumph of Islam did not bring magical prosperity or a new utopian order. Not only did Khomeini have to sacrifice revolutionary doctrine in practice, but in 1988 he was forced to admit openly that he was doing so. Preserving the regime, he confessed, took priority over even implementing Islam.

By such measures, the government saved itself from Iraq's invasion; its excessive—often paranoid—fears of foreign intervention did not materialize. But the threat to the country's stability came more from division within its ranks than from domestic enemies or outside powers. Khomeini's passing could free surviving leaders to battle among themselves. They may reach some agreement, though Iran's history does not encourage hope that such an arrangement could last.

If recent experience is any guide, Iran's future will be fraught with dangers and full of surprises.

The author would like to thank Professor David Menashri for his excellent insight, which was helpful in the preparation of this article.

7

Syria's Quest for Arab Leadership: a Period of Retreat and Retrenchment

ITAMAR RABINOVICH

Hafez al-Asad seized full power in Syria in November 1970. Within a period of less than five years he succeeded in establishing a comparatively stable and effective regime and in transforming his country's foreign policy. From a passive object buffeted by domestic forces and ambitious neighbours, he turned Syria into a regional power vetoing the acts of others and intervening in the affairs of weaker Arab states. This spectacular success gave rise in the mid-1970s to rationalization and conceptualization. There had to be a design or at least a purpose to guide Asad's external efforts.

A British journalist with access to Asad, in fact his future biographer, in an article he wrote in 1977 was ambiguous in his characterization of Asad as building a virtual Greater Syria as a stepping stone on the road to a larger Arab Union:

> Asad has been a member in the Ba'th Party, dedicated to Arab unity for 30 years. Moreover, the fact that he rules in Damascus, the heartland of Arabism, makes him heir to a remorseless drive to reach out beyond Syria's boundaries. His current unionist campaign is two-pronged. First he sees Syria's two immediate neighbours, Lebanon and Jordan, as a natural extension of its territory, vital to its defence. This three nation grouping is already a *fait accompli*, although in the low key Asad style, without fanfare. Asad now rules by proxy in Lebanon, while the progressive integration with Jordan is well advanced. If the Palestinians ever recover a West Bank homeland, they will inevitably join the complex.[1]

Itamar Rabinovich is Ettinger Professor of contemporary Middle Eastern history at Tel Aviv University and director of that university's Dayan Center of Middle East and African Studies. Among other works, he is the author of *Syria under the Ba'th—1963–1966* (1972) and *The War for Lebanon, 1970–1985* (1985).

Syria's Minister of Information was bolder when he explained to an American correspondent that Syria possessed the necessary qualifications for replacing Egypt as leader of the Arab world. In addition to her special place in Arab history and to Asad's leadership, he said, 'Syria has increasing support and confidence of other Arab states, excellent international relations with East and West, a population united behind the regime and a popular army of 150,000 with the latest Soviet weapons; it is the largest Arab army after Egypt.'[2]

A non-partisan and a particularly astute student of Arab politics saw the same trends in more cautious terms: 'From Syria's vantage point this success [in Lebanon] was another reminder that the politics of compromise does not pay, that the center of gravity in the Arab world may have shifted away from Cairo, that Nasser's mantle has been picked up and claimed by Asad.'[3]

Buoyed by the unusual success of his regional and foreign policies in the 1975–77 period, Asad may indeed have been carried away to the point of believing that Syria could replace Egypt as leader of the Arab world. Shortly thereafter he discovered the limits of his country's potential. A series of domestic and external set-backs reversed the trend in Syrian politics and pushed Asad and his regime into a defensive corner.

But in any event the notion of 'leader of the Arab world' was anachronistic. Arab leadership in the style developed by Nasser in the 1950s was not possible in the 1970s. Nasser in his heyday (1955–61) combined messianic leadership with the resources of a state much more powerful than all other Arab states. In the 1970s there was no Arab leader with Nasser's personal charisma and the differences between Egypt and the other Arab states were to a considerable extent obliterated. The oil-producing states acquired, after 1973, enormous financial resources while Syria and Iraq built powerful armies. The decline in Egypt's relative strength was matched by Egyptian disenchantment with the Arabs which led to a weakening of the Egyptian commitment to Arab causes. Other Arab states, Saudi Arabia, Syria and Iraq, tried to fill the vacuum and succeeded one another as the lynchpin of the Arab system. Each had its day in court and played the role for a brief period until the limit of its power and the pretentiousness of its claim were exposed.[4]

It is against this background that the evolution of Syria's Arab policy during Hafez al-Asad's tenure of power should be seen.

By the end of 1980 at the conclusion of its first decade in power the Asad regime had come full circle. In domestic politics the new regime sought in the early 1970s to find a modus vivendi with the urban Sunni population. Its domestic strategy collapsed in 1977/8 under the impact of the anti-Ba'th Islamic rebellion. By the end of 1980 the rebellion's backbone had been broken but at a heavy price; the regime survived and its ability to crush its opponents had been proven (and then reinforced in Hama in 1982) but the patina of popular consensus had been removed. Thereafter Asad had ruled by the sword.

The domestic crisis of the late 1970s was exacerbated by a series of setbacks in the regime's regional and foreign policies. Syria played a major role in pushing Sadat towards opening direct negotiations with Israel and then was hard put to contend with the ramifications of Egypt's new policy. The limits of Syria's power and influence in Lebanon had become apparent and the costs of maintaining its Lebanese patrimony seemed to outweigh its benefits. The rival Ba'th regime in Iraq was exerting effective pressure on Syria and the intimate alliance with Jordan (of the mid-1970s) was transformed into active hostility. Internationally, Syria lost its ability to manoeuvre between the two superpowers.[5]

Having stabilized the domestic situation in Syria in the summer of 1980 Asad began also to regain the initiative in foreign policy. The recovery was temporarily arrested by the war in Lebanon in 1982. The war's immediate results were catastrophic from a Syrian point of view. Syria was defeated militarily and was about to lose its immense Lebanese investment and to face instead a hostile Lebanese regime under American and Israeli influence.

What followed instead was an amazing Syrian recovery and a period of just under three years (September 1982-June 1985) during which Syria defeated its rivals in Lebanon and used its exploits in the Lebanese arena in order to advance the larger goals of its regional policy.[6] Within this period Syria fomented an anti-Arafat rebellion in the ranks of Fath and had Arafat and his loyalists expelled from Lebanon, brought about the abrogation of the Lebanese-Israeli Agreement of 17 May 1983, played a role in obstructing President Reagan's initiative of 1 September 1982 and normalized its relationship with Jordan. Syria took part in the Fez Arab Summit conference in September 1982. There, still under the impact of its recent defeat in Lebanon, it endorsed the Fez Formula, a modified version of the Saudi proposal for a new Arab approach to the issue of a political settlement with Israel. Having recovered soon thereafter Syria did not formally withdraw its endorsement of the Fez formula, but it did use its new power and position to prevent another Arab summit from being convened (until November 1987).

If his successes in the Lebanese arena were one pillar of Asad's revised regional influence, his alliance with Iran was the other. The partnership with Khomeini's regime gave Asad a measure of religious legitimacy and some economic advantages but its main benefits were the neutralization of Iraq and Syria's positioning as a mediator, actual or potential, between Iran and the conservative Arab oil producers. Iraq's virtual elimination as rival and competitor was particularly welcome to Syria given the effectiveness of the Iraqi pressure in the late 1970s.

Asad's conduct at the height of his renewed success in the mid-1980s reflected some of the lessons he drew from the setbacks of the previous years. The Asad of 1983, as distinct from that of 1976, was aware of the limits of his country's intrinsic power and resources and of the underlying weakness of his regime's political base. He knew that the weight Syria acquired in inter-Arab relations was to a great extent a product of Iraq's weakness and Egypt's absence. It was by definition a temporary state of affairs, bound to be changed by yet another shift in the regional balance of power.

One measure of Asad's caution was the trepidation of his Lebanese policy. Following the American and Israeli withdrawals he did not dispatch his own troops to Beirut. Sizeable Syrian troops were stationed in eastern and northern Lebanon but not in the capital. This would involve Syria in the most minute intra-Lebanese bickerings and would cause Syrian casualties. Syria still wanted hegemony in Lebanon but it understood now that more patience was needed. She had the military but not the political power to quash her rivals.

Nor was Asad thinking, let alone speaking, in terms of Arab leadership. Syria of the mid-1980s did not seek to lead as it sought to block. She presented herself as the keeper of the Arab nationalist flame and standards and set out to block and undo any policy which, in Syrian eyes, deviated from the accepted lines. Policy towards Israel remained the touchstone of genuine Arab nationalism. As the Syrians saw and put it, they remained the last defenders of the Arab trench in the historic conflict with Israel. Sadat and Egypt had deserted it in 1977. The Lebanese-Israeli agreement of May 1983 was another step in the same direction. King Hussein and Arafat were contemplating the same and the conservative Arab states as well as Iraq were willing to support them. It was up to Syria to stem the tide and every measure taken or not taken was significant within that larger scheme. A typical Syrian statement at the height of the offensive against the Lebanese-Israeli agreement exemplified this state of mind:

> When Arafat sheds tears about independent decision making, he certainly wants to lend legitimacy to the independent decisions of others. Sadat's treasonous decision was also an independent decision and an expression of sovereignty. Hussein's decision to sell out the cause is also an independent decision and an expression of sovereignty. Consequently the Lebanese Phalangist decision to conclude an agreement with Israel is an independent decision and an expression of sovereignty according to the Arafatist concept of independent decision making. Wasn't the Lebanese regime's main excuse for concluding the submission agreement that it was an independent Lebanese decision emanating from Lebanese sovereignty?[7]

Syria's rhetoric was backed by its actual ability to block or help block some of the policies it objected to. It also played the decisive role in preventing an Arab summit from meeting subsequent to September 1982. Furthermore its policy and rhetoric won support and admiration, albeit grudging and ephemeral, from bitter opponents who objected to practically everything that Asad's regime stood for but had to admit that it alone stood up successfully to both the United States and Israel.

Yet the Syrian claim to be the foremost custodian of the Arab nationalist cause was seriously weakened by the Syrian alliance with Iran. Siding with a non-Arab, albeit Islamic, state at war with another Arab state and posing a threat to several other Arab states was a serious deviation from the tenets of Arab nationalism. This was one of the principal themes used by Iraq in its propaganda campaign against Syria and the theme was also taken up, though in a less strident fashion, by Syria's other rivals. Syria's own propaganda machinery developed a response to these charges but even the most sophisticated argumentation could not eliminate the tension between a radical Arab nationalist posture and an anti-Iraqi alliance with Iran.

In any event, the heyday of Syria's renewed success and effectiveness as a regional actor was over by 1986. Several factors and developments accounted for the change—Asad's illness and its domestic and external ramifications, Syria's position and role in Lebanon, the crisis of the Syrian economy, Syria's discomfort with Gorbachev's new policies—but it was the new configuration in Lebanon that had the greatest effect on Syria's standing in the region.

Syria exploited its success in Lebanon in the 1982–85 period and the centrality of the Lebanese arena in the region's politics to the full. During this period Syria was in the advantageous position of heading a coalition directed against three easy targets—Israel, the United States and the Maronite militias. When Israel completed its withdrawal from Lebanon in June 1985 Syria found herself confronted with an entirely different set of circumstances. She was the hegemonial power in Lebanon and it was up to her to keep public order and effect political reform. The diverse coalition that had been kept together against common enemies disintegrated. Syria was allied with part of the Shi'i community (Amal's militia), part of the Maronite community (former President Faranjiyya) and the reluctant Druze leader Kamal Jumblatt. It faced the enmity of the other parts of the Shi'i (Hizballah) and Maronite (the Lebanese Forces) communities, the PLO and the pro-Israeli militia of General Lahad in the South. Iran, a former ally, became a competitor in Lebanon and President Jumayyil, if not hostile, was unreliable. By 1986 Syria's position in Lebanon had again been transformed from a springboard for attaining regional influence into a source of weakness and embarrassment draining the Ba'th regime's dwindling resources.

In 1986, then, a new phase began in the evolution of the Asad regime's foreign policies. It was marked by retrenchment, not the sharp set-backs and the acute sense of crisis and siege of the late 1970s, but certainly a loss of initiative and a defensive mood, as a survey of the main developments in the principal areas of Syrian foreign policy during the past three years should clearly show.

Inter-Arab Relations

The dominant pattern of inter-Arab relations in recent years has been a division into two loose coalitions. The two coalitions of the 1980s can be dubbed 'pragmatic' and 'radical', and their composition has been determined by attitudes toward the two major conflicts in the region—the war between Iran and Iraq and the Arab-Israeli conflict.

The 'pragmatic' coalition was composed of Egypt, Iraq, Jordan and the conservative Arab states. It supported Iraq against Iran and a continuation of the Arab-Israeli peace process under American auspices. The radical coalition, made up of Syria, Libya, the People's Democratic Republic of Yemen, Algeria and, a non-Arab state, Iran, took Iran's side in the conflict with Iraq and objected to a continuation or revival of the Arab-Israeli peace process along its familiar lines.

As the lynchpin of the radical coalition, between September 1982 and November 1987 Syria successfully aborted all efforts to convene a full Arab summit, the supreme and most important forum in inter-Arab relations. It was the most notable measure of Syria's blocking power in inter-Arab relations. Syria's opposition to a summit meeting derived from the realization that the agenda of an Arab summit was bound to be embarrassing—a discussion of the Gulf War, the Lebanese crisis, the PLO's position and Egypt's return to the Arab fold.[8]

By November 1987 Syria could no longer stem the tide and attended the Amman summit. The spirit of the meeting and several of its resolutions were, indeed, unpalatable to Syria. The Amman summit placed the Gulf War and the Iranian challenge at the head of the Arab agenda. It chided Iran for its conduct and it sanctioned the renewal of diplomatic relations with Egypt. Syria's acquiescence can be explained in part by the loosening of her alliance with Iran but the principal motive must have been the financial assistance promised by the conservative Arab oil producers.

A second Arab summit met in June 1988 in Algiers. It marked a total change of direction under the impact of the Palestinian uprising, the *intifada*, and Iran's weakening. The Algiers summit restored the Arab-Israeli conflict to the top of the Arab agenda, strengthened the Palestine Liberation Organization's standing *vis-à-vis* Jordan and thus rendered the prospect of an Israeli-Jordanian agreement on the West Bank still dimmer. This was certainly welcome to Syria but the gain was offset by the larger gains accruing to the PLO.

There was, indeed, a close interplay between Syria's relationship with the two chief contenders for the right to represent the Palestinian cause. Syria herself claimed a role in the custodianship of the Palestinian cause and knew full well that progress towards a settlement made by either Jordan or the PLO would have serious repercussions on the Ba'th regime's own position in the conflict. In the late 1970s and early 1980s Syrian-Jordanian relations were at their worst while Damascus mended fences with the PLO in a joint effort to obstruct the implementation of the Camp David accords. The situation changed in the aftermath, and to some extent as a result, of the 1982 war in Lebanon. Syria's rivalry with Yasser Arafat was revived as Syria sought to exploit the war's outcome in order to destroy Arafat's power base and leadership. Syria's rivalry with Jordan was quelled and their relations were normalized. This did not prevent King Hussein from taking advantage of the PLO's plight. By offering Arafat a haven from Syrian persecution, he acquired, at least temporarily, a hegemonial position in their relationship.

Following the formation of the Israeli National Unity government in September 1984, the new Jordanian-PLO relationship was formalized into the Amman Agreement of February 1985. That agreement was to produce a Jordanian-Palestinian delegation authorized to negotiate the future of the West Bank with Israel. Such negotiations were most undesirable to Syria which gave every indication that, should they proceed beyond a certain point, she would seek to obstruct them. The shadow of Syrian opposition was thus cast on the prospective negotiations. In the event, though, Syria was not required to make good her threats. There were sufficient difficulties inherent in the Israeli-Jordanian/Palestinian relationship to prevent the effort from taking off. In February 1986 King Hussein suspended the Amman Agreement and all subsequent attempts in 1986 and 1987 to proceed with the settlement process failed.

The quest for settlement was in any event transformed by the Palestinian uprising that broke out on 9 December 1987. It weakened the positions of Israel and Jordan and strengthened Palestinian nationalism and the PLO as an organization. Syria relished Israel's and Jordan's political losses and was relieved by the decline in the prospect of a Jordanian-Israeli settlement. Syrian spokesmen and the Syrian media endorsed the Palestinian uprising during its first few months and presented it as a vindication of Syria's own position in the conflict with Israel—struggle was the key to success and capitulation to the US and Israel was not merely illegitimate but also unwarranted. Asad himself addressed the subject in two important speeches. The first was delivered on 8 March 1988 to mark the 25th anniversary of the Ba'th seizure of power. He lavished praise on the Palestinians in the West Bank and Gaza and sought to present his own generation's struggle against the French as foreshadowing the *intifada*: 'I was a student during the era of French Imperialism in Syria,' he said, 'these were years during which half of the school year was spent in street demonstrations . . . we were suddenly fired upon. We would scatter in the streets and hide behind walls. We would not run away . . . We would stand facing these barracks, curse, shout and throw any object held in our hands.'[9]

The second speech was delivered on 12 May before a group of Muslim men of religion. Appropriately for the occasion Asad spoke about martyrdom, but the interesting part of the speech dealt with the relationship between might and right. 'Everybody speaks about rights and about international conventions and about international protocols and resolutions,' he stated, 'but you will find out that in every international event it is force alone that ultimately decides the issue.'[10]

Asad's speeches in March and May 1988 reflected also a concern that the

Palestinian uprising could lead to a revival of the Arab-Israeli peace process albeit in a different fashion and with a different accent. In February the US Secretary of State, George Shultz, produced a new initiative seeking, partly under the pressure of the uprising and partly in an attempt to take advantage of it, to inject new life into the moribund plans of 1987. This time Damascus was included in the Secretary's agenda, but Syria remained suspicious. On 8 March Asad warned his listeners by saying that 'I do not want to enter into the details of the proposals being discussed. I will only say briefly that their spirit and essence is like the spirit and essence of all the programmes which had been raised many years ago, though in different words. There is nothing new in this matter.'[11]

Syria's suspicions were exacerbated by the growing indications in the summer of 1988 that Arafat and the PLO's mainstream were seriously considering a bold change of orientation that would facilitate the PLO's direct participation in a new round of negotiations. On 24 June Arafat's spokesman Bassam Abu Sharif wrote an article in the *New York Times* that included such sentences as 'the PLO accepts Security Council resolutions 242 and 338'. Later in the summer it was suggested that the PLO was about to announce the formation of a Palestinian state or at least a provisional government. The pressure for such a dramatic move came from within the West Bank and Gaza. The local leadership and the population who had been carrying the load of the uprising were clearly expecting a political breakthrough that would constitute an achievement and would earn them a respite.

For Syria this was as dangerous a threat as the prospect of a Jordanian-Israeli settlement. She suspected that a declaration of independence or statehood would, as the Soviet Union and several European states indeed advised, be integrated into a larger strategy addressed toward negotiations and settlement with Israel. Consequently, in August 1988 Syria launched a full-blown propaganda campaign designed to abort the PLO's plans. A typical Syrian commentary argued:

> The Arafatist deviationist gang offers concessions to the Zionist enemy and marches on a path which exposes the face of the Palestinian right wing: It is an attempt to turn the Arafatist gang into a party acceptable to the US and Israel at the table of direct negotiations, because in the aftermath of Abu Sharif's document of conciliation and submission and exchanges of letters and consultations with the enemy's leaders ... they came to us with the new-old idea of a government in exile.[12]

These were not mere denunciations. When another Syrian newspaper[13] warned that 'we will not allow the Arabs to be subdued and the Palestine problem to be liquidated', the threat resonated against the background of the recent blows inflicted by Syria in Lebanon. In January 1988 Amal, the pro-Syrian Shiite militia, finally lifted its siege of the PLO's strongholds in Beirut. It was not a magnanimous concession but an admission of failure. But in May another Syrian proxy, Abu Musa's PLO secessionists, were more successful and expelled Arafat's supporters from Sabra and Shatila. Syria did not pursue the anti-PLO drive but, implied in its propaganda campaign, was the threat to do precisely that.

Syria's expected reaction was one of the considerations that led the PLO to blunt the cutting edge of the declaration of a Palestinian state in Algiers in November 1988 with the complex formulations of the attached political document. Under these circumstances Syria was denied the opportunity to denounce the PLO's 'submission' and 'sellout'. Nor did it wish to be cast in the role of the one Arab state formally and explicitly opposing the notion of Palestinian statehood. Syria's way out of the dilemma was to match the ambiguity of the Algiers statements with another form of ambiguity. Thus on 17 November 1988, two days after the Algiers declaration, a 'responsible Syrian source' issued a statement on Radio Damascus that expressed Syria's support of the Palestinian people's rights, and in the first place 'its right to establish the Palestinian state.' But the statement also paid tribute to Syria's leading role in the conduct of the struggle against Israel and warned against concessions to Israel. It did not explicitly recognize the Palestinian state, and in that respect was the correct expression of a Syrian policy that refused both to recognize the Palestinian state and to say so explicitly.

Syria and the Gulf War

Syria's alliance with the Islamic Republic of Iran has been mentioned above as one of the two pillars of her regional policy and success in the 1982–85 period. But with the passage of time the alliance became increasingly problematic. When Iranian troops crossed the border into Iraq and threatened to rout the Iraqi army, Arab fears of Iran and of a swelling wave of Islamic radicalism grew and with them criticism of Syria's position and conduct. Syria itself was wary of the prospect of a sweeping Iranian victory. It was one thing to have an alliance with an Iran exerting pressure on Iraq from the east and quite a different matter to have a victorious revolutionary Iran as a neighbour.

But it was in the Lebanese arena that Iran presented Syria with the greatest and most immediate difficulties. During the early years of their co-operation Syria afforded Iran with easy access to Lebanon's Shi'i community and enabled her to build Hizballah as a virtual instrument of Iranian policy. Syria and Iran continued their co-operation in the 1982–85 period and directed their joint efforts against such common enemies as the US, Israel and the Maronite militias. But in the aftermath of their success their paths began to diverge. Syria's concept of hegemony in Lebanon extended to the Shi'i community, the country's largest. She cultivated Amal as her ally and client in the Shi'i community and was soon in conflict with Hizballah. The Syrians treaded softly in their conflict with Hizballah knowing full well that a crackdown on the Shi'i radicals could seriously undermine their alliance with Iran.

Syria's trepidation, Amal's weakness and Hizballah's boldness and co-operation with the PLO led to a new loss of Syrian control in Beirut and forced Asad to dispatch an army division to Beirut in February 1987. This was a deviation from his post-1982 policy in Lebanon but he understood that it was essential if Syria's position and prestige were to be saved. The Syrian troops did not enter the Dahya, Hizballah's stronghold in southern Beirut, but the move had a clear anti-Hizballah and anti-Iranian edge.

The move's significance was enhanced by Asad's willingness to meet with his arch-rival Saddam Hussein and to sanction an effort to seek a Syrian-Iraqi reconciliation. Asad acted under the impact of Arab pressure and entice-ment. Indeed, having alleviated Syria's economic plight by a grant in aid from the oil-producing Arab states of the Gulf, he terminated the dialogue with Iraq. And yet the very fact that such a dialogue was held gave further indication of a growing distance between Syria and Iran.

In the spring of 1988 Syria took advantage of Iran's military weakness in the Gulf War in order to complete the move begun in 1987 and sent its troops into the Dahya. Asad acted with his customary patience and caution and avoided an overt rift with Iran and a clash with Hizballah but the goals of consolidat-ing Syria's hold over Beirut and the release of Western hostages were not accomplished.

A few months later Iran's military weakness led it to agree to a ceasefire in the Gulf War on terms which amounted to a slight Iraqi victory. The resulting change in Syria's position was not dramatic. The ceasefire was tenuous and the future course of the Iran-Iraq conflict uncertain. One could assume that the conflict would continue and that Iraq would not be free to devote its full attention and resources to the larger Middle Eastern arena. But even a partial relief sufficed for Iraq to indicate that it intended to settle its accounts with Syria and that it considered Lebanon a suitable point of departure. Iraq began by providing weapons to the Lebanese Forces, the Maronite militia most vehemently opposed to Syrian domination in Lebanon, and continued with aid to the PLO. Iraq's support stiffened the back of the Lebanese Forces and was instrumental in their decision and ability to prevent Syria in August 1988 from imposing its candidate as Lebanon's president. Iraq's leader was quite explicit when he addressed the Lebanese issue in November:

> In Lebanon, we live in a tragic situation, in the full sense of the term and it is a tragedy when one Arab occupies another ... We are delighted by Taba's return to Egypt but at the same time the Israelis are violating Lebanon's entire territory because of the Syrian occupation ... We are open to dialogue with our brethren in Lebanon and to help anyone who seeks to expel the occupier whether he comes from Syria or from Israel.[14]

Syria in Lebanon

Syria's decision to seek the election of its most trusted Lebanese client, Suleiman Faranjiyya, as Lebanon's president represented yet another deviation from Asad's post-1982 strategy in Lebanon and as such was a symptom of distress.

When Asad undid the results of the 1982 war and re-established Syria's hegemony in Lebanon he also modified the principles that had guided his Lebanese policy prior to 1982. The lessons drawn from the first phase of Syrian preeminence in Lebanon indicated that a massive military presence in Beirut and intimate involvement in the minute details of Lebanese politics were counterproductive. It seemed preferable to pursue Syria's goals by relying on her military presence in eastern and northern Lebanon, on her clients, on her ability to manipulate the remaining institutions of the state and on the deterrent effect of her record in Lebanon. Asad knew that Lebanon could not be brought fully under Syria's control. He had come to realize his own limitations, the complexity of Lebanon's politics and the constraints imposed by other external actors in Lebanese politics. Yet he still assumed that Syria could gradually consolidate and further extend her preeminence, introduce some reform and change, maintain a reasonable level of public order and draw additional political dividends from her Lebanese patrimony.

But in 1985 and 1986 it transpired that the resources available to Syria in Lebanon were insufficient. She could not effect any reform, and public order in Beirut deteriorated rather than improved. Amin Jumayyil as president and Michel Awn as army commander were uncooperative and Syria's rivals proved to be more numerous and more effective than her clients.

In 1987 Asad had to abandon one tenet of his new policy and to dispatch his army into Beirut. He did so to avoid a dangerous erosion of Syria's position but his success was limited. He went deeper into southern Beirut in 1988 and the results were equally meagre. The Hizballah and the PLO networks were not uprooted and Syria's soldiers were even more exposed to attacks by Shi'i and Palestinian opponents. In this context, it is important to explain Asad's outlook on the question of Western hostages in Lebanon. As the power claiming a preeminent position in Lebanon, Syria felt that the kidnapping of new Western hostages reflected badly on her international standing. As for hostages already held in captivity by the radical Shi'is, their release could be used as an asset in negotiations with the relevant Western powers.

In 1988 Lebanon's politics were governed by the presidential elections to the extent that the term can apply to the election of a new president by a 'rump' parliament, whose mandate should have expired in 1976, and held under the shadow of rival military threats. Amin Jumayyil's term was to expire on 23 September and according to Lebanon's political tradition his successor was to be chosen at some point between May and September.

Syria faced three principal options: to accept a nationalist-Maronite candidate; to try to impose one of her Maronite clients; to settle on a compromise candidate. Syria never seriously considered the first option. In the course of 1988 she discussed various compromise ideas with the United States but finally decided to force the election of Suleiman Faranjiyya. The Syrians knew that it would be difficult to impose an old candidate who aroused strong opposition in many quarters, primarily because he was so totally identified with Syria. But they assumed that the election could be arranged and that the immediate costs of this arbitrary act would be dwarfed soon thereafter by the immense advantage of having a pliable president in Lebanon. Three years of successive challenges and difficulties in Lebanon and the spectre of vigorous Iraqi intervention must have reinforced this frame of mind.

But the Syrian gambit failed. Syria's opponents headed by the Lebanese Forces were able to obstruct Faranjiyya's election by preventing a quorum at the parliamentary session. There followed a formal round of American-Syrian negotiations when Assistant Secretary of State Richard Murphy visited Damascus in September. The US agreed to support another pro-Syrian candidate, Mikhail Daher. But the US could not prevail upon Asad's Maronite opponents and Daher's election was foiled in a similar fashion. The Lebanese crisis became still more entangled and Syria suffered a humiliating failure.

Syria and the Superpowers

Mr Murphy's visit to Damascus in September 1988, and Washington's willingness to endorse a pro-Syrian candidate for the Lebanese presidency, were illustrative of the complex nature of Syria's relationship with the United States and, in a larger way, of her international orientation.

Since 1972, Syria had been the Soviet Union's most important Middle Eastern client and had, in turn, depended on the Soviet Union for political support, military supplies and aid, some economic aid and a vague security umbrella. But the importance of this relationship for both parties had not been matched by its closeness or warmth. There is no ideological dimension to the relationship; both sides seem to be motivated by a cool calculation of interest. In the past, tensions arose over policy differences and as a result of Asad's determination to preserve Syria's independence and his ability to decide freely over national security questions against Soviet encroachment in these matters. In recent years relations have been marred by differences of opinion over such issues as attitudes toward the PLO, the development of Soviet relations with the conservative Arab states, Soviet refusal to supply certain weapon systems and insistence on proper payment, and the application of glasnost to the Middle East. The Syrians feel uncomfortable with Gorbachev and his policies and suspect that their extension to the Middle East would be conducted at their expense.

It was a measure of the limits of his relationship with the Soviet Union that, since coming to power, Asad had consistently sought to develop a dialogue with the United States. Asad's drive was motivated by a desire to reduce his dependence on the Soviet Union as well as by recognition of Washington's crucial role in the region. A dialogue with the United States was opened in December 1973, in the immediate wake of the October War. Then, and on several subsequent occasions, a rapport was established between Asad and his American interlocutors, and a sense prevailed that the US and Syria could not only improve their bilateral relations but co-operate also in the implementation of a larger regional policy. But in the event the 1974 Syrian-Israeli disengagement agreement was the only product of these efforts. All other attempts ended in failure and led to periods of antagonism and conflict. During these later periods Syria strove to demonstrate to the US that whilst it was difficult to reach agreement with Syria it was impossible to implement a regional policy in the Middle East in the teeth of Syrian opposition.

Between 1982 and 1984 the US and Syria were on opposite sides of the Lebanese conflict. That episode ended with a clear cut Syrian victory which left the Reagan-Shultz administration with a residue of anti-Syrian sentiment but also with some grudging admiration for Asad's skill and tenacity. Washington's subsequent efforts to promote an Israeli-Jordanian-Palestinian agreement never advanced sufficiently to draw serious Syrian opposition, but the shadow of that expected opposition was clearly visible. It was correctly assumed that should such an agreement become feasible and imminent Syria should be either brought in or neutralized.

The quest for an Arab-Israeli settlement was abandoned in 1987 but the success of the Palestinian uprising led to its renewal in 1988. When Secretary of State Shultz launched his initiative in February 1988 and came to the region to advance it, he included a visit to Damascus in his programme. Syria was clearly pleased that her relevance and role were recognized but made no secret of her opposition to the plan itself. In any event the initiative soon collapsed and the accent of the Syrian-American relationship again shifted to the Lebanese issue.

As has been described above, Richard Murphy's visit to Damascus in September resulted in an agreement on the candidacy of the pro-Syrian Mikhail Daher. It was an American concession and it is still not known what was promised in return. If Syria promised to help with the release of Americans held by Hizballah, her efforts to produce American hostages were foiled by the radical Shi'is. Whether Arab-Israeli issues were discussed as well has yet to be seen.

Syria and the Arab-Israeli Conflict

It is on her role and position in the Arab-Israeli conflict that Syria's claim to Arab leadership has rested most firmly. Syria participated in the post-1973

Arab-Israeli settlement process and accepted the 1982 Fez formula, but since 1975 she has led the opposition to any Arab agreement with Israel that deviated from her definition of the proper Arab nationalist position. While still adhering to the principle of a political resolution of the Arab-Israeli conflict, Syria's definition of a legitimate political settlement is such that the prospect of her actual endorsement of one seemed very dim.[15]

Syria's policy in the Arab-Israeli conflict since the early 1980s had been conducted under the doctrine and slogan of 'strategic parity with Israel'. The doctrine holds that Syria should have sufficient military strength to stand on her own against Israel in a future confrontation. Under that doctrine an impressive build-up took place in the aftermath of the 1982 war that turned Syria's armed forces into a large and well equipped military machine.

This military machine did not have 'strategic parity' with its Israeli counterpart. But the rapid pace of its development against the backdrop of Syria's achievements in Lebanon in 1982–85 and the self-confidence they generated created an anxiety in Israel and elsewhere that Syria was planning to launch at least a limited war against Israel. Ironically, the Syrian leadership itself was worried by the prospect of a pre-emptive Israeli attack as well as by the political damage at home that exaggerated expectations were creating. The stage was set for a classic case of mutual misperception.

Thus in February and March 1986 speculation concerning a planned Syrian attack on Israel was fuelled by two speeches in which Hafez al-Asad spoke about 'strategic parity' and used threatening language against Israel. A close reading of the same speeches revealed that Asad was actually telling his people that 'strategic parity' had yet to be achieved and was in fact a long term goal. But the wave of speculation which emanated from Israel had a curious mirror effect on Syria. Since Syria did not, in fact, plan an attack at that time her leaders tended to interpret the Israeli statements as the preparatory political groundwork for an attack on Syria. The American raid on Libya in April 1986 and a visit by the Israeli Defence Minister to Washington exacerbated Syrian anxiety in the spring of 1986 that the US and Israel were indeed planning an attack on Syria.[16]

In 1987 much of this tension was dissipated by Syria's economic difficulties. In an effort to reduce expenditure the order of battle of the Syrian army was reduced. The military significance of this reduction was a matter of debate, but its psychological impact was unquestionable. The Israelis became persuaded that an army preparing to launch war would not be reducing its order of battle and a much calmer atmosphere came to prevail in Syrian-Israeli relations. But the underlying instability and tension were not addressed and not removed, and in 1988 the pendulum began to swing in the other direction. News of Syrian success in purchasing precision guided medium range missiles from China and Syrian efforts to develop chemical weapons pointed to a new source of tension. If Syria were to obtain such weapon systems her leaders might be tempted to believe that a significant advantage over Israel would have been acquired.

There was a weakness built into Syria's policy in the Arab-Israeli conflict. Syria's definition of an acceptable political settlement coupled with Israel's own view of a settlement with Syria made such a settlement a remote possibility. Syria's role as the standard bearer of Arab nationalism and the criticism she levelled at all Arabs seeking a settlement with Israel exposed her role to close scrutiny. The question was asked, what Asad intended to do in practice *vis-à-vis* Israel if he opposed all available modes of settlement on the one hand and was not ready to go to war on the other?

It was in order to counter such criticism that Syria devised ways to promote anti-Israeli activities in an indirect fashion which gave Syria political benefits without exposing her to Israeli retaliation and without running the risk of an undesirable escalation. Recently this strategy focussed on South Lebanon where Syria encouraged pro-Syrian Palestinian organizations and the Lebanese Syrian Social Nationalist Party to operate.

Conclusions

A study of Syria's regional and foreign policies reveals an almost rhythmic oscillation between phases of success and retreat. Syria's inability to sustain her successes over time seems to be the product of her limited intrinsic power and resources, the underlying weakness of the regime's political base and the shifting nature of Middle Eastern regional politics.

Syria has been at once part of the regional political system and an actor seeking to shape it to its own liking. Her ability to do so has naturally depended on the attitudes and relative strength of the other actors.

The recent period has clearly been one of retreat and retrenchment for Syria in the Arab world. Her main rivals—Iraq, Egypt and the PLO—have all registered considerable successes. In the three principal arenas of Syria's regional policy—Lebanon, inter-Arab relations and the Arab-Israeli conflict—Syria faces uncertain odds. It will be up to Hafez al-Asad to take advantage of the weaknesses which do exist among his rivals and of the opportunities that the unstable politics of the Middle East are bound to provide in order to swing the pendulum one more time in the other direction.

Notes

1. Patrick Seale, *Observer* (London), 6 March 1977.
2. The Associated Press from Damascus, 21 November 1975.
3. Fouad Ajami, 'Between Cairo and Damascus', *Foreign Affairs*, April 1976, pp. 444–61.
4. See the various essays in G. Luciani and G. Salame (eds.), *The Politics of Arab Integration* (London 1988).

5. Itamar Rabinovich, 'Full circle—Syrian politics in the 1970s', in G. S. Wise and C. Issawi (eds.), *Middle East Perspectives* (Princeton, NJ 1981), pp. 129–40.

6. Itamar Rabinovich, 'The changing prism: Syrian policy in Lebanon as a mirror, an issue and an instrument', in M. Maoz and A. Yariv (eds.), *Syria under Assad* (London 1986), pp. 179–90.

7. *Tishrin* (Damascus), 9 July 1983.

8. See Bruce Maddy-Weitzman's chapters on inter-Arab relations in *Middle East Contemporary Survey*, vols. 7–10 (Tel-Aviv, 1982–86).

9. Radio Damascus, 8 March 1988.

10. Radio Damascus, 12 May 1988.

11. Radio Damascus, 8 March 1988.

12. *Al-Thawra* (Damascus), 7 August 1988.

13. *Tishrin*, 6 August 1988.

14. *Al-Thawra* (Baghdad), 18 November 1988.

15. Itamar Rabinovich, 'Syria's quest for a regional role', Working Paper No. 79, International Security Studies Program, Woodrow Wilson International Center for Scholars.

16. Ibid.

Part C
THE USA

8
The Presidential Election of 1988

STUART E. EIZENSTAT

The 1988 presidential election underscored one of the most remarkable political events of modern American political history—the continued romance between American Jewish voters and the Democratic Party.

American Jews continued to vote contrary to others in their income range and to buck the conservative tide which, since 1968, has continued to be the major undertow in America's national elections. Thus, for example, in Ronald Reagan's landslide 59–40 per cent 1984 victory over former Vice-President Walter Mondale, President Reagan won 78 per cent of the white fundamentalist Christian vote, 72 per cent of the white Protestant vote, 54 per cent of the Catholic vote, but only 31 per cent of the Jewish vote. This came despite an excellent record of support for Israel and for Soviet Jewry—two causes dear to American Jews.

In 1988, Republicans mounted an enormous effort to woo the Jewish vote, even surpassing their 1984 activities. A formal Jewish Republican coalition group, headed by Chris Gersten, had been operating for several years. A strong pro-Israel platform was drafted by the George Bush loyalists and approved by the Republican Convention in New Orleans. Thomas Dine, Executive Director of the American Israel Public Affairs Committee, proclaimed the Republican platform the 'best platform ever on US-Israel relations by either political party'. The platform condemned antisemitism, supported strategic co-operation with Israel, and stated that the US should have no dealings with the Palestine Liberation Organization.

In addition, an intense and often vitriolic campaign was launched by Jewish Republicans close to Vice-President Bush to raise the spectre of Jesse Jackson against the Democrats.

Stuart Eizenstat, a lawyer and a lecturer at the Kennedy School of Government in Washington, DC, was President Carter's Chief Domestic Policy Adviser at the White House. He is active in a variety of local and national Jewish organizations.

Jesse Jackson was a very controversial figure among American Jews. His past association with avowed antisemite Louis Farrakhan, his offhand remark in his 1984 presidential campaign that New York City was 'Hymie town', his pro-Palestinian position and meeting with Yasser Arafat combined to make him *persona non grata* in parts of the Jewish community. His strong second place finish in the Democratic primaries and his dominance of the Democratic Convention in Atlanta only heightened anxieties, upon which Republicans played.

Max Fisher, long a pillar of the American Jewish community and a leading Republican, flatly accused the Dukakis campaign of antisemitism in agreeing to permit Jesse Jackson to name three persons who had anti-Israel backgrounds to the 450-member Democratic National Committee. Gordon Zacks, perhaps Vice-President Bush's closest adviser from the Jewish community, claimed that the Democratic Party had decided to trade Jewish support for blacks. As he put it, 'The Democratic Party, to which we Jews once entrusted the protection of our interests, has told us that what we say does not count any more. With the rise of Jesse Jackson and his confidants, our views are expendable, a price the Democrats are willing to pay to keep Mr. Jackson happy.'

An additional factor which should have helped the Bush candidacy among Republican voters was voting patterns by income class. The United States likes to see itself as a classless society; indeed, there is considerably less class-consciousness in America than in most European societies. Virtually everyone thinks he or she is 'middle class'.

But in point of fact, voting heavily follows income. Thus, for example, in the 1980, 1984 and 1988 presidential elections, each won overwhelmingly by the Republican candidate, the Democratic nominees, Jimmy Carter, Walter Mondale and Michael Dukakis, actually won among lower income voters, those earning under $12,000 annually. In the 1988 election, Dukakis beat Bush among those voters with a household income under $5,000, those between $5,000 and $9,999, and those between $10,000 and $19,000. He virtually broke even with those between $20,000 and $29,000. But as household income increased, so too did the Republican vote, in perfect step with income.

Jewish voters, with average household income in the $40,000 range, should have voted with their income. Yet, despite all of this, the Jewish vote in the presidential election went overwhelmingly for Governor Michael Dukakis, the Democratic nominee. While the estimates varied, they all fell in a range which indicated that Jews voted from two to two-and-a-half-to-one for Dukakis. Thus, for example, the CBS-*New York Times* exit poll indicated 64 per cent of American Jews voted for Dukakis. The *Washington Post*-ABC exit poll had 71 per cent for Dukakis to only 28 per cent for Bush. The NBC poll also was 71 per cent. The CNN-*Los Angeles Times* was 74 per cent and an exit poll taken by the American Jewish Congress was 77 per cent. Even the poll taken by Robert Teeter, George Bush's own pollster, indicated a split at 69–31 among Jewish voters for Dukakis.

This disproportionate Democratic support was not an aberration. Thus, in 1984, Vice-President Mondale won 67–70 per cent of the Jewish vote, despite being swamped by Ronald Reagan. The high water mark of American Jewish support for a Republican was in the 1980 Reagan-Carter election when Reagan got 39 per cent of the Jewish vote, a percentage which has slipped in the two elections since then.

Where there is now a virtual 50-50 split in party identification between Democrats and Republicans, American Jews are four-to-one Democratic in their registration. Where by a two-to-one margin American voters in general identify themselves as conservative rather than liberal (with a great bulk who identify themselves as moderates), Jews identify themselves by a three-to-two margin as liberal.

What then explains this extraordinary identification by the American Jewish community with the Democratic Party, an identification all the more amazing when one considers that among white voters in general Dukakis received barely over 40 per cent of the white vote and Mondale in 1984 under 40 per cent?

There are several reasons for this extraordinary attachment. The first is simply history. The identification of American Jews with the Democratic Party was locked in by Franklin Roosevelt, who reached out to the disadvantaged and extended the hand of government protection to all minorities. FDR attempted to bring those outside the mainstream of American life into the mainstream, Jews among them. First generation American Jewish immigrants thus developed a powerful identification with the Democratic Party, an identification that has been passed on to a second, third and now fourth generation of voters. According to a humorous phrase, Jews in the 1940s talked of three things: *Die Velt* (this world), *Yenna Velt* (the world to come) and Roosevelt!

And yet this cannot be a full explanation. For many groups, such as union workers, blue collar workers, other Eastern European immigrants, the attachment to the Democratic Party that Franklin Roosevelt initially created has been diluted over the years and those voters have tended to vote more along economic lines.

There is a second reason why Jews have remained loyal to the Democratic Party when other groups have not: American Jews take a broad view of their own self-interest. In the end, most voters vote according to what they believe is in their own best interests, and then interpret that to mean that it is necessarily in the best interests of the United States. For most voters that self-interest comes down to economics. It has been said that American Jews live like white Anglo-Saxon Protestants, but vote like low income minority groups. This is because of a most expansive notion of self-interest. From Jewish history, there is a recognition that ultimately Jews do best when all segments of society are treated fairly and brought into the economic and political mainstream. Indeed, when this does not occur, it is the Jews who will become the scapegoats in the end. There is a powerful sense of community among Jewish voters, a community of interest across economic, race and class lines.

There is a third reason: Jewish values. Certainly, the Torah nowhere tells American Jews to vote Democratic. However, the values of the Democratic Party—the use of government to protect the disadvantaged and to reduce barriers to full opportunity for everyone, the emphasis on helping the poor and downtrodden rather than benefiting the rich—are all values which resonate with traditional Jewish values of justice and charity. The Bible admonishes us to leave a portion of our field untended for the poor. It tells us, in the words of Leviticus, that 'if thy brother waxen poor and his means fail, then though shalt uphold him.' Abraham's offer of bread and shelter to the three strangers underscores the Jewish commitment to social justice and to the equality of all people in God's eyes. Isaiah's words, that we should 'feed the hungry, clothe the naked, and let the oppressed go free', resonate with the philosophy of the Democratic Party.

Maimonides, one of the greatest Jewish sages of all time, wrote a lengthy tractate on the orders of charity, the highest being to help a person to help themselves—the very essence of the ethic of opportunity embodied in Democratic presidents from Roosevelt to Carter.

A fourth reason for the lasting identification of American Jews with the Democratic presidents is that Democratic presidents have been the champions of Israel. It was President Harry Truman who extended the crucial American recognition of Israel in 1948 at its time of maximum vulnerability. It was President John Kennedy who ended the arms embargo and sold defensive arms for the first time to Israel. President Lyndon Johnson sold the first offensive weapons to Israel and ended the diplomatic embargo of Israel by inviting the Prime Minister, Levi Eshkol, to the United States in 1965 for the first state visit by an Israeli prime minister. And it was another Democratic president, Jimmy Carter, who helped Israel achieve its first peace with an Arab neighbour.

Support for Israel is a litmus test all candidates for the presidency must pass before they can be seriously considered by the American Jewish community. Once a Democratic candidate passes this litmus test, Jewish voters will consider other domestic issues in which the Democratic candidates seem more congenial. Indeed, one of the reasons why Jimmy Carter's support in the Jewish community slipped so badly was the perception—I strongly believe an incorrect one—that he had leaned on Israel too heavily.

Governor Dukakis passed this litmus test and thus American Jews were able to vote on broader issues. Perhaps among the most important of these additional issues was church-state and abortion. Vice-President Bush and the Republican platform had supported prayer in public schools—a position supported by 71 per cent of the general population, but only 18 per cent of American Jews. Likewise, on the issue of a woman's right to abortion, Mr Bush and the Republicans took a very hard stand in opposition to abortion under virtually every circumstance. Yet, 87 per cent of the American Jewish population—compared to only 45 per cent of the general populaton—supported a woman's right to an aborton.

With respect to Vice-President Bush, there had been some questions raised about the depth of his commitment to Israel. Former Secretary of State Alexander Haig recounted in his book that Vice-President Bush had led the charge to condemn Israel for its attack on the Iraqi nuclear plant and had urged withholding arms to Israel in retaliation. Others stated that Mr Bush had been the prime proponent condemning Israel at the United Nations after the Israeli invasion of Lebanon. He had also been perceived as using Israel as a scapegoat in the Iran-contra scandal, telling the Tower Commission that 'US policy was in the grasp of the Israelis'. Nor was the Bush campaign helped by the charge levelled a few weeks before the election by Secretary of Defence Frank Carlucci that pro-Israel groups 'have sought to impede virtually every Administration initiative to provide reasonable and responsible military assistance to our Arab partners . . . causing billions of dollars in jobs to go abroad instead of sustaining our key defense industries.'

Yet, it is not that American Jews voted against Bush because they thought he was antagonistic to Israel. In fact, he was not, and has been friendly to Israel. Rather it is simply that when a Democratic and Republican presidential candidate are both acceptable on Israel, most of the Jewish community moves to other issues in which Democrats have an advantage.

The last factor which held Jews to the Democratic ticket in 1988 is simply the background and personality of the candidates. Governor Dukakis's background as the son of a Greek immigrant is one with which American Jews readily identify. Like Governor Dukakis and his father, they had made it in America. Vice-President Bush's background, on the other hand, was one with which American Jews felt less comfortable, coming as he did from an old line New England family, with a prep school and Yale education and a Texas oil industry background. Many American Jews simply did not relate to his background.

This was reinforced by the unfortunate fact that on an ethnic advisory committee created for Mr Bush, there were a few neo-Nazis, who subsequently resigned when their backgrounds were disclosed. Fred Malek, whom Mr Bush selected to be his convention manager and deputy chairman of the Republican party, was also required to resign when an old Watergate-era report surfaced that while on the White House staff of President Nixon, he supplied the names of Jewish employees in the Labor Department's Bureau of Labor Statistics at President Richard Nixon's request, when Nixon was angered at the unemployment figures coming from the Bureau of Labor Statistics, and believed that Jews had been responsible.

One interesting sidelight was that the presence of a Jewish wife, Kitty Dukakis, active and visible in Jewish activities, such as the Holocaust Commission and Soviet Jewry, according to poll data had very little influence on Jewish support for Dukakis. While this may be true, her presence as a potential First Lady contributed to the overall feeling of being comfortable with Dukakis.

There were two potential bright spots for Republicans. The first is that among younger American Jews, a survey taken by News Combo, a syndicate of three independently owned Jewish newspapers, indicated that younger Jews were twice as likely to have voted for Bush as middle aged and older Jews, thus giving some hope for the future to Republicans.

Second, the same survey found that nearly half of orthodox Jews backed Bush. A poll taken by Robert Teeter, Mr Bush's own pollster, indicated an even higher figure for orthodox Jews—75 per cent. By contrast, the News Combo poll found that conservative Jews gave 81 per cent of their vote to Dukakis, reform Jews 76 per cent, and unaffiliated Jews backed Dukakis by 83 per cent to only 16 per cent for Bush.

But even these potential bright spots in an otherwise gloomy result on the Jewish side for Republicans was tempered by other realities. One was that Jews are an ageing community and younger Jews made up only a small portion of the overall Jewish electorate. Whilst orthodox Jews, more conservative in their political attitudes, tended to vote more heavily Republican, they composed only about 10 per cent of the American Jewish community.

The fact that Bush failed to do better in the Jewish community was caused in significant part by defections of almost half the Jews who voted for President Ronald Reagan in 1984 against Walter Mondale, while Dukakis inherited fully 95 per cent of those Jews who voted for Mondale, the 1984 Democratic nominee.

One question frequently asked in the American Jewish community was whether the continued overwhelming support of American Jews for the Democratic Party would mean less Jewish influence on the Bush administration and, consequently, less Jewish clout on behalf of the state of Israel. My belief is that this will not be the case. Republicans for years have targeted the Jewish community as a major constituency group both for their financial contributions and their enthusiastic involvement in the political process— whilst only 50 per cent of the overall American public voted, it is likely that some 80 per cent of the American Jewish population voted. The Bush administration, like the Reagan administration before it, will continue to woo the American Jewish community and is unlikely to turn its back on the Jewish community because of its relatively poor showing in the election. Moreover, support for Israel is so broad-based that the Bush administration's Middle East policy will not turn simply on election returns.

But, the bottom line is that Republican efforts to obtain American Jewish support for their presidential candidates is like chasing the proverbial pot of gold at the end of the rainbow. Just when they think they are close, the prize remains out of reach.

9

US Jewry's Response to the *Intifada*

CHARLES FENYVESI

Since the outbreak of the *intifada* in December 1987, American Jews have run through a gamut of reactions that began with shock and disbelief, and blame put on the news media for creating the crisis. The painful experience of seeing television images of Israeli soldiers beating up Arab civilians eventually turned into a deep, throbbing anguish, with reports of drops in synagogue attendance and involvement in Jewish organizations. The current mainstream response may be best characterized as battle fatigue. To the left-of-centre, a deepening despair has set in, and to the right-of-centre there is only a quasi-fatalistic hope that somehow some Israel will eventually come up with a solution in the years to come.

Following the first searing television images of Israeli soldiers in full battle gear hitting and shooting Arab youths, committed American Jews feared an imminent open break between American and Israeli Jewries. Across the spectrum of American Jewry, parallels were drawn with the protest against the Vietnam war and the riots in black ghettoes.

The initial revulsion against Israel's attempt to crush the *intifada* ran so high that in the first days of 1988, two reform rabbis called upon their national organization to cancel immediately its meeting scheduled to be held in Jerusalem later that year. Speaking separately, the two rabbis protested that 'honouring Israel' with a meeting at this time of 'tragic and inexcusable Israeli brutalities' would not be right. Their suggestion was eventually rejected, but not dismissed outright as it doubtless would have been at any other previous time in the past four decades.

Charles Fenyvesi is a reporter with *US News & World Report* responsible for the weekly column 'Washington Whispers'. At various times in his long career, he served as the Washington correspondent of the *Jerusalem Post, Ha'aretz* and the London *Jewish Chronicle*. He also worked as a feature writer for the *Washington Post* and as an editor of the *National Jewish Monthly* and the *Washington Jewish Week*.

In February 1988, at a meeting in the conservative and emphatically establishment synagogue Adas Israel in Washington DC, author Milton Viorst expressed his 'horror' at what Israel was doing in the occupied territories. He was discussing his new book, *Sands of Sorrow*, which was sharply critical of what he called Israel's refusal to make peace with the Arabs. At any other time since Israel's rebirth, Viorst would have been given the verbal equivalent of tar and feather. But much to his surprise—and to the rabbi's, who introduced him and asked everyone 'to be calm, please'— Viorst's condemnation of Israeli policies occasioned a few sceptical questions but no hostility. Following his speech and the question-and-answer session, he received hearty applause. Viorst, the rabbi and the audience itself were astonished.

Organized American Jewry's first significant statement on the *intifada* was published in February 1988, following three days of telephone argument and marathon negotiations. The first draft suggested a reiteration of the kind of traditional endorsement that American Jews give to Israel's policies. But this time, as many as four key organizations refused to sign unless Israel was also taken to task. Because Jewish unity in that hour of crisis was judged to be all-important, Morris Abram, then chairman of the Conference of Major American Jewish Organizations and an amiable lawyer from the South, finally cobbled together a compromise: the 51 national Jewish organizations affiliated with the conference expressed 'unity and identification with the embattled nation of Israel', but at the same time voiced 'concern' at 'any departures' from Israel's long-standing 'policy of restraint' in dealing with the Arabs. 'There is no question that the community supports Israel', said Abram at the time.

> Everyone is agonized and anguished with what Israel is faced with. These people [the Palestinians] have a grievance, but that grievance is misdirected and the means are improper. The overwhelming majority [of Palestinians] also know that their means of protest are improper. It's not civil disobedience, such as sit-ins at lunch counters. It's revolutionary violence, with lethal slingshots and Molotov cocktails.

Moreover, the Presidents' Conference ignored the objections of Prime Minister Yitzhak Shamir and sided with Israel's Foreign Minister, Shimon Peres, in welcoming US efforts 'to move the peace process forward to a just and lasting peace.' In the past, opposition to any US peace initiative that did not have the complete and unambiguous support of the Israeli government came under the category of 'imposed peace' and was condemned by US Jewish organizations.

For the first time in the 30-odd year history of the Presidents' Conference, it issued a statement that clearly and unmistakably implied criticism of Israel's government. Also for the first time, in a matter affecting Israel's security, there was an angry split instead of congenial unanimity among conference members.

'We signed only after Alexander Schindler spent many hours on the phone to change the statement from a total defence of Israel', explained Rabbi Eugene Lipman, then president of the Central Conference of American Rabbis, the reform rabbinical association, and an ally of Schindler, president of the Union of American Hebrew Congregations, the reform movement's lay body, with a membership of more than one million. 'The occupation is impossible and has been for a long time', said Lipman who called Arab unrest 'an event that was waiting to happen. It blew the top off a festering, cancerous sore. The territories have been anything but peaceful.'

Rabbi Schindler was once credited with the considerable public-relations feat of improving the image among American Jews of Menachem Begin shortly after he became prime minister. 'Schindler made Begin kosher in America', sums up one veteran observer of the reform movement and its rabbis. 'That means he can also do risky things from the left as well.' In 1988, Schindler took the risk and stood out as the first important national Jewish leader in the US who publicly protested Israeli policies. In a January 1988 telegram to President Chaim Herzog, Schindler called Israel's policy of 'indiscriminate beating' of Arabs 'an offence to the Jewish spirit' and a 'betrayal of the Zionist dream'.

Statements by American Jewish intellectuals have been even less restrained. 'We read with shame reports of hundreds of beatings and broken bones of the aged and children', wrote Irving Howe and other Jewish intellectuals in a statement carried in the *New York Times*. The *New Republic*, one of America's leading intellectual weeklies with many Jews among its contributors and readers, has adopted the epithet 'the mad settlers'.

For Ted Mann, then chairman of the American Jewish Congress, the watershed event which spurred his and other public criticisms of Israel was the beating of shopkeepers by Israeli soldiers to force the opening of stores. Mann called these incidents 'inhumane and unacceptable'. He explained that the 75,000 members of the activist organization he heads had been 'very solidly' behind the following argument: Israel is right to be in the territories because it has no one to negotiate with—because it has to be in the territories. But the moment Israel has a choice, as it now appears, it should leave because the alternative is a worsening cycle of riots and repression. According to Mann, once that policy was announced last spring, the American Jewish Congress lost some 20 members, 'but a lot more people joined'.

Statements such as Schindler's and Mann's raised the ire of traditional Zionists. 'We are seeing a surprising lack of sophistication on the part of people entrusted with high positions in Jewish life', said Paul Flacks, executive director of the Zionist Organization of America (ZOA) whose 120,000 members are considered firm supporters of Israel. 'I don't know of a time when the Jewish community acted as emotionally as now—as full of self-doubt, as unsure of itself.' Flacks charged that critics of Israel have 'their own private agendas' and suggested that there would not have been 'such an outburst' if Labour's Shimon Peres headed the government, rather than Likud's Yitzhak Shamir. Conceding that the Presidents' Conference declaration offered criticism of Israeli policies for the first time, Flacks expressed pride that he and his organization were able to delete a phrase which would have referred to Israel's 'harsh treatment' of Palestinian demonstrators.

To Mann, the first round of the American Jewish argument with the Israeli government over the *intifada* had an important consequence. 'Now it is a given that American Jews have the right to speak out', Mann said in March 1988. 'I don't want to talk about the issue. I just do it. Whether people like it or not, American Jews are part of the peace process—a factor in what the American government decides to do, a factor in what Israel decides to do. But it is no longer a silent factor. The American Jewish community is now an active factor—and that is terribly self-evident.'

A year after that statement, Ted Mann, a Philadelphia lawyer and a frequent contributor of opinion pieces to major metropolitan newspapers, felt even stronger on the issue of freedom to criticize. The onus attached to public criticism of Israel was 'much, much less' than it was only a year ago, he said. What contributed to the new mood was the 'Who is a Jew?' issue, which upset many Jews even more than the *intifada*. As a result, Mann concluded, 'I am not getting anywhere near the flak I would have gotten a year ago. And in terms of membership, the American Jewish Congress has gained far more than it has lost.'

To Paul Flacks of the ZOA, Mann's ideas smacked of treason. Flacks argued that American Jews did not really want to condemn Israel but they did it because of what they saw on television. 'If it were not for the TV scenes showing Arabs and Israelis', Flacks said, 'American Jews would be going about their business as usual—as would the rest of the world.' As for the point about American Jews speaking up, Flacks said that 'Jewish over-reaction' is what bothered him most in the current crisis. 'The worst thing is Jews condemning Jews', he summed up.

The Presidents' Conference and mainstream Jewish organizations have made no significant public statements on the *intifada* since the Presidents' Conference declaration in February 1988. A principal reason is that there was little to say, and there was no particular reason to rekindle the heated arguments of 1988. Another reason is that a large part of American Jewry was confused and did not wish to commit itself one way or another, and the organizations were sensitive to that feeling. 'We are very quiet', says Rabbi Lipman, a retired rabbi in the Washington DC area. 'There is no consensus. There is only a fragmentized consensus, with a lot of polarization and name-calling.' From the other end of the spectrum, Flacks found the status of Jewish unity 'sad' and agreed that polarization had increased. He said that on the left, the rhetoric had become sharper, describing Israel in words that should never be used, such as 'brutal'.

Among members of the Presidents' Conference only the ZOA stood up forcefully and publicly for Israel, with occasional help from the Anti-Defamation League. The others were either 'quiet or hedging or are helping Israel's enemies.' Flacks believed that those who voiced their opposition to Israel's policies on the *intifada* did 'incalculable harm' to Israel, with effects that are 'far-reaching and long-lasting'. The rhetoric they produced is 'absolutely perfect for the anti-Israel forces'.

Between Lipman and Flacks, but closer to Flacks, is Seymour Reich, the president of B'nai B'rith, the current chairman of the Presidents' Conference and a centrist. A New York lawyer, Reich described the American Jewish community as 'uneasy with the nightly television screen showing young Palestinians throwing rocks at Israeli soldiers.' He acknowledged being 'unhappy' with Israel's handling of the *intifada*, but, he added, the Palestinian problem must be put in the context of the Arab refusal to make peace and Israel had the responsibility to maintain order. Reich said he found that the tide had turned: criticism of Israel in and out of the Jewish community had diminished, and Shamir's proposal for elections had 'the overwhelming support' of Americans, Jews and Gentiles alike.

At the same time, Reich's B'nai B'rith also protested, in its fashion, against Israeli government policies. For instance, B'nai B'rith did not respond to the Israeli government's request to lobby the US government against its opening of talks with the Palestine Liberation Organization (PLO) in Tunis last year. In the years before the *intifada* such an important Israeli appeal for assistance would not have fallen on deaf ears.

Reich spoke for the centre, which ached for an Arab-Israeli accommodation —and that centre may well be the majority or at least the plurality of American Jewry—and his phrases had the strong flavour of public relations caution. In contrast, Lipman and Flacks represented the critical minorities of strongly committed Jews and their statements were blunt. Which of these forces will gain strength depends on the success of Israeli policies. There is little doubt that if Israel bungled the proposed election for the occupied territories, or the elections did not take place, the consensus would shift to the left, and Israel's government would have something of an *intifada* in America as well.

What set in, gradually, and particularly since the first anniversary of the *intifada*, was the perception that whatever Israeli officials would like to see as reality, the intensity of Palestinian extremism would not diminish, but that American Jewry had no choice but to continue to commit itself to a steady and stable relationship with Israel. American Jews said they were losing patience with Israel—but the process had gone on for so long that a loss of patience had lost its edge. In the annual survey of the Jewish community, conducted by the sociologist Steven M. Cohen for the American Jewish Committee, a critical conclusion was that 82 per cent of respondents in 1988 agreed with the following statement: 'Even when I disagree with the actions of Israel's government, that doesn't change how close I feel toward Israel.'

Cohen's study found 'some disaffection' among some subgroups over 'Israel's rightward tendencies'—of which handling of the *intifada* is but one part—but 'no broad trend of alienation from Israel, or, for that matter, intensification of support.'

Cohen's surveys, taken annually since 1981, have established that American Jewry is divided into three roughly equal groups: those indifferent or hostile to Israel, those claiming strong commitment to Israel but without active involvement and those who are indeed passionately involved with Israel. Others would add that the liberal left and the Zionist right each claims 10 to 15 per cent of the people in the first category, with the rest being centrists.

Cohen's research points to the following danger signals: a new lack of enthusiasm in defending Israel's cause in Jewish communities across the land; 'a sluggish' response to United Jewish Appeal-Federation fund-raising campaigns; a fall-off of American Jewish tourism to Israel.

Whilst reliable figures are not easy to obtain, UJA fundraising does not seem to have suffered significantly as a result of reactions to the *intifada*. Unverifiable rumours speak of an up to 10 per cent fall-off in the number of contributors. But, UJA professionals said privately, committed Jews upset by the defection of that 10 per cent increased their contributions to make up for what would have been a shortfall. On the record, UJA executives firmly denied suggestions that negative political developments such as the *intifada*—or the incursion into Lebanon in 1982—have had any effect on the philanthropy of American Jewry, which is, after all, charity helping Israel's social programmes and not military campaigns.

That UJA professionals might not have been telling the whole truth is suggested by the large increases in contributions to such politically-charged philanthropic enterprises as the New Israel Fund, which focuses on programmes such as Arab-Jewish co-operative projects. In fiscal 1987, the Fund raised $2.5 million, then the *intifada* prompted a jump to $3.3 million in 1988, and 1989 is expected to bring in $5 million. The number of contributors increased from 4,300 a year in 1987 to 6,000 in 1988. While the Fund's political appeal includes support for religious pluralism in Israel—which prompted contributions from Jews unhappy with the 'Who is a Jew?' controversy in Israel—Fund professionals saw opposition to Israel's handling of the *intifada* as the single most important component in spurring contributions.

Cohen and others noted a significant growth in 'specialist' philanthropy, which includes American organizations of friends of Israeli political parties and movements. There is little doubt that in the long run, the UJA is the likely loser in such a development.

In the idiom of today's divorce-ridden American society, one might say that the world's two largest Jewish communities were 'drifting apart' and were 'feistier' than ever before in expressing their disagreements, but that they would not 'split'. They might have had their 'rows', shouting at the tops of their voices and not caring about the neighbours overhearing, but that openness was 'a relief valve'. Thanks to 'the useful conflict' over the handling of the *intifada*, American Jewry was no longer 'a doormat'; nor could the Israeli government ever again play 'macho'. Both partners had 'too much invested in the relationship' to risk a break-up.

The American public and government went through a less passionately-felt but essentially similar evolution of reactions, albeit with one significant difference: whilst many American Jewish leaders promptly and repeatedly vented their rage in private conversations with Israeli officials and took Israel to task in a restrained way in public statements, makers of American policy and opinion often tended to be sharply critical in public and somewhat more understanding in private meetings with Israeli leaders. Not surprisingly, this none-too-subtle asymmetry of reactions was quickly perceived as encouraging by Israelis arguing for a go-it-alone, hard-line position.

In the tortuous language of public statements and in direct private comments, some American Jewish leaders privately critical of Israel expressed a most cautious hope: that while the problem would not go away, it might drop out of sight, and that Israeli officials had learned their lesson and were working on the case.

The departure of Ronald Reagan from the White House did not seem to increase pressures on Israel. Like many of his American Jewish friends from Hollywood and other places in the West, Reagan found it extremely difficult, if not impossible, to be critical of Israel. However, Vice-President George Bush comes from a different political milieu. His ties to the oil lobby and big business, which in turn have ties to the Gulf states, as well as his tenures at the Central Intelligence Agency and the UN, suggest that he might attempt to revert to the traditional pre-1967 American policy of evenhandedness in the Arab-Israeli conflict. This mind-set, as well as the emergency pressures of the Palestinian uprising, seem to argue for renewed demands on the Israeli government to 'come up with a plan' that the US could support. Ever since Bush became the Republican candidate for president and he chose his lifelong friend James Baker as his principal advisor, there were widespread rumours about the 'coolness' of both of these Texas gentlemen towards Israel and their eagerness to seek favour in Arab capitals by nudging Israel along the road to Palestinian self-determination. And Palestinian self-determination means a Palestinian state, which Bush's friends and Baker's State Department staff considered inevitable. There is little doubt that Secretary of State George Shultz's decision in late 1988 to open negotiations with the PLO was approved, and probably approved enthusiastically, by his successor, Baker.

With President Bush and his Secretary of State having put themselves on record as giving the Israeli government another chance to deal with the Palestinians, not many American Jews were about to mount the rostrum— and even fewer to take to the streets for demonstrations—to protest Shamir's old-new plan to hold elections in what he calls Judea and Samaria. One exception was the liberal group centred around the California-based monthly intellectual magazine *Tikkun*. In its March-April issue, the editor of *Tikkun*, Michael Lerner, defined the task of American Jews as 'simple: to make clear to Israel that Shamir does not have a blank check from us to continue the occupation. Israel must negotiate with the PLO about the conditions under which Israel would allow for Palestinian self-determination and the creation of a Palestinian state.' His conclusion, a reference to one memorable line in a Bush campaign speech about new taxes: 'Mr Shamir, can you read our lips? Negotiations now.'

Tikkun's editorial board includes nationally known rabbis from all three branches of American Judaism (Wolfe Kelman, Michael Berenaum, David Saperstein), as well as prominent writers and publicists (Letty Cottin Pogrebin, Abraham Brumberg, Martin Peretz), and top executives of such leading Jewish organizations as the American Jewish Committee and B'nai B'rith. Lerner argued that American Jewish organizations did not represent the majority of American Jewry and that his group was representative of 'a new Jewish thinking' that was winning adherents.

Nevertheless, at the time of writing, among the official spokesmen and veteran leaders of the American Jewish community—as well as in the White House and the State Department—the tendency was to avoid confrontation with the Israelis. Perhaps Shamir had a formula that would work. American officials and mainstream Jewish leaders used nearly identical words—and they all hoped something would turn up.

Strengthening the position of those who were prepared to give Shamir a chance was the widespread perception, by no means limited to the American Jewish community, that Yasser Arafat, chairman of the PLO, was a liar at best and a psychopath at worst, and some of his allies were worse. As long as he was heading the Palestinian movement, it was unlikely that strong US government pressure would be exerted on Israel to recognize a Palestinian state.

Nevertheless, the confidence in Shamir's strategic wisdom and tactical finesse cannot be compared to the confidence once placed in the skills of Golda Meir or Levi Eshkol. (Though, one ought to add, Shamir did not provoke the kind of instant and often enduring animosity that used to dog Menachem Begin.) Moreover, the once-high prestige of Shamir's rival—and possible future ally—Yitzhak Rabin had plummeted. Rabin's initial confident projections of a quick end to the *intifada* and his famous order to break the bones of Palestinians were remembered on this side of the Atlantic. Shamir was blamed for the overall policy, but he seemed to have been able to escape the odium of direct responsibility for 'Israeli brutality'. To many Americans, the man held accountable in the line of command was Rabin, as Defence Minister, and as such operationally in charge of order in the territories.

It was impossible to determine whether Israel's critics who went public and their sympathizers who expressed similar views only in private conversations indeed formed the majority. However, the critics were undoubtedly eloquent and passionate, and in op-ed articles and in debates in front of television cameras they tended to do better than their opponents, who dutifully defended Israel's tough positions.

On the right, there was hope that the American public, Jewish and Gentile, would learn to live with the new reality by essentially ignoring it and turning off the television set—just as the public had learned to live with the Lebanese civil war, the madness of Ayatollah Khomeini's Iran and South Africa's efforts to maintain apartheid, or the drug culture and other examples of lawlessness in American cities. After a while, even the most exciting news story becomes old news when it is repeated night after night, and the most bloodthirsty editor as well as the audience will get tired of seeing the same images. Some centrist Jewish leaders like Seymour Reich pointed out to journalists and State Department officials that Israel ought to have been praised for not going as far as South Korea's riot police and Soviet army troops in Tbilisi in suppressing demonstrators. Compared to what they were doing, Reich argued, Israel was mild and restrained.

On the left, there was nothing but contempt for such a comparison because, it was argued, such a comparison robs Israel of its moral pedestal. There was also mounting fury with the increasingly routine acceptance of Israel's harsh response to the *intifada*. One modest yet not insignificant factor in keeping a lid on outrage was that, both in Washington and New York, Israel's diplomatic missions happened to be headed by soft-spoken, non-confrontational professional diplomats. While presenting the official line, Ambassador Moshe Arad and the Consul-General, Uri Savir, made certain to keep their lines of communications open, offended no one and talked to everyone.

However, many of the emissaries sent from Israel since the *intifada* began did not do a good job in reporting and explaining. Particularly at the beginning, they predicted an imminent end to what they initially termed 'the troubles' or 'riots'. The emissaries did not seem to be embarrassed that their predecessors' prophecies turned out to be wrong, and many of them kept repeating the line that Israel was in control of the situation and the *intifada* would come to an end soon. Some of them sounded as if they really believed what they were saying. But the audiences, whether American Jews or State Department officials, tended to be openly sceptical. The emissaries reminded them of the American officials of the late 1960s and early 1970s who kept predicting that the war in Vietnam would soon be over. Confronted with the comparison, Israel's emissaries did little more than shrug.

One consequence of this new credibility gap and Israel's failure to stem the tide of the *intifada* was that the Jewish state's quasi-biblical image of omniscience and invincibility was in tatters. The 20-year era of high Israeli prestige seemed to be over. Born in the straight-out miracle of the 1967 Six Day War, tested in the bounce-back of the 1973 Yom Kippur War and dented in the confusion of the 1982 Lebanese incursion, the image of Israel's military, intelligence and moral superiority may have suffered serious damage in the hands of Arab teenagers throwing rocks. What remains to be seen is whether that damage is irreparable.

10

The Voices of the American Jewish Community

JEROME A. CHANES

Nineteen-eighty-eight was a year in which the organizational dynamics of the American Jewish body politic experienced strain, and in which a number of long-held assumptions were called into question. Nonetheless, the mainstream Jewish organizations—and the community—remained strong. The capacity for the Jewish community to accept, work with, and benefit from diversity was demonstrated once again as a fundamental fact of Jewish organizational life. Moreover, the organized American Jewish community, even with its multiplicity of agencies and 'umbrella' bodies, remained an effective forum for discussion of issues of concern to the community, and a vehicle for acting on those issues.

A number of issues have been raised in recent years—and particularly during 1988—that cut across the organizational board. The question of whether the 'establishment' organizations are representative of the Jewish electorate became a vocal—sometimes shrill—issue; the changing demographic pattern of the Jewish community sharpened questions surrounding affiliation, funding patterns and other issues;[1] relations between professional and volunteer leadership (including questions involving decision-making) came under scrutiny; the issue of duplication of function and service on the part of organizations remained; and the reality of consensus in the Jewish community on key issues was called into question.

These issues raise the question of the organizational voices of the community. Is there a 'voice' of or for the American Jewish community? Ought there to be a single voice? Are there not, in fact, many voices, some overlapping,

Jerome A. Chanes is Co-Director for Domestic Concerns of the National Jewish Community Relations Advisory Council in the USA. He is the author of numerous articles and papers on a range of Jewish public-policy issues.

that produce expressions along a broad continuum of ideologies, views and needs, but that cohere on questions of Jewish security and survival?

These and other questions must be viewed against the backdrop of the associational and voluntary nature of the American Jewish community. The associational base of the community, and its federated structure, have permitted and indeed have depended upon affiliation—with a synagogue, a federation, a community-relations agency, a Zionist organization—to a far greater degree than at any other time in Jewish history. Any and all connections with Jewish organizational life in the United States depend on some degree of voluntary association. The sum total of these associations determine, define, and inform American Jewry's organizational structure.[2]

The organizational matrix of the community, national and local, consists of entities that come under five general rubrics or spheres of activity: social service; community relations; religious; Israel/Zionist/International; and educational.

Communal Service and Social Welfare Agencies

Of central importance in the organizational matrix of the Jewish community is its communal welfare structure. The organizational focus of this structure, the federation, is a paradigm for the way in which much of the American Jewish community itself is structured, on a voluntary associational basis, run by the co-operative actions of lay board and professional staff.

The federation is the funding vehicle on the local level for community needs, national needs, and overseas needs. Historically, the idea of the local federation derives from an extension of the *kehilla* and congregational/synagogal system of establishing voluntary fellowships—the *hevra* system—in order to provide community services. The motivating force in the genesis of the federation movement in the United States was the desirability of pooling community resources. The earliest federations, organized towards the end of the last century,[3] were essentially volunteer-directed associations that linked philanthropic institutions with whatever Jewish social services then existed. The purpose was joint fund-raising, with an idea that a centralized budget process was necessary. Over time, the commitment to a history and tradition of voluntarism, and the increasing size and complexity of the community, yielded today's federations that undertake major responsibility for community planning and co-ordination of social services, in addition to their fund-raising and allocations functions. With these functions concentrated in the organization, the federation has become the Jewish 'address' in a community, and the federation—and federation leadership—consequently wield significant power. Collectively the federations around the country raise more than $700 million per year. But while the federations are the most powerful community instrumentalities, there are other significant power

centres, namely certain umbrella organizations and national agencies that will
be discussed below.

Under the federation umbrella in a community are member beneficiary
social service agencies that agree to follow certain rules of fund-raising. In
many cases this means that they do not engage in independent fund-raising,
other than from their own leadership.[4] National defence agencies, boards of
Jewish education, umbrella agencies and other organizations receive federation allocations. In terms of fund-raising for Israel, a major activity in every
Jewish community, the merger of federation and United Jewish Appeal
(UJA) campaign structures has been a reality for a number of years. The UJA
campaign channels money to the Jewish Agency in Israel via the United Israel
Appeal and to the American Jewish Joint Distribution Committee.[5]

Council of Jewish Federations

The Council of Jewish Federations (CJF) is a confederation that acts as the
umbrella organization for the federations in the United States and Canada.
Established in 1932, CJF now has a membership of approximately 200
federations. The founding of the Council of Jewish Federations came in large
measure as a response to the need for programmatic exchange among the
federations. CJF's fundamental mission has been to provide guidance to
federations in their community-planning work and in budgeting, and to
represent the federation movement in the US, Canadian and Israeli capitals.
Over the years CJF has developed as one of the significant voices of the
community, not only on issues strictly related to social service planning and
delivery. CJF's power derives directly from that of the federations, from
which the council draws its leadership, which is the top leadership in the
community. Among the reasons for the growth of CJF's role is that it provides
an annual forum, the General Assembly, that has become the gathering place
for individuals and groups at every level of decision-making in the Jewish
community. It is no exaggeration to suggest that CJF is the point at which the
co-ordination system of the American Jewish community comes together. Its
influence goes far beyond social-welfare and other public-policy issues; it
extends to areas basic to Jewish survival, and the CJF process makes every
effort to represent the views of the widest possible segment of the Jewish
polity. While this effort has not always been entirely successful, there is
acknowledgement of its necessity.

Large City Budgeting Conference

The funding of national agencies, and particularly of those organizations that
were created by the CJF, has been both a priority and dilemma for the
community. In 1948, frustrated by the increasing difficulty in their ability to
sort out budget demands from national organizations and umbrellas, nine
federations created the Large City Budgeting Conference (LCBC) for the
purpose of national budgetary review and planning. LCBC, now comprised of

34 federations, and staffed by the CJF, is to budgeting and national-agency allocations essentially what the National Jewish Community Relations Advisory Council (NJCRAC) is to community relations and CJF is to federations. Its role is to review and analyse national agency budgets, programmes and finances; to 'validate' these agencies' budgets; and in effect to provide a recommendation to the federations for their allocations.

The LCBC process has not been free of problems, especially as the budgeting process for national agencies becomes increasingly competitive for a share of a dwindling portion of funds remaining after social service and overseas allocations are made. More to the point is the fact that less than 2 per cent of all funds raised by federations goes to national agencies. There has therefore been a movement towards an integrated process, indeed towards a national budget 'authority'. This movement has resulted in the proposal, coming out of the CJF and the 'Big 19' federations, for a Joint Budgeting Council that, using the LCBC recommendations, will actually make allocations. The Joint Budgeting Council will go into operation in 1990, with at least 10 major federations participating, and will be limited in the beginning to engaging in the allocation process to four national entities.[6] The process is designed to strengthen the principle of accountability to the federations; it could also provide the means for strengthening what the federations regard as their national service bodies.

National Jewish Welfare Board

The other co-ordinating body in the social welfare area is the National Jewish Welfare Board (JWB), established in 1917. JWB's function is the co-ordination of Jewish community centres around the country. The JWB is to the community centres what CJF is to the federations and the NJCRAC is to community relations. One of JWB's functions has been to serve the needs of Jews in the armed services, and, to this end, it co-ordinates chaplaincy activities.

Emerging Organizations

It is important to note the development of energetic and creative organizations in a number of spheres that individually and collectively constitute an emerging voice in the Jewish community. Organizations such as the Jewish Fund for Justice, a foundation to support social services at the local community level; the American Jewish World Service, for social service needs internationally; Mazon, to combat hunger in America; the Shalom Center, for disarmament causes; the New Israel Fund; Americans for a Safe Israel; the Wiesenthal Center; and the older Union of Councils for Soviet Jewry and the North American Conference for Ethiopian Jewry—these and other agencies have responded to the needs of those Jews who felt that 'establishment' organizations were not sufficiently responsive on certain issues or needs, or who felt that those organizations needed supplementing. It ought to be noted in this regard that most of these emerging agencies are viewed today by leadership elements in a somewhat different light than originally; for the most part they are no longer seen as competitive but as complementary to the mission of the federation and of national agencies. The New Israel Fund especially will continue to have an increasing impact in the Jewish communal world.

Community Relations

National Agencies
During the nineteenth and early twentieth centuries, as Jewish communities around the country were gradually evolving in terms of their communal structures, national Jewish organizations developed in order to respond to national communal needs. As early as 1859, the Board of Delegates of American Israelites, a group arising largely out of the reform Jewish movement and modelled on the Board of Deputies in Britain, was acting as the social action and community relations arm of the American Jewish community. But the model of a central organizational structure was not one appropriate to the federated, voluntary nature of American-Jewish society.

The American Jewish Committee was formed as one response to the search for a basis upon which a central representative organization of American Jews could be built. Established in 1906 in response to concerns about conditions in Czarist Russia, such as the 1905 Kishinev pogrom, the Committee initially consisted of a small group drawn from the established German-Jewish community, who viewed their purpose as being able to mobilize American Jews to respond to matters of concern.

For many years the American Jewish Committee was precisely what its name implies, a committee with a membership of some 50 individuals. It was small, self-selected, and had a sense of 'elitism'. Enlarged after 1943, it developed into a highly professional organization in which the leadership have played the critical role in decision-making, and has been an effective voice on public-policy issues. The agency has a special interest in ethnicity, pluralism and Jewish family life, and in a broad range of interreligious affairs, and is significantly active in these areas. Nonetheless, the Committee's leadership suggests that the organization is undergoing a necessary process of redefinition of mission and function within the community.

The Committee's orientation has long been that of a thoughtful and deliberative organization. Indeed, it has viewed itself as the 'think tank' of the Jewish community. In addition to its regular sponsorship of a range of studies and conferences, two influential periodicals are produced under the Committee's auspices, *Commentary* (with a completely independent editorial policy) and *Present Tense*, plus the annual *American Jewish Year Book*.

The origins of the American Jewish Congress, founded in 1918, provide an important lesson in the dynamics of American Jewry. The American Jewish Congress was established by a group that felt dissatisfied with the American Jewish Committee. This group, largely of Eastern European origin, felt that the 'aristocratic' German-Jewish leadership of the Committee was a self-appointed, self-perpetuating body with no mandate from American Jewry. The debate, largely between East European and German Jews and between Zionists and anti-Zionists, was primarily over the establishment of a congress that would represent American Jewish interests at the peace conference following World War I. The result was an ad hoc congress. While the Committee and other organizations wanted Congress to go out of business— and indeed it did formally dissolve itself in 1920—the pressure for a permanent representative organization resulted in the formation of the present Congress, which came into being in 1922, originally as a council of agencies. (It evolved into a membership organization in the 1930s.) The initial constituency of the American Jewish Congress was mainly Zionist, other voices coming into the body after a 1928 reorganization.

The American Jewish Congress was the only community relations agency that has been pro-Zionist throughout its history, and, on a number of issues (including a boycott of German goods in the 1930s), was arguably more representative of the views of the grass-roots than the other agencies. The American Jewish Congress pioneered the use of law and social action as tools in combatting prejudice and discrimination. This led to Congress having viewed itself as being the 'lawyer' for the American Jewish community; indeed, it took a pioneering stance and leading role in Jewish community involvement in landmark Supreme Court cases on First Amendment (especially church-state separation) and civil rights issues. It is viewed as being relatively 'liberal' on most social justice issues.

B'nai B'rith is an international fraternal and social organization that has become increasingly active in community relations issues. Founded in 1843 by German-Jewish immigrants, it provided oportunities outside the synagogue for association, and developed, successively, into a fraternal order, social service facilitator and community relations agency, an area in which it has become increasingly active under its current leadership.

The Anti-Defamation League of B'nai B'rith (ADL) was originally created in 1913, as a commission of B'nai B'rith, to combat antisemitism. This focus on discrimination and Jewish security has remained ADL's most salient feature.

Unlike the American Jewish Congress, American Jewish Committee and other community relations organizations, the ADL is not a membership organization. It has evolved from being a commission of its parent body to an organization with independent board and fund-raising structures, and in reality it is fully autonomous.

While the primary focus of the ADL has traditionally been combatting antisemitism and discrimination, it has over the years developed a broad agenda that includes Israel and international affairs, civil rights and interfaith activity. During the 1980s ADL became increasingly active in legal activity in such areas as church-state separation.

The ADL suggests that the threats to Jewish security come from an antisemitism that appears in new forms and guises, such as anti-Israel activity and radicalism of right and left. The league views itself as being an 'active' organization, responding in a timely manner to what are perceived to be threats to the rights and security of Jews. It sees itself as taking a pragmatic, rather than an ideological, approach to issues. The ADL, by virtue of its budget and its varied activity, is considered to be a significant voice among the community relations agencies.

A number of other national community relations agencies were established to respond to a variety of needs and service different constituencies.

The National Council of Jewish Women has functioned (as have the other two womens' community relations organizations, Womens' American ORT and Hadassah) as part community relations and part social service agency. Founded in 1893, NCJW is the oldest American Jewish womens' organiza-tion, and has a national membership of approximately 100,000. It views its mandate as working on behalf of the disadvantaged in both the Jewish and general communities. Although womens' rights are high on the agenda of NCJW, the organization is most active on many other issues.

Womens' American ORT is the most visible and active of those agencies associated with international ORT, an agency that sponsors vocational training programmes throughout the world. Womens' American ORT was founded in 1928 and has a membership in excess of 100,000 and is the support organization for the worldwide ORT network. Its agenda addresses a range of social concerns in the US. ORT plays an active role in trying to influence policy on its social concerns.

Although Hadassah is primarily a Zionist organization, it has in recent years given a higher priority to the agenda of its American Affairs Committee, and is also fairly active in the area of community relations. Important is the fact that Hadassah is the largest membership organization of its kind in the United States, with a membership of 385,000. Hadassah is thus able to mobilize a large cadre of members around issues advocacy, thereby en-hancing its significance as a potential actor in the community relations sphere.

The congregational organizations of orthodox, conservative, and reform Judaism also have significant community relations functions. These bodies will be discussed in the section on religious organizations.

Community Relations Councils/National Jewish Community Relations Advisory Council (NJCRAC)

The issue of the co-ordination of community relations within the Jewish community has long been a sensitive one, and calls for examination. Prior to the end of World War II the American Jewish community did not play the role that it plays today as an advocate on public policy issues. Deep divisions existed within the community—between 'Uptown' and 'Downtown' Jew, between 'Litvak', 'Galitzianer' and 'Yekke', between Hasidim and Misnagdim, between Bundist, Zionist and religionist. These divisions did exist, but probably more compelling reasons for the relative inability of the Jewish community to act on public policy issues were the following: first, there was the very real insecurity felt by the Jewish community, essentially an immigrant community struggling to survive in a depression-racked society, *vis-à-vis* the larger community. Second, in addition to all of the divisions within Jewish society, the Jewish community did not have a network of agencies, national and local, that was able to articulate the needs of the community and to act in a co-ordinated manner in addressing those needs.

Until the 1930s and the Nazi threat, federations had been more or less content to satisfy the community relations needs of their communities by allocating some funds to the three 'defence' organizations, the American Jewish Committee, the American Jewish Congress and the Anti-Defamation League. The viciousness of Nazi antisemitism, however, had an impact upon every community and virtually every Jew, with a result that communities were no longer content to leave activity entirely to national organizations which rarely consulted with one another or with local leadership.

Community relations councils (CRCs) were established, beginning in the 1930s, in order to provide a means for co-ordination of defence activity within a community, and thereby mitigate the effects of this national disarray, and to serve as forums for the discussion of varied views. Contrary to a popular view, early CRCs were not spearheaded by the federations. There were two parallel impulses at work in the creation of CRCs: community councils were in large measure the outgrowth of grass-roots democratic urgings; and the view, a conceptual framework of the American Jewish Committee, that each community should be able to respond immediately, in the manner of a fire brigade, to antisemitism. These two impulses began to coincide in the creation of CRCs. Indeed, a number of CRCs were organized as counter-organizations to their community federations, to be more representative than their respective federations. In terms of resources, some of the early CRCs were funded almost in their entirety by the ADL and the American Jewish Committee. Thus the CRC movement developed as result of two separate drives: to democratize the Jewish community on the local level in response to what was perceived to be oligarchic control by those representing federation wealth; and to co-ordinate, on the local level, the fight against antisemitism.

An important result of this effort at local co-ordination was a concomitant pressure for co-ordination on the national level. In 1944, the General Assembly of the CJF created the National Jewish Community Relations Advisory Council (NJCRAC) (originally the National Community Relations Advisory Council, NCRAC). In the agreement hammered out by the CJF, the absolutely crucial addition to NJCRAC membership was membership of

CRC representatives, who served for the first time, together with national agencies, on a co-ordinating and planning council. The NJCRAC has grown from 4 national and 14 community agencies to 13 national and 117 local community agencies.

The creation of the NJCRAC was the first significant indication of the federation world moving, as it were, into the community relations sphere. Indeed, following the creation of the NJCRAC, federations have charged the NJCRAC with the responsibility of creating new CRCs.

Over the years, the NJCRAC has been an effective vehicle not only for the sophisticated discussion of public policy and community relations issues, but for enabling the network of national and community agencies to bring the message of the Jewish community to the centres of power, in the US Congress, by means of legislative advocacy; and in the federal courts, by submitting *amicus curiae* ('friend of the court') briefs. The NJCRAC's activity in community relations includes the world of coalition relationships, including the often tangled realm of interreligious relations; issues relating to Jewish security and antisemitism; constitutional issues, especially those involving civil liberties and the separation of church and state; and issues of social and economic justice. The Israel Task Force of the NJCRAC has been a significant vehicle for the co-ordinated shaping of strategy on issues involving Israel, including America's relationship with the state of Israel. The NJCRAC is the body that provided the first staffing of an agency that responded to the plight of Soviet Jews.

In the area of community relations the question of who acts as the voice for the American Jewish community is particularly sensitive. The NJCRAC is a planning and co-ordinating body, whose charge it is to co-ordinate the community relations activities of its national member agencies and the CRCs, in an effort to reach consensus on the public policy issues facing the community; and to act as a resource for the CRCs and federations. NJCRAC's 'Statement of Purpose' bars the council from engaging in functional activity. The NJCRAC is an enabling mechanism, and, as such, is a vehicle for the co-ordinated activity of member agencies. The council's agencies jointly identify the critical issues before the Jewish community, determine the policies of the Jewish community, and shape the strategies on how these policies should be implemented. Nonetheless, an umbrella body such as the NJCRAC is an instrumentality through which communities and national agencies speak collectively, and can maximize the potential of these agencies working together. Thus the NJCRAC can be and has been a significant force in the shaping and implementing of public policy, while maintaining a low profile.

Continual tension has resulted from the forces generated by the three actors in the process: national agencies, legitimately concerned about their institutional interests and prerogatives; CRCs, who regard the NJCRAC as their institution and are impatient at the low profile that the NJCRAC usually maintains; and federations, particularly large city federations, who also regard the NJCRAC as their instrumentality and feel that the council should be more responsive, especially on those issues the federations regard as of priority concern, including those related to fund-raising, and who themselves occasionally enter the community relations sphere. This tension notwithstanding, the co-ordinated activity of national and local community relations agencies is a significant voice of the Jewish community in the public affairs arena.

Religious Organizations

The Jewish community in America is in large measure a synagogue-centred community. Notwithstanding the independence of each congregation, national religious organizations—rabbinic and lay—speak for the denominational groupings of American Jewry. These bodies represent the expression of the philosophies and approaches of the denominations to Jewish life in America.[7]

Rabbinical Bodies

The professional rabbinic association of the so-called 'modern' or 'centrist' orthodox community in America, the Rabbinical Council of America (RCA), represents those rabbis who are associated with (and who are, in the main, graduates of) Yeshiva University's Rabbi Isaac Elchanan Theological Seminary. Their Zionist political orientation and affiliation tends to be that of Mizrachi. The RCA was founded in 1935 because the existing orthodox rabbinical organization, Agudas Horabbonim, enjoying a relationship with Eastern European Yeshivas, refused to accept rabbis who had been ordained at Yeshiva University. The RCA today is the largest and most geographically representative of the orthodox rabbinical organizations.

The present leadership of the RCA, confronted with the suggestion that the moderate centre has dropped out of the orthodox world, asserts that what has happened among the orthodox is a microcosm of the general movement to the right of all Jewish religious bodies, and that all of the religious organizations are responding to the lead of their constituencies. This assertion is worth examining in that it has profound implications in terms of a number of important issues, such as the 'Who is a Jew?' controversy.

The once-influential Agudas Horabbonim (Union of Orthodox Rabbis) represents those rabbis educated in yeshivas that are considered to be to the religious 'right' of Yeshiva University, and are allied with Agudat Israel. Other rabbinical organizations include the Satmar-associated Hisachdus Horabbonim and Lubavitch's Rabbinical Alliance of America.[8]

Neither the conservative movement nor the reform is as variegated as is the orthodox in America. The Rabbinical Assembly represents rabbis educated for the most part at the conservative Jewish Theological Seminary of America. (This seminary was originally established as an orthodox—or 'conservative'—counter to the inroads of reform.) The (reform) Central Conference of American Rabbis celebrates its centennial year in 1989, and is the oldest rabbinical organization in the United States. Its rabbis are educated at the Hebrew Union College in Cincinnati and New York.

Synagogue (Congregational) Bodies

Each of the denominations has a corresponding lay organization, representing the congregations in that denomination. The congregational bodies deal with a broader range of issues, including community relations concerns, than do their respective rabbinical associations.

The Union of Orthodox Jewish Congregations of America (UOJCA or the 'Orthodox Union', 'the OU'), established in 1897, claims a membership of some 1,000 orthodox synagogues in the US. Its monitoring of kashrut, active involvement with youth (through the National Conference of Synagogue Youth (NCSY)) and increasing activity in public affairs make the union the closest thing to an 'address' in the United States for the orthodox world.

Representing the so-called 'Yeshiva' world of the more orthodox, non-Hasidic 'right', is the increasingly influential Agudat Israel, founded in 1922. Enjoying a relationship with both Aguda and the UOJCA is the National Jewish Commission on Law and Public Affairs, COLPA (established 1965), a group of lawyers whose charge it is to represent the legislative, judicial and other public affairs interests of the traditionally observant community.

The United Synagogue of America was founded in 1913 as the congregational arm of conservative Judaism. This body (together with the well-organized Womens' League for Conservative Judaism) is strongly supportive of constitutional principles such as the separation of church and state, and is renewing its active interest in public affairs. The conservative youth organization is United Synagogue Youth (USY).

The congregational body for reform Judaism, the Union of American Hebrew Congregations, is also the prime mover of the denomination's significant social action activity, whose main vehicle is the UAHC/CCAR Religious Action Center in Washington.[9] The UAHC, founded in 1873, moved by the reform movement's ideological commitment to social justice, is a vocal and active proponent on civil rights, civil liberties and other social justice issues, and views itself as the 'liberal' and 'activist' force among the religious bodies. Affiliated with UAHC and CCAR is the National Federation of Temple Youth (NFTY).

The UOJCA, USA and UAHC each play an important role in the NJCRAC.

Reconstructionism, whose main voice remains the Reconstructionist Rabbinical College in Philadelphia, is an offshoot of the conservative movement, but considers itself to be a fourth denomination. Its activist rabbinate and constituency, and operations such as the Shalom Center, give reconstruction-ism a decidedly liberal cast.

Synagogue Council of America

The Synagogue Council of America was set up in 1926 for the purpose of serving as the co-ordinating body for the rabbinic and congregational bodies of the three denominational movements. The council was created in order to act as the religious 'face' of the Jewish community *vis-à-vis* the non-Jewish religious world.

The Synagogue Council's remit does not include dealing with sensitive internal religious questions. Additionally, the Synagogue Council has often been frustrated in efforts to deal with religious issues (even though it is an umbrella of religious organizations) because of the council's rules of pro-cedure, which include veto power—which can block the adoption of a policy[10]—that may be exercised by any one of its six constituent organiza-tions. The threat of veto is not merely implicit; it is frequently invoked, and it has the effect of preventing discussion of difficult religious issues. It has been suggested that the Synagogue Council of America is an umbrella that has difficulty opening. Nonetheless, the Synagogue Council does satisfy an important need in terms of the other religious co-ordinating and umbrella bodies (National Council of Churches, National Conference of Catholic Bishops and so on), who can relate to the council, and through it to the Jewish community.

Zionist Organizations/International Concerns

UJA

The United Jewish Appeal (UJA) is the agency responsible for receiving and disbursing funds from community campaigns for Jewish needs in Israel and overseas. UJA has a critical fund-raising function. The history of UJA's genesis is an important example of an ongoing process of consolidation and co-ordination that takes place in the American Jewish community. In the first decades of this century there were a number of social service campaigns that grew out of the necessity to provide funds for Eastern European communities in distress. American Jewish leadership concluded that, in the interests of efficiency, these campaigns ought to be consolidated. During World War I they were brought under the Joint Distribution Committee.

At the same time, there were a number of campaigns, under a variety of organizational auspices, for Palestine. These campaigns were consolidated under the United Palestine Appeal. In 1939, specifically in response to Kristallnacht, the two consolidated campaigns of the 'Joint' and UPA were merged into what is now known as the United Jewish Appeal. UJA campaigns around the country have become incorporated into local (federation) campaigns, and the integration on the local level of UJA campaigns into federation structures has been a fact of community life in recent years. Most Israelis and many Americans believe that most of the money raised by annual appeals goes to Israel, but this is not always the case. Allocations to Israel have tended to follow a wave pattern: the percentage to Israel normally drops during periods of calm, and rises sharply during periods of crisis. Israel now receives more than 40 per cent of the total raised.

From a structural point of view, the UJA is an entity that assists federations in their fund-raising efforts. UJA's members are the United Israel Appeal (channelling money to the Jewish Agency in Israel) and the Joint Distribution Committee.

Zionist Organizations
Most American Zionist organizations are either directly or loosely affiliated to Israeli political parties. Sixteen Zionist organizations and movements comprise the American Zionist Federation, a non-partisan umbrella that acts as a co-ordinating body for the promotion of Zionist programming and public information. Compared with 1948, the Zionist movement is relatively weak in terms of its collective influence, many of its activist and public functions having been taken over by the American-Israel Public Affairs Committee (AIPAC), NJCRAC, the Presidents' Conference and other national bodies.

Included among major national Zionist organizations are the Zionist Organization of America (ZOA), a centre-to-right organization deriving from the old General Zionists and represented by the Liberal wing in Likud, and once a dominant force in American Zionism; the Religious Zionists of America, coming out of Mizrachi and Hapoel Hamizrachi, supportive of National Religious Party positions; Labor Zionist Alliance, a merger of Farband, Poalei Zion and Habonim, and affiliated with the Labor Party; Hadassah; Americans for Progressive Israel, Mapam-affiliated and adopting a 'dovish' stance; Herut USA, affiliated with the Herut wing of Likud; Association of Reform Zionists of America (ARZA), with a platform based on principles of religious pluralism; Mercaz, affiliated with the conservative movement; and other groups.

Conference of Presidents of Major American Jewish Organizations
The Conference of Presidents of Major American Jewish Organizations serves as the vehicle to the American administration when American Jewish organizations wish to express themselves collectively on international affairs, and particularly on Israel-related issues. The Presidents' Conference (as it is known) consists of representatives of some 46 major Jewish organizations comprising all of the spheres of communal activity. Of all American Jewish organizations, the Presidents' Conference has the highest visibility in the American media. It meets on a regular basis for the purpose of receiving

briefings from Israeli and American government officials, the contents of which are useful for the leadership and constituents of member organizations. Ideally the Presidents' Conference carries the message of the government of Israel and the American Jewish community to the administration in Washington, and vice versa.

The Presidents' Conference, founded in 1954, arose out of a coincidence of interests: the Israelis were eager to have a table at which they could present and discuss their concerns with the American Jewish community; the US State Department, under Secretary John Foster Dulles, was not delighted with the idea of many Jewish organizations coming to it with messages from the Jewish community, and was therefore receptive to the idea of a single instrumentality with which it would relate, and that would represent the multiplicity of Jewish agencies. Additionally, Nahum Goldmann, who was also President of the World Jewish Congress (which had no real base in the United States other than the American Jewish Congress, which did not really serve as a vehicle for the WJC), wanted more of a voice on the American scene. He played a key role, together with Philip Klutznick, then-President of B'nai B'rith, in the creation of the Presidents' Conference.

Conventional wisdom has it that the Presidents' Conference languished until the Six Day War, but this is not so. In fact, the conference was launched at a time when the Eastern Bloc began shipping heavy arms to Egypt, and arms sales became an issue for the first time. Fedayeen activity across Israel's borders was also of increasing concern for the Jewish community and was on the conference's agenda. The 1956 Sinai Campaign, and the need to respond to the threat of sanctions from the White House, was the first critical issue facing the Presidents' Conference. The conference, together with the NJCRAC, convened regional conferences around the country during those years. Over the years, the Presidents' Conference has remained a significant vehicle for the Israeli government to communicate to American Jews, and for the American Jewish community to speak with one voice to the administration.

Nonetheless, for the most part the Presidents' Conference is not responsible for the deliberative process of shaping strategy on public policy issues facing Israel. This process is a function of the delivery agencies, many of which are under the NJCRAC umbrella and play an active role in NJCRAC's Israel Task Force.

American-Israel Public Affairs Committee (AIPAC)

AIPAC, founded in 1950, is arguably the most influential voice in Washington on Israel-related issues. From its very beginning AIPAC was a highly-effective instrumentality even though in its earlier years it maintained a low public profile. Since 1975 AIPAC has been a very high-profile agency.

Originally an umbrella organization and not a membership organization,

AIPAC is an officially-registered lobby with headquarters in Washington but with a growing network of regional offices, whose function it is to develop support for the state of Israel in the American government. (As a lobbying organization, contributions to AIPAC are not tax-deductible.) Its activity includes high-quality research, legislative liaison and public information. The weekly *Near East Report*, an autonomous publication, has very close ties to AIPAC.

AIPAC, unlike most other Jewish organizations in America, is a single-issue agency; its agenda is limited to Israel and Israel-America relations. It normally presents the case for most Israeli government policies, and there is significant respect in the administration and the Congress for AIPAC's skill. The important debates within the Jewish community during the past year over a variety of Israel issues, however, have encouraged AIPAC to re-examine some of its own approaches.

National Conference on Soviet Jewry

The National Conference on Soviet Jewry (NCSJ) is the co-ordinating body for the campaign for Soviet Jewry in the United States. This often-troubled body grew out of the American Jewish Conference on Soviet Jewry, established in 1964 by the Presidents' Conference, and originally staffed on a rotating basis by the conference, the American Zionist Youth Federation and the American Jewish Committee. The NJCRAC took over responsibility for the staffing of the American Jewish Conference in July 1965, other agencies having been willing to subordinate their own institutional needs in order to service this growing issue. Under the NJCRAC, the American Jewish Conference was responsible for the first national public demonstrations on behalf of Soviet Jewry.

In 1971, with NJCRAC no longer able to provide the resources necessary for the American Jewish Conference, the NCSJ was created with funding primarily from the federations. With the NCSJ as the policy making body on Soviet Jewry issues, and the NJCRAC as the instrument of the communities spearheading Soviet Jewry activity, there was defined a special relationship between the two bodies. While the two bodies have been very close, the relationship has not been without tension. There are conflicts between the two agencies on particular issues. The Council of Jewish Federations, in order to enhance the resources for Soviet Jewry and to have the National Conference be more responsive to community needs, have recently called for a reorganization of the Conference, and for a redefinition of the relationship between the NCSJ and the NJCRAC. How this reorganization plays itself out in terms of the NCSJ and the NJCRAC, and in the context of a 'new generation' of Soviet Jewry and immigration issues, will have important implications for the Jewish community relations field.

Educational Organizations

The crucial cluster of issues surrounding the functional literacy—or as is more often the case, illiteracy—of the Jewish community, has often been discussed. Each denomination has its own network of day schools, yeshivas and synagogue-based supplementary schools, loosely co-ordinated and inconsistently funded within the community.

JESNA

The co-ordinating body for the boards of Jewish education (BJEs) in communities around the United States is the Jewish Education Service of North America (JESNA). A creation of the CJF in 1981, JESNA replaced the American Association for Jewish Education (AAJE). JESNA's purpose was to enhance the resources for Jewish education and serve as a national service agency for boards of Jewish education. It provides materials and teacher placements, and engages in long-range planning. It is primarily an advisory body, and is limited in terms of its functional activity.

CAJE

The Coalition for the Advancement of Jewish Education (CAJE) is one of the more creative organizations on the American-Jewish scene. CAJE developed as an outgrowth of the North American Jewish Students' Network and began convening a series of national conferences on alternatives in Jewish education in 1976. It became an organizational entity in 1977 and is at present the largest membership organization of Jewish educators in North America, with a membership that crosses the board ideologically and religiously. Its curriculum development and annual conferences serve as an important support system for Jewish educators at every level.

Holocaust Survivors' Organization

The American Gathering and Federation of Jewish Holocaust Survivors was established in 1983 as an outgrowth of the World Gathering of Jewish Holocaust Survivors. The American Gathering is essentially a merger of the original American Gathering and the American Federation of Jewish Fighters, Camp Inmates and Nazi Victims. The American Gathering serves as an umbrella for a number of organizations, including the World Federation of Bergen-Belsen Associations and the Warsaw Ghetto Resistance Organization (WAGRO).

The International Network of Children of Jewish Holocaust Survivors was founded in 1981. The Network has provided the means for 'second generation' groups around the world to have a voice in Jewish affairs. It was the prime mover in such activist expressions as the Bitburg protest in 1985.

The day-to-day workings of the American Jewish communal system, described in this article, involving the local community, the national Jewish polity and Jewry worldwide, suggest approaches to the questions of representativeness and consensus that were identified earlier.

The boundaries of the American Jewish body politic are not pre-set; the Jewish community is not a classical Greek polity, in which every citizen automatically has a vote. In the Jewish community everyone is born into eligibility, but affiliation requires some kind of voluntary action, even if the act is nominal, that represents a conscious decision on the part of the individual to be part of the community.

The fact is that no self-identifying group in the United States offers as many institutional forms that provide opportunities for expression as does the American Jewish community. The question of whether the organized Jewish community is representative is assessed, not on the basis of 'direct elections', but on another criterion: if people feel that there is a vehicle for expression, and if by means of their choice (through affiliation) of that vehicle they can cast a vote on policy issues, then the community is representative. Thus the multiplicity of Jewish organizations is the strength, and not the burden, of the Jewish community.

Moreover, the basic institutional format of the community, with its abundance of organizations, is one that provides for active debate on a range of issues. The structure today is one in which lay leaders do not remain as presidents of their organizations for more than a few years. This is an important departure from the patterns of the previous age of the 'giants' of the community, when, however effective their leadership may have been, there was often little pretence at democracy in their organizations.

A good indicator of the representativeness of the agencies is that over the years the resolutions passed by the CJF, the positions articulated in NJCRAC's annual *Joint Program Plan*, and the policies adopted by a range of national Jewish organizations across the political spectrum, almost completely parallel the views that are observed in the periodic polls of the grass-roots of the American Jewish community, and that are consistently expressed in the voting patterns of the Jewish polity. The grass-roots certainly does let the leadership know if their expressed positions are out of step with what Jews generally are thinking and saying.

Nonetheless, there is a degree of asymmetry between the grass-roots and the organizations, and that raises questions about the fundamental consensus in the community. There have been a number of events and issues—the *intifada*, trends in antisemitism in the United States, Soviet Jewry and so on—that have raised questions about some *components* of the consensus.

The Jewish community consensus has been shaped over the years on the basis (generally) of pragmatic considerations, and not as a direct result of conceptual frameworks. (There was, of course, a high degree of consensus on general conceptual formulations.) Questions of values and priorities, while they always underlay the community's approaches, were rarely at the forefront of the debate. During 1988, a year of serious decision-making, these questions were sharpened. The 'Who is a Jew?' issue forced Jews into defining and re-defining themselves. The Soviet Jewry issue moved the American Jewish community to ask if it ought to function on the basis of long-held freedom of choice positions, or on the basis of the well-being of a Jewish national movement—again, a question of values rather than responding pragmatically to an issue. This defining of the debate on the basis of values rather than pragmatically has added an important dimension to the question of consensus.

There have been a number of approaches to the question of consensus and dissent. Some have suggested that issues on which there is a lack of consensus among American Jews are those on which in *Israel* there is no consensus, but on other issues the consensus is solid. But the core of the issue is not whether consensus is unravelling. The judgement of many observers is that it is a sign of increasing maturity that the American Jewish community can handle the degree of dissent that exists on some issues without becoming defensive.

Further, an important distinction must be made between those issues in which there is some gap of perception or judgement between the grass-roots and the organizational leadership—the extent of antisemitism in the United States, for example—and real dissent on core issues. The former does exist on a number of issues; the latter is rare.

An additional point. The Jewish community is not in danger of being 'balkanized'. Most Jews in America do not concede to any one organization the right to express their views; they may look to a number of different organizations, and this dynamic is very important in shaping the voices of the community. Thus American Jews are willing to accept a fair amount of elasticity on views and positions, as long as basic, elemental consensus positions (such as the security of the state of Israel) are at their core. These basic positions remain strong and secure.

Having said this, we might note that there are issues on the American domestic agenda in which, as we enter the twenty-first century, there could be an unravelling of consensus. The funding of social welfare services is increasingly—and legitimately—a public sector function. The issues surrounding social service funding are likely to result in a widening gap between the federation world, that wants to protect public funding of its facilities (even if many of those facilities are under sectarian auspices), and the community relations sphere, committed to the pluralistic ideals of the separation of church and state.

The strength of the Jewish community lies in its pluralistic communal structure. The Jewish community does not seek unity merely for the sake of unity, but in order to enable the community to achieve collectively its shared goals. The co-ordinated national and local organizations can and do reach the American Jewish community, and provide a collective voice for the community.

One perception has it that the American Jewish community, with its multiplicity of organizations, is chaotic. The reality is that the community possesses the institutions that are capable of getting these disparate organizations to work together. The resultant voice is an effective one in terms of its impact on public policy and its fostering of a dynamic and creative Jewish life in America. It is not hyperbole to suggest that it was the collective voice of the American Jewish community, by virtue of its activity in shaping the civil rights movement, in immigration reform (the repeal of the National Origins Quota System), in the separation of church and state and in providing the models for social service federations, that was a major force in changing the face of American society. The vitality demonstrated in this co-ordinated activity and voice of the Jewish communal structure is strong, and presages well for the best interests of Jews everywhere.

Notes

The author expresses his appreciation to Albert D. Chernin and Dr Donald Feldstein for their helpful suggestions.

1. This article will not address questions of demographic patterns in the Jewish community. A useful summary of these questions, and review of recent findings, is Sidney Goldstein's 'Demography of American Jewry: implications for a national community', *The Emergence of a Continental Jewish Community: Implications for the Federations*, The Sidney Hollander Memorial Colloquium of the Council of Jewish Federations (New York 1987). See also recent articles on demography in the *American Jewish Year Book* and Nathan Glazer, 'New perspectives in American Jewish sociology', *American Jewish Year Book, 1987* (New York 1988), pp. 3–37.

2. For discussion and analysis of the federated nature of the American Jewish community, see Daniel J. Elazar, *Community and Polity: The Organizational Dynamics of American Jewry* (Philadelphia 1976).

3. The first established federation was the Boston Federation of Jewish Charities, organized in 1895.

4. Some larger federations have so-called subvention agencies, which can raise money independently.

5. The Joint Distribution Committee, known as the JDC or the 'Joint', was established in 1914 as a result of a merger of a number of organizations. Its function is to provide for social-service needs in overseas Jewish communities.

6. The organizations are: the National Jewish Community Relations Advisory Council (NJCRAC), the National Conference on Soviet Jewry, the Jewish Education Service of North America (JESNA), and the National Foundation for Jewish Culture.

7. Those wishing to explore the history of Jewish denominationalism in America will find an abundant literature on the topic. For example, Nathan Glazer, *American Judaism*, second ed. (Chicago 1972); Marshall Sklare's classic *Jewish Identity on the Suburban Frontier* (New York 1967), chapter 4, pp. 97–178; and Daniel J. Elazar, *Community and Polity*, pp. 99–113.

8. A fine review of contemporary American orthodoxy is Wolfe Kelman, 'Moshe Feinstein and postwar American orthodoxy', in *Survey of Jewish Affairs 1987* (Cranbury, NJ/London Toronto 1988), pp. 173–187.

9. The RAC, an important Jewish voice in the discussion of the social justice agenda, was born out of a bitter four-year struggle during the early 1960s within the reform

movement, in which a number of leading reform congregations were deeply opposed to the idea of any public-issue 'lobby'.

10. The NJCRAC, in contrast, adopts policy by majority vote. National member agencies of the NJCRAC can veto only the *public expression* of a policy. The threat of veto is therefore not an inhibiting factor in debate on issues. This crucial difference in organizational procedure between the two umbrella bodies informs their relative effectiveness.

11

New Jewish Immigrants in the United States
(i) Israelis

MOSHE SHOKEID

There is no agreement as to the number of Israelis living in the United States; estimates vary from 100,000 to 500,000. Conflicting figures have been produced by the Israeli Central Bureau of Statistics, the Jewish Agency, American Jewish organizations (such as the Federation of Jewish Philanthropies of New York) and independent researchers. The wide disparity on estimates of the Israeli immigrant population is indicative, *inter alia*, of the obscurity of the position of Israeli ethnicity in the United States.

The increasing influx of Israeli immigrants has generated a growing interest in the subject.[1] Nevertheless, no research to date has produced a representative sample of this population, and it is doubtful whether the standard procedures of sampling are feasible in this case. Moreover, the definition and registration of Israelis abroad is not clear. Thus, for example, apart from those born and raised in Israel, there were immigrants who, though not born in Israel, lived there for many years, and others who lived there only for a short period.

Israeli demographers infer about 250,000 Israeli immigrants in the United States (including a considerable number of Israeli citizens born elsewhere). Lower estimates are suggested by those researchers who rely on American official sources (particularly the US Census of Foreign-Born Population). Israeli politicians, concerned officials and the Israeli media tend to put forward alarming estimates of the rapidly growing population of Israeli emigrants.

The Israelis are remarkably different from previous major waves of Jewish

Moshe Shokeid is professor of anthropology at Tel-Aviv University. His studies among Moroccan Jews in Israel and among Israeli Arabs have been published in many articles and books. His most recent study among Israelis in America has been published in his book *Children of Circumstances: Israeli Emigrants in New York* (1988).

immigration to the United States (as well as from the concurrent immigration of Russian Jews). The early waves of Jews left an 'old country' where, for many generations, they had retained the status of sojourners, and to which they had no wish to return. On arrival in the United States they were almost unique among immigrants in their determination to remain. Although they might have missed some elements of the culture of the shtetl, they did not yearn to go back 'home'. Nevertheless, they established numerous *landsman-shaften* to commemorate the society and heritage of their shtetls and soon founded the influential and continuously viable national and communal Jewish organizations. The Israelis, in contrast, are expatriates from an 'old country' which they continue to regard as their homeland. For the first time in 2,000 years of exile, 'wandering Jews' constitute a section separated from a compact majority in a territorial base.

From the point of view of their home society, these immigrants represent an egoistic type of behaviour. Most Israelis perceive themselves as called upon to sacrifice their material resources, daily comfort, and sometimes even their lives for the sake of national survival. The phenomenon of Israeli emigration has come to be known in Israel as *yerida*—'descent'—and its participants are derogatorily nicknamed *yordim*—'those who go down'. These terms are the opposite of *aliya* and *olim*—'those who go up'—to Israel.

The homesick Israelis refrain from recreating a substitute Israeli environment. But this does not imply that their prospects of staying or returning home are different from those of the more visibly organized societies of sojourners in the various past and present American 'ethnic towns'.

Furthermore, unlike the great waves of Jewish immigration in the latter decades of the nineteenth century and the new ethnics who have arrived since the late 1960s, the Israelis have not developed easily identifiable economic enclaves. While the Koreans, for example, who have recently arrived in America, rapidly took over a considerable portion of the fresh produce market in New York, the Israelis do not seem to have evolved an economic basis of ethnic solidarity.

The *Harvard Encyclopedia of American Ethnic Groups* (1980) devoted two paragraphs to Israeli immigrants, considered as part of the category of Jews. This same source (p. 597) estimated that 300,000 Israelis had immigrated to America since the founding of the state of Israel in 1948, half of whom settled in New York and another large contingent in the Los Angeles area. Israeli nationals have also been observed, in smaller or larger numbers, in many other American cities. Most published studies are based on small samples of specific Israeli populations (mostly students) and executed by formal research techniques. In the following discussion, I shall mainly relate to my two-year (1982–84) anthropological research among Israeli immigrants in the Borough of Queens, New York, which hosts one of the largest concentrations of Israelis in the United States.[2] However, the major characteristics of this population have also been confirmed in other studies.

Motives for Immigration

Observing the motives or situational constraints which affected the immigration of Israelis, we find four major causes according to the following order of
importance: (1) economic and professional problems or temptations; (2) an
inner drive to get out and see the world; (3) professional and graduate
studies; (4) pressure or desire to join their own or their spouses' relatives.

Apart from these four major factors which initiated the departure from
Israel of 80 per cent of the couples and single men, there were also other more
specific reasons for particular individuals. Contrary to a common assumption,
only very few left because they were fed up with or worried by Israeli security
problems and the duty of service with the reserve forces.

Only a minority of the *yordim* were aware at the time of their departure
that they were going to stay on, acquire a new citizenship and possibly never
return to Israel for permanent residence. Even among those who wished to
join their relatives in the United States, not all grasped the finality of their
move. Most students planned to go back to Israel with a degree which would
better their chances of finding a good job. Tempting opportunities as
stimulants for departure were often considered as a break in routine, which
would enable the men to make their fortunes, gain professional experience
and satisfy their curiosity. In fact, most immigrants looked back nostalgically
and many regretted the circumstances which made them leave Israel. 'We got
stuck' (*nitka'nu*), was a common expression they used to describe their
situation. The longer the stay, the more difficult became the possibility of
going home. Not only did they themselves change, but Israel also changed—
in their perception and in reality.

Age and Occupation

While all ages were represented, the large majority of emigrants were
relatively young: more than two-thirds were in the 20–40 age group and more
than half of the population were under 36 years of age. Ashkenazi immigrants
were considerably more represented in the older age groups, while Sephardi
men were more concentrated among the young age groups, a phenomenon
related to the later arrival of Sephardi Israelis in America. There can be no
doubt, however, that Israelis of Middle Eastern extraction have gradually
become a considerable section of the *yordim* population.

The majority of the research population were economically comfortable.
Thus, a third of the male population were employed in professional, scientific
and academic occupations (engineering, computer sciences, accountancy,
medicine, psychology etc.); 20 per cent were engaged in business and
commerce (garment boutiques, diamond and jewellery dealers, electronic
retailers and wholesalers); 12 per cent were small industrial entrepreneurs

and craftsmen who had set up shops for mechanical works, carpentry, clothing; and 7 per cent were self-employed taxicab licence owners. Thus, altogether 70 per cent of the male population were either well-paid salaried professionals, established in a privately owned business or self-employed in a craft or service. If we add to these figures those engaged in the performing arts and managerial and bureaucratic jobs, and students, we find only a minority of males employed in lower status positions such as shop assistants, mechanics, taxi drivers and so on. Most of these considered their present jobs as a first step.

Contrary to popular stereotypes, the Israelis were not concentrated in a few specific occupations, but were dispersed in various occupational fields and economic strata. They often possessed educational and technical skills (and frequently also financial assets) which facilitated easy integration into the American economy.

Comparing the occupational status of *yordim* of Ashkenazi extraction with the status of those of Sephardi extraction, we find some differences. There were considerably more Ashkenazim in the professions. Ashkenazi men were also more often engaged in professional studies. But there were more Sephardim engaged in business and small industries.

Most studies among Israeli immigrants have emphasized their successful economic integration in America. But recent research by Y. Cohen suggests that despite their high educational level, not all Israelis attain high-status occupations. His data, based on the 1980 US Census of Population (confined to Israeli-born immigrants), reveal a duality within the occupations of Israeli-born Americans. 'While Israeli Americans are twice as likely as other American workers, including European-born, to hold one of the top occupational categories, Israeli-born Americans are also concentrated in an occupation inconsistent with their high educational level—sales. Nearly one-fifth of all Israeli-born American men were in this occupation, compared to less than eight percent among European-born and six percent in the American male labor force'.[3]

Cohen's research reveals the complexity of the Israeli situation in America. There are some indications, for example, that the socio-economic status of Israeli residents of the Borough of Brooklyn was somewhat lower than that of the Queens residents.

Yordim and American Jews

Although most Israelis I observed had little, if any, contact with American Jews, they usually assumed that American Jews resented them. The major arena of conflict, though rarely expressed explicitly, was in the field of personal and national identity. In Israel, secular Israelis consider themselves Jewish regardless of their alienation from any form of orthodoxy. They are usually unaware of American Jewry's attachment to Jewish religious traditions (such as the American style of modern orthodoxy, as well as the conservative and reform movements which bring together the majority of organized American Jewry). These are often very different from those represented by Israeli orthodoxy. Israelis arriving in America immediately perceive a wide disparity between themselves and American Jews. The Israelis discover the central role of the synagogue (or temple) in the life of American Jews, while the latter are stunned by the ignorance and complete withdrawal of Israelis from Jewish tradition and Jewish communal organizations. Synagogues in Israel are perceived as specialized institutions for religious services, fulfilling fewer social functions than those in America. It is therefore much easier in Israel to join a synagogue congregation on a casual basis without making an immediate commitment. This uncommitted association does not cause embarrassment or give rise to a sense of humiliation. The Israelis in America resented the expectation that they become full members.

The issue of synagogue and school affiliation relates to a major structural difference between American Jews and the *yordim* population, namely, the establishment of community and nationwide organizations. American Jewry, probably more than any other ethnic group in America, has created a proliferation of viable communal and national institutions. In striking contrast, Israeli immigrants in New York, while disassociating themselves from active participation in Jewish communal and national organizations available to them, have not initiated even one viable institution of their own. Israelis in New York, the only committee organized during the early 1980s in order to promote cultural activities among New York's population of *yordim*, survived for a very short time and was restricted to the organization of a few parties associated with the festivals.

American Jews and Israeli *yordim* regard each other with little sympathy. The *yordim*, striving to achieve the economic and social position gained by their American brethren are, nevertheless, inhibited by their inherent disdain for Diaspora Jews and their aversion to being identified as such. The Israelis' contempt for Diaspora life has most recently been expressed by A. B. Yehoshua, a leading Israeli author. According to his emphatic argument,[4] the Jews' continuing existence in the Diaspora, which entails much suffering and humiliation, represents the most acute symptom of a national neurosis. Israelis are brought up to believe, as A. B. Yehoshua does, that the Jews could have escaped the Diaspora much earlier had they had the courage to break the chains of bondage which were at least partly forced on them by the Jewish religious belief in redemption by the Messiah. Religious passivity and the priority of economic security are to blame for the Jews' endurance of Diaspora existence.

Reaching out to American Jews, by joining their synagogues and other organizations, demands the transformation of a crucial part of the *yordim*'s identity and self perception *vis-à-vis* Diaspora Jews. Their sense of real or assumed rejection by American Jews supports the self image of *yordim* as closer to the Israeli axis of identity, despite their present status as Diaspora Jews.

American Jews, for their part, are bewildered by the presence of Israelis in their midst. For many of them, particularly the less orthodox, Israel has become a new symbol of Jewish identification. They have, however, in effect rejected prospects of their own immigration to Israel. Instead they have adopted the role of guardians and supporters of Israel while preserving the slim hope of a move to Israel in the unspecified future. In the meantime, many have made Israel a site for pilgrimage and visits, which usually confirm their beliefs about the well-being and special quality of life in the Promised Land. The arrival of skilled and often affluent Israeli immigrants who have left the Jewish homeland raises doubts as to the *raison d'être* of Zionism and, at the same time, appears to threaten the viability and security of Israel.

Israeli citizens wishing to settle in America introduce an anomaly with which it is difficult to come to terms. For many generations Jewish communities everywhere have extended help to their brothers in bondage or at physical risk. American Jews have been particularly generous in regard to this responsibility. Russian Jews are the most recent group to have received such support, although they are the least 'Jewish' in their education and religious outlook. The *yordim*, on the other hand, introduce a total revision in the definition and categories of Jews in the Diaspora. They indeed have a most peculiar identity. On the one hand, they openly repudiate Jewish tradition, assuming instead a superior Hebrew culture; on the other hand, they have forsaken the Jewish homeland and cradle of the culture which they claim to represent.

While the religious disparity between 'Jews' and 'Israelis' seemed unbreachable, particularly with regard to secular Israelis of Ashkenazi extraction, both sides viewed the related field of Jewish education as a matter of great importance and urgency. Both *yordim* and American Jews became gradually aware that the chances of the children of *yordim* remaining either 'Israelis' or 'Jews' were greatly dependent on their exposure to some kind of parochial education. There is no definitive data about the extent of the enrolment of Israeli children in Jewish educational programmes. The representatives of the Federation of Jewish Philanthropies and the Jewish Board of Education in New York claimed that the rate of enrolment was very low, 25 per cent at most.[5]

Israeli parents were extremely uncertain about the right action they should take concerning their children's education. Many expressed a wish for an Israeli-style secular school, but this option seemed to be the least likely possible development. The Israeli authorities were reluctant to support a service which would make life easier for the *yordim*. The Jewish organizations were doubtful about the value and substance of a 'religion-free' education which, they argued, would not be much different from a school whose curriculum was taught in Italian or Spanish. The *yordim* themselves were neither able nor willing to finance the establishment of their own schools. Moreover, some *yordim* doubted whether many Israeli parents would register their children at an Israeli school were this alternative actually available.

The dilemma confronting the Federation of Jewish Philanthropies of New York was clearly expressed in the first recommendation concerning Israeli adults put forward in the 1983 final report prepared by the sub-committee on services to Israelis:[6] 'The *delicate balance* [emphasis in text] of not losing Israelis to the Jewish community yet not creating a support system for Yerida must be maintained'.[7]

But in spite of the mutual avoidance of *yordim* and American Jews observed during the 1980s, some new attitudes may take root in the future. It is already noticeable that although Israeli immigrants have not yet joined American Jewish institutions, they seem to prefer Jewish neighbourhoods, being attracted to the safety and congeniality of a Jewish environment. At a later stage some may indeed enter into more active patterns of mutual relationships with American Jews. For their part, American Jews may reconcile themselves to the presence of these unwelcome newcomers who might also compensate for the demographic shrinkage of American Jewry.

Yordim Among Themselves

Israelis who remain abroad cannot escape being penalized by their compatriots in the old country and their representatives in the United States. The Israeli-stigmatized *yored* responds to this designation by his home society and by American fellow Jews, as well as to his own sense of inadequacy, by a style of behaviour which is not dissimilar from that of other stigmatized groups. He often perceives other *yordim* as morally inferior and unworthy of his company.

Many *yordim* were unhappy with the apparently growing numbers of Israelis in New York. The early *yordim* in particular emphasized the deteriorating image of Israelis in the United States, who are often associated with bad manners, drug-trafficking, bankruptcies and other illegal activities. Thus, for example, a woman who came to New York during the 1950s, after marrying an American student whom she had met at the Hebrew University, told me: 'When I myself left, Israelis were leaving for other reasons than those which motivate them today, such as economic or security pressures. At that time people left in order to broaden their intellectual horizons and see the world'. Another man told me:

> When we arrived here fifteen years ago, there were not many Israelis around. Everyone who came at that time had a special personal reason for leaving Israel [he himself had left because of a matrimonial dispute]. But the second generation of *yordim* are completely different. They come over because they've heard about the prospects of success in America. Whenever I used to see an Israeli I escaped immediately to the other side of the street.

While the oldtimers were often sensitive to the worsening image of Israeli immigrants, the more recent arrivals seemed less worried by the growing number of their compatriots and sometimes described the newcomers in more positive terms, which naturally reflected on their own position. Their view of the oldtimer was, however, less favourable. Thus, for example, a woman who had arrived seven years previously with an American spouse, claimed that up to 1973 the Israeli arrivals were those who had not been able to find their place in Israel and were ashamed to acknowledge the fact. But since then Israelis have been leaving because Israel cannot offer them the opportunities they are looking for.

The growing Israeli community in the city of New York and its suburbs has encouraged the establishment of restaurants and coffee bars which advertise Israeli food (mainly Middle Eastern favourites such as *falafel*, *houmous* and *techina*). These establishments have become meeting places for Israelis where, apart from the 'ethnic cuisine', they can also seek out information or advertise apartments, furniture, cars, babysitters or jobs. Among these, Naomi's Pizza on Flushing's Main Street in Queens is a good example. The place carries the name of the lady of the house, who is of Yemenite extraction and who runs the restaurant together with her husband, other family members and hired workers, all of whom speak Hebrew. Its strategic location, the spicy food and its variety, the cosy atmosphere and the convenience of a spacious additional dining room make Naomi's Pizza attractive at all hours of the day (it is closed on Friday evenings through the sabbath). Although many Israelis visit the place, it lacks the stereotypical characteristics of an ethnic club and caters both to an Israeli and American clientele. Some restaurants also offer Israeli entertainment programmes, and a few Israeli nightclubs (Hafeenjan for example) operate in Manhattan. For a few years, the Federation of Jewish Philanthropies of New York supported an Israeli cultural establishment, B'Tsavta, also located in Manhattan.

Although the number of *yordim* in Queens and Brooklyn has greatly increased within a short period, and although some shops carry Hebrew names, the Israelis have not set up a little Tel Aviv or an Israel-town. The image of a lively ethnic community as a common characteristic of both early and more recent waves of immigration to New York, certainly could not be applied to the Israelis. The Israelis in Queens avoided the display of noticeable communal designations. Though many Israelis did live in close proximity, there were no visible signs of this population density. Thus, for example, there were no concentrations of shops in Queens carrying Israeli merchandise or catering mainly to an Israeli clientele. Israeli residents might consult Israeli professionals (medical experts in particular) and use Israeli services, but this specific reliance did not entail communal significance. Most important, neighbourhood was not conducive to social interaction and friendships, a mode of interaction prevalent in the old country.

My observations at the Israeli club at the Central Queens YM and YWHA in Forest Hills clearly demonstrated the reluctance of *yordim* to support Israeli institutions. The club was designed to offer a more stable and intimate environment for continuing social and cultural activities. Its geographical location made it easily accessible to the residents of some of the densely Israeli-populated neighbourhoods in Queens, particularly Forest Hills, Rego Park, Flushing and Kew Gardens. The club, which was launched in June 1982 with the financial support of the Federation of Jewish Philanthropies of New York, was open to both members and non-members of the Y.

Despite the efforts invested in advertising the club's programmes and its accessibility to a major concentration of Israelis, the pattern of attendance at the club was often unsatisfactory (in terms of the sponsors' expectations). Moreover, after two years of operation it had not developed a strong core group which could support its activities. Attendance was somewhat erratic: one week 50 participants might show up while no more than 20 people would attend over the next two weeks, but a festival celebration might attract nearly 200 old and new faces.

Most participants maintained few close social ties. They were unable to sustain the extensive close-knit networks of relatives and friends that many had had in Israel. Nevertheless, to the extent that they looked for Israeli company beyond the small circle available, they were reluctant to become involved in social ties which might entail obligation and commitment. At the club, the majority preferred the 'one night stand' type of participation. Moreover, those who attended Israeli activities more regularly did not develop close ties with other regulars. The intimate ambience which engrossed most participants was left behind once the visitors left the building.

The reluctance to acknowledge the finality of their move to America, which inevitably implies a threat to their self-definition as non-Diaspora Jews, made an accommodation with American Jews' communal lifestyle particularly difficult, if not impossible, for most secular Ashkenazi Israelis. This self-definition not only held them back from finding their way even into the less religiously demanding streams developed by American Jewry, but also inhibited the establishment of their own ethnic associations. Instead, they have been left with the local Hebrew weekly newspapers, the Israeli daily newspapers and the Hebrew radio station. The holiday parties, organized by private entrepreneurs, occasional volunteers or by public organizations, offered them a festive reminder of the Israeli-national calendar. They were also able to express their Israeliness through attending performances given by visiting Israeli artists as well as through the ecstatic occasions of communal singing of Israeli folk songs. The visits to Israel, frequent phone calls, and the invitations extended to relatives from Israel to come and visit, were also effective mechanisms of preserving the integrity of their self-image as Israelis.

The pattern of the *yordim*'s accommodation with the conflicts and the stigma related to their position may prove, however, conducive for the acculturation of the younger generation into the American mainstream. Most noticeable is the rapid demise of Hebrew among the younger generation, particularly among those born in America. Although Hebrew is the major vehicle of identity and of cultural and sentimental expression, the majority of Israeli parents do not insist on speaking Hebrew to their children. Educated at public schools, unbound by close-knit networks of relatives and friends and lacking an Israeli (or Jewish) communal organization which would support and display an Israeli ambience, the Israeli children grow up under little pressure to conform to their parents' social commitments and cultural heritage. A similar observation was also reported in a study of Israeli immigrants in Australia.[8]

This somewhat pessimistic evaluation of the prospects for the survival of an Israeli identity in America should not be viewed as a final verdict. The history of our century has recorded the rise and fall of Jewish fortunes to the highest peaks and the lowest depths. Circumstances of the 1990s and of later decades may encourage or slow down further emigration from Israel. Likewise, circumstances and attitudes may change among the Israeli Diaspora in America. A revival among *yordim* of a Jewish or an Israeli ethnic identity and the emergence of Israeli-American communal organizations are not inconceivable in the near or more remote future. A new generation may be searching for the roots cut off by their parents, who could neither acknowledge nor reconcile themselves to their break from Israel.

(ii) Soviet Jews

SYLVIA ROTHCHILD

In 1971, five years after the announcement that requests for emigration to unite families would be taken under consideration, 20 Soviet Jewish families with visas for Israel arrived in Vienna and asked to be reunited with their families in the United States. They began a trend that continued to this day. The Jewish Agency tried to dissuade them from 'dropping out' (not emigrating to Israel). The Israeli government deplored the misuse of the visas they had sent, and many American Jews believed that Soviet Jews who left their country with visas for Israel were obliged to go there.

At the end of 1988, the Hebrew Immigration Aid Society (HIAS) in New York reported that about 125,000 Soviet Jews had been settled in American cities

Sylvia Rothchild, a novelist, essayist, book columnist and short-story writer, is also the author of two works of oral history, *A Special Legacy. An Oral History of Soviet Jewish Emigres in the United States* (1985) and *Voices from the Holocaust* (1981).

with the help and support of American Jews and the American government. After many years of curtailed immigration, the gates reopened. In Boston, where there were only 29 Soviet immigrants in 1984, 1,500 came in 1988.

The restrictive American immigration laws that kept emigrés out in the 1930s and 1940s, when Jews were trying to escape Nazi persecution, were rescinded in 1965. In July of 1988, the Soviet Union agreed that Soviet Jews could receive invitations from family members in the United States, Canada, Great Britain and other countries, finally releasing them from the subterfuge of asking for a visa to Israel when they did not plan to settle there.

Despite the many changes and shifts of policy since 1971, the actual process of emigration remained the same. It was designed to be an ordeal that would discourage people from leaving and it remained a risky and anxiety-provoking experience. Emigrés have described the numerous documents required, the permission needed from parents, supervisors at work, Communist Party officials. The most painful consequence of applying for an exit permit was the immediate loss of jobs, housing and friends while waiting for permission. The ultimate disaster was to be refused without reason and for an indefinite length of time. The most recent arrivals in the United States were men and women who had been 'in refusal' for eight or nine years, years without work in their professions, years in limbo out of the mainstream of Soviet life.

Information about the Soviet Jewish emigrés who came to the United States in the last 17 years was acquired through interviews with the emigrés themselves and also with the social workers, vocational guidance counsellors, English language teachers and administrators who worked with them directly. Though there has been no time for formal studies, a large body of information exists about a heterogeneous group of men and women of different ages, educations and Jewish identification who shared only the fifth line of their internal passports that marked them as Jews and also the experience of a Soviet upbringing, a socialization that did not prepare them for American life.

In 1978 the William E. Wiener Oral History Library of the American Jewish Committee, with a grant from the National Endowment for the Humanities, taped 176 oral memoirs of Soviet Jewish emigrés. An overview of the findings, by this writer, was published by Simon and Schuster in 1985, under the title, *A Special Legacy*. The memoirs included the stories of men and women old enough to remember the 1917 Revolution, of devoted Communists who described their disillusion with the system that failed to produce the promised good life and of rebellious young people who could not and would not conform to what they perceived to be an unreasonably oppressive society. Their stories revealed the consequences of 70 years of Soviet indoctrination, the loss of Jewish traditions and loyalties and also their lack of information about Israel and the United States.

All of this had a bearing on their ability to make a place for themselves in American Jewish communities. It gradually became clear to the caseworkers and guidance counsellors trying to be of help to the newcomers that they knew nothing about them, their background and their expectations. They were no longer the 'Jews of Silence' Elie Wiesel had written about so poignantly in 1965. Nor were they the heroic 'Jews of Hope', in Martin Gilbert's phrase. They were highly individualistic in spite of their socialization in a conforming society. They seemed unusually assertive and manipulative—important survival techniques in the Soviet system. Those who did not have such skills were unlikely to have received permission to leave.

Soviet Jewish emigrés confused those who tried to be their benefactors by retaining their affection for Russian culture, the books, music and art they had enjoyed all their lives. They also tended to be non-religious, if not anti-religious, on arrival. In the Soviet Union, they were separated from other Soviet citizens by their Jewish nationality. Living without Jewish religious observance, education and community made Jewish nationality something mysterious and inexplicable, 'a matter of blood', that could not be altered.

There were many different responses to the fact of being Jewish. Emigrés described families that had consciously inculcated pride in the 'Jewish heritage'. Others hated the Jewish names and faces that set them apart from Russians and diminished their professional opportunities. Still others maintained that they kept their Jewishness a secret as much as possible. A small minority spoke of growing up in families where Jewish holidays and sabbaths were kept in spite of the official prohibitions. They were all, however, challenged and confused by the expectations of the Jewish communities that welcomed them in the United States. They found it ironical that they had been conscious of being Jewish in the Soviet Union, where they had wished to be accepted as Russians, only to be perceived as Russians in the United States where they had come as Jews.

The Jewish Federations in six large American cities were responsible for the resettlement of 80 per cent of the Jews coming from the Soviet Union. In the process, the men and women working with Soviet Jewish emigrés learned that resettlement does not automatically result in integration. American Jews, concerned about Jewish survival and still feeling remorse for the millions of Jews they had been unable to save from the Holocaust, were sincere in their efforts to 'save Soviet Jewry'. Their emotional involvements with the plight of dissidents, refuseniks, and 'prisoners of conscience' did not prepare them for the majority of the emigrés, ordinary people who had experienced losses and known great frustration, but who were not heroic figures. They might be older parents following their children, rebellious young people escaping their parents. They might be intensely Jewish and determined to 'restore their Jewish souls' among the Lubavitch, or relieved finally to put Jewishness behind, even to attend services at the Russian Orthodox church for the pleasure of hearing Russian.

In spite of the enormous challenges and the lack of preparation, the resettlement programme run by the American Jewish community could be considered a great success and become a model for all resettlement programmes. After a brief stay in Vienna and a longer wait in Rome, where their refugee status is established, Soviet emigrés, with the help of HIAS and the New York Association for New Americans (NYANA), made their way to the city where family or friends awaited them. They were expected to find their own housing, which would be subsidized for four months. They received food stamps, Medicaid, information about schools for children, vocational guidance and English lessons. Special courses were arranged for those who needed help in order to continue in their professions. They were expected to find work within four months. Most of the emigrés needed seven to ten months to settle in. A few highly skilled scientists and engineers who were also fluent in English managed to find work while in Rome. The majority found housing and work within a year. Friendships and even marriages were made. The children learned English quickly and the older people learned according to their ability to learn a new language and the amount of English they had studied in the Soviet Union.

Soviet emigrés often spoke of immigration as a kind of sickness from which they had to recover. They experienced America as a 'powerful psychological shock'. Those who had waited a long time as refuseniks imagined that everything was possible 'in freedom', and were not prepared for the insecurities and responsibilities that are normal in a free society. Many emigrés described passing through a period of mourning for the people and places they would never see again. They also grieved for the loss of confidence and competence, for the reflexes that have to be retrained to fit a new environment; there was inevitable anxiety about their ability to create a new life for themselves.

The new wave of immigrants in the 1980s received a more sophisticated welcome than the earlier arrivals. The social workers were no longer surprised to find that Soviet Jews cannot be compared to the Russian Jews who came at the turn of the century, the German Jews who came to escape Hitler, or the refugees from concentration camps in the late 1940s and early 1950s. In Boston, most of the resettlement workers were themselves Soviet emigrés who understood both the experience of emigration and acculturation. Joel M. Carp, who helped direct the work of the Jewish Federation of Metropolitan Chicago wrote in *Sh'ma* magazine (11 November 1988) about the successes of their programmes. The willingness to learn from the emigrés, rather than assume that they could be easily Americanized, bore fruit. Young adults who 'were literally torn out of their Russia as children and, often, not told they were leaving until the night before they were to board the plane, because their parents did not feel they could be trusted', are now taking leadership roles in the Russian emigré community. He reported that several thousand Jews from Russia were involved in the Jewish community. More than 350 Jewish Russian households contributed to the Jewish United Fund. Hundreds of children were Bar and Bat Mitzva in a special programme, preceded by six months of Jewish education which included four months of classes for their parents. Close to 200 married couples decided to have a Jewish marriage ceremony since their arrival. Thirty adolescents travelled to Israel as participants in special missions sponsored by the Jewish community and another 30 went with their families.

The report from San Francisco, where 6,000 Soviet emigrés represent more than 10 per cent of the entire San Francisco Jewish population, was a similar success story. Anita Friedman, the director of the Jewish Family and Children's services, found many former Soviet Jews involved in various aspects of Jewish community life, working in the agencies, attending day schools, going to Jewish summer camps and Jewish community centre activities. A Russian speaking Hadassah chapter had a membership of close to 100. Five hundred Russian emigrés attended the Passover Seder at the Jewish community centre, and a local Russian-language Jewish newspaper was delivered to 3,000 households and was supported in large part through advertising by emigré-owned businesses.

In New York City, the largest site of Russian resettlement, the Brighton beach neighbourhood was the most visible Russian Jewish enclave. A decaying old neighbourhood along the shore was revived by Odessa Jews and turned into a lively centre of Russian life and entertainment. Some emigrés thought it a mistake to live in Brighton Beach and speak Russian as if one were still in Odessa. The more reserved emigrés from Moscow and Leningrad were uncomfortable in the presence of Odessans, whom they perceived to be 'lower class', less cultured and too volatile. 'Little Odessa by the sea', however, is in the tradition of immigrant communities in New York City and was surely a comfort to newcomers between worlds as well as an interesting place for Americans who wanted to learn about Russian Jews.

Boston was the city most requested by scientists, academics and engineers. Mathematicians and computer programmers found their way into the universities and high-tech industries. The newest emigrés lived close to Jewish neighbourhoods and sent their children to public schools or to the Jewish day schools where they received scholarships. The emigrés who came in the middle and late 1970s were by now out in the suburbs, in their own homes, integrated into the general community and sometimes the Jewish community as well. In Boston, like other cities, Soviet emigrés chose different ways to express their Jewish feelings. 'I am good earth in which to plant Jewishness', said one woman. 'It was not possible for me to be Jewish in Moscow. Here it is possible'. Others maintained that it was too late to begin and that it would be more possible for their children. In spite of a pervasive reluctance to get involved in community affairs, there were exceptions. An older Soviet emigré in Boston who had been an English translator in Moscow became the president of the Russian branch of the Workman's Circle. She organized concerts, lectures, holiday celebrations and trips around the city for the 'lonely' older generation that would never speak English properly, never find themselves in the new world. Russian musicians created a chamber orchestra of their own. Artists from Moscow and Leningrad arranged group shows. Slowly, in their own time and in response to their own needs, Soviet Jewish emigrés were reaching out to each other and sometimes to the wider community as well.

Their greatest challenge came in the form of requests for sponsorship from the new wave of emigrés. Such requests came from family, old friends and sometimes even from strangers, and they were almost always accepted. Contact with new arrivals from the Soviet Union made the earlier emigrés aware of how much they have been changed by American life. They inevitably compared themselves to their contemporaries who had spent eight to ten years in refusal. They found their old friends and relatives disturbed and depressed by their long battle with the Soviet government and unprepared to discover that the hard work of acculturation was still ahead of them. The older emigrés were loath to give up the privacy of their newly acquired homes and yet found it difficult to refuse to share their spacious quarters with families that had been living in the traditionally cramped Soviet apartments.

The newcomers, in turn, were exhausted and anxious. They may or may not have been openly envious. They found it hard not to feel bitter about their lost years and were disappointed in old friends who were unwilling or unable to take care of them. Many gave up hope of ever coming to terms with America and stopped taking the English lessons they could not afford. Many had also become religious Jews during their years of refusal and that separated them from American friends and relatives who had remained secular.

There were also new arrivals who had not experienced the ordeal of refusal and who had not dared to apply until it seemed certain that they would get permission to leave. Some left so precipitously that they had not learned English or acquired enough information about where they were going or what to expect.

The social workers who received and helped the new arrivals, and the many volunteers who tried to help them through the disorientation and anxiety of the early days in a new country, saw them at a time of triumph and tragedy. They were called 'new Americans' long before they knew what that could mean. They were invited to tread a 'New Freedom Trail' before they knew where that would lead. The emigrés who came before them became their models and teachers. The Jewish communities who supported their resettlement had faith that it was worth doing and would ultimately succeed. Meanwhile, the Russian-speaking social workers were discovering America, and the Jewish American volunteers who were in close contact with Russian Jewish emigrés were discovering themselves, their Jewish lives and their Jewish community.

Notes

1. See, for example, Paul Ritterband, *Education, Employment and Migration: Israel in Historical Perspective* (New York 1978); Aharon Fein, 'The Processes of Migration: Israeli Emigration to the United States', Ph.D Thesis, Case Western Reserve University, 1978; Dov Elizur, 'Israelis in the United States: motives, attitudes and intentions', *American Jewish Year Book 1980* (Philadelphia 1980), pp. 53–67; Drora Kass and Seymour Martin Lipset, 'Jewish immigration to the United States from 1967 to the present: Israelis and others', in M. Sklare (ed.), *Understanding American Jewry* (New Brunswick 1982); Marcia Freedman and Joseph Korazim, 'Israelis in the New York area labor market', *Contemporary Jewry*, no. 7, 1986, pp. 141–53; Yinon Cohen, 'Education, occupation and income: Israeli and European immigrants in the United States', *Sociology and Social Research*, no. 72, 1988, pp. 173–6.

2. *Children of Circumstances: Israeli Emigrants in New York* (Ithaca 1988). It is commonly assumed that the great majority of Israelis in New York City reside in Queens and Brooklyn. Considering the various estimates of the Israeli immigrant population in the United States, and in New York in particular, the Queens' Israeli population may range from 35,000 to 40,000.

3. Cohen, 'Education, occupation and income', p. 174.

4. *Between Right and Right* (Garden City, NY 1981).

5. Steven M. Cohen and Linda G. Levi, 'Sub-Committee on Services to Israelis in New York: Final Report to the Communal Planning Committee', Federation of Jewish Philanthropies of New York, 1983, p. 9.

6. The sub-committee on services to Israelis was first appointed in 1977 to gather information about the characteristics and needs of the Israeli population in Greater New York.

7. Cohen and Levi, p. 16.

8. See Tim F. McNamara, 'Language and social identity: some Australian studies', *Australian Review of Applied Linguistics*, no. 10, 1987.

Part D
WORLD JEWRY

12

Fading Shadows of the Past: Jews in the Islamic World

NORMAN A. STILLMAN

Barely a generation ago, approximately one million Jews lived in the Islamic countries from Morocco to Afghanistan. Some of the Jewish communities in this region were large and important. Many had their roots in antiquity, going back long before most of what today are called the Arab countries had any Arabs, before Turkey had any Turks. Today only a small, vestigial and for the most part moribund remnant is left behind. The great majority of the Jews who had lived in these lands emigrated mainly to Israel and France—but also to other European countries and the Americas—during the two decades following the founding of the Jewish state. Any survey, therefore, of the Jewish communities in the contemporary Islamic world is little more than a picture of fading shadows.

The Arab Countries

The most dramatic demographic decline of all the Islamicate Jewries has been in the Arab countries. There are no Jews left in the former British Crown Colony of Aden, now the Democratic Republic of Yemen. Half a dozen individuals are known to remain in Libya, some 60 in Lebanon, and about 200–300 each in Iraq, Egypt, and Algeria. Most are elderly. Only four Arab countries can boast a Jewish population of more than a thousand souls: Morocco (less than 10,000), Tunisia (a little over 2,000), Syria (about 4,000), and the former Imamate of Yemen, now the Yemen Arab Republic (perhaps over 2,000).

Norman A. Stillman is professor of history and Arabic at the State University of New York at Binghamton. He is a specialist on the history and culture of the Jews in the Islamic world and is the author of numerous books and articles in English, French and Hebrew, including *The Jews of Arab Lands* (1979) and *The Jews of Arab Lands in Modern Times* (forthcoming).

The situation of the Jews who remain in the Arab world varies greatly from country to country. In Morocco and Tunisia, for example, Jews enjoy considerable freedom and may come and go at will—even to Israel. In Syria and Yemen, on the other hand, they are virtual prisoners, living in a state of constant fear under strict surveillance in Syria, and under considerably less oppressive, but even more isolated conditions in Yemen. However, in all of these countries a pall of apprehension and uncertainty about the future hangs over the dwindling Jewish communities.

Morocco

The Jews of Morocco enjoy a unique position within the Arab world. No other Arab government has shown such consistent and open cordiality to its Jewish citizens. It is not surprising, therefore, that Moroccan Jewry remains the largest, the best organized and certainly the most vibrant Jewish community in any Arab country, despite the fact that the present Jewish population is only about 3–4 per cent of what it was at the end of the Second World War.

The majority (about 6,000) of Morocco's remaining Jews reside in the modern commercial metropolis of Casablanca. There is still a sizeable community in Meknes (about 1,000), and smaller but still viable communities in Rabat, Kenitra, Tangier, Fez, and Marrakesh. Each community is headed by a legally recognized committee of officers which administers communal properties and local charity and social services. The committees are federated in a national body known as the Conseil des Communautés Israélites du Maroc, headquartered in Rabat, the capital. The leaders of the Conseil des Communautés are all wealthy businessmen and professionals with close ties to the royal family and the governing elite. In addition to their administrative duties, they serve as representatives of Moroccan Jewry before the authorities and in many respects are 'court Jews' of the traditional type. The president of the Conseil des Communautés, David Amar, a Casablancan industrial tycoon, has been a partner with members of the royal family in many business ventures and until June 1986 was chairman of the board of directors of Omnium Nord Africain, the giant holding company whose chief stockholder is none other than King Hassan himself. Another Jewish notable, Robert Assaraf, who is managing director of Omnium and a close friend of Muhammad Rida Guedera, the king's chief adviser, is reputed to have been the behind-the-scenes intermediary at the historic meeting between King Hassan and the then Israeli Prime Minister, Shimon Peres, which took place at the king's mountain retreat in the Central Atlas town of Ifrane in July 1986.

Over the years, King Hassan has been a consistent and courageous voice of moderation in the Arab-Israeli dispute. Although Morocco is a member of the Arab League and the king chairman of that organization's al-Quds (Jerusalem) Committee, the Sherifan monarch has on numerous occasions urged the Palestinians to negotiate with Israel and has extolled the great potential benefits of an Arab-Jewish entente. He has not only permitted

Moroccan Jews to maintain close contact with international Jewish organizations and with their relatives in Israel, France and Canada, but he has allowed Israelis of Moroccan origin to visit the country both individually and in organized groups, especially during the Hilloula, or pilgrimage to the graves of saintly rabbis which takes place each spring at Lag B'Omer. In addition to Shimon Peres, the king has openly received Israeli politicians, communal leaders and intellectuals of North African ancestry, including Rafael Edri, Shaul Ben Simhon and André Chouraqui.

Under Hassan II's benevolent rule, which has lasted for over a quarter of a century, Jewish religious and cultural life has been virtually unhampered in Morocco. The American Joint Distribution Committee, the Lubavitcher movement, ORT, the Sephardi religious educational organization Ozar Hatorah, and Ittihad-Maroc (the local successor to the Alliance Israélite Universelle), operate schools, clubs, old age homes and other service institutions. Modern Hebrew is taught in all Jewish schools, and most young people are quite fluent in the language. Israeli songs are sung openly and unabashedly along with Judaeo-Arabic and French ones at Jewish gatherings, even when Muslims are present. Matters of personal status such as divorce and inheritance are decided according to Halakha by a rabbinical court that is a branch of the Moroccan judiciary.

But in spite of the official tolerance shown to Jews which goes well beyond that of almost any other Arab—or for that matter, Islamic—country (Tunisia and Turkey being the only exceptions), Moroccan Jewry is anything but thriving. There is a disproportionate number of the very old and the very young. About half of Morocco's Jews receive some sort of assistance from the Joint Distribution Committee. The community is steadily dwindling as families send their older children abroad to seek better educational, professional and social opportunities—and no less importantly, a greater sense of security. For there is a pervasive air of uncertainty and apprehension that clouds the future of the Jewish community in Morocco just as in less favoured Arab countries.

Moroccan Jews are only too well aware that their relatively enviable position depends almost exclusively upon the reigning monarch who has survived several attempted coups, the two most notable being in 1971 and 1972. The Jews are equally well aware that Morocco is an Arab country with strong commitments to Arab and Islamic causes. The country is plagued by poverty, high unemployment and an exploding population. Islamic fundamentalism and secular revolutionary ideologies have made inroads among the young and other discontented elements of the population. The news media give continual coverage of events in Israel and the occupied territories. During periods of heightened tension, which invariably accompanies the outbreak of Arab-Israeli hostilities, some elements of the Moroccan press, such as the nationalist Istiqlal Party's newspaper *al-'Alam*, have published inflammatory articles inciting the population against local Jewry. Throughout such crises, however, the monarchy has steadfastly maintained the distinction between local Jews and the state of Israel and has provided police protection to Jewish institutions and neighbourhoods. It has even shut down various newspapers when it has judged their rhetoric as posing a danger to public order in general and to the Jewish minority in particular. Although there have been minor incidents of harassment of Jews—pebbles thrown at individuals by children, garbage dropped in the doorways of Jewish homes, anti-Zionist grafitti scrawled on the walls of Jewish homes and buildings, and even occasional threats against Jews by telephone or mail—outright violence has been extremely rare in the more than three decades of Moroccan independence (the last pogroms in the country took place in 1948 under French rule). One such isolated incident occurred in 1983, when Eli Gozlan, a wealthy jeweller, was murdered at his home in Fez. However, the perpetrators and their motives remain unknown to this day. There is no reason to believe on the basis of this or any other incident that the Jews in Morocco are in any imminent danger or that there is any widespread or focussed hostility against them.

For the foreseeable future, the Moroccan Jewish community seems secure. Its numbers will continue to decrease slowly but steadily as the elderly die off and the young people who have completed their secondary education depart. Few Moroccan Jews in Israel and abroad have responded to King Hassan's oft-repeated invitation for them to return and re-establish themselves in the land of their birth. On the other hand, it is noteworthy that while Jewish life in Morocco is waning, Moroccan Jews in Israel and the Diaspora are undergoing a strong reassertion of their cultural identity. This revival is viewed favourably by both the leaders of the Jewish community in Morocco and by the Moroccan government. Addressing the first World Assembly of Moroccan Jewry held in Montreal in October 1985, Morocco's Ambassador to Canada, Ahmad Mahmoud, told 150 delegates representing the estimated 750,000 Jews of Moroccan ancestry who now live outside Morocco that their action would 'guarantee the preservation of the links between the Muslims and Jewish communities of Morocco, ties which contributed greatly to our national heritage'.

Algeria

Only about 300 Jews remain in Morocco's socialist neighbour Algeria. Prior to the bloody Algerian Revolution, the Jewish population numbered around 140,000. French citizens by virtue of the Crémieux Decree of 1870, most Algerian Jews have settled in France. Less than 10,000 emigrated to Israel. The majority of those who have remained in Algeria are concentrated in the capital, Algiers. A smaller number reside in the port of Oran, 300 miles to the west, and there are individual Jews scattered throughout the country. As late as the early 1980s, a Jewish lawyer was still practising his profession in the interior town of Batna. Those Algerian Jews who have opted to remain behind are primarily elderly, native-born bourgeois. According to a recent report by George Gruen of the American Jewish Committee, 'the majority are over 60'. There is no functioning Jewish communal organization to speak of in Algeria today. The last Talmud Torah in Oran closed in the 1970s.

Despite Algeria's militantly anti-Zionist stance, there is no official harassment of Jews or public expression of antisemitism. The government has in fact welcomed visits by Algerian-born Jews. The intellectual Henri Chemouilli writes that he was warmly received during his visit to the land of his birth in 1975. The government even provided kosher food and temporary prayer facilities for a large organized group visiting the country in 1978. However, the sole functioning synagogue in Algiers has twice been vandalized in a little over a decade, first in January 1977 and again recently in May 1988. In both instances teenagers were apprehended for the crime. In 1983, a delegation of rabbis from France conducting a survey of abandoned Jewish synagogues and cemeteries found that the former had all been confiscated or destroyed and that some of the latter had been desecrated.

While Jewish life in Algeria is quietly approaching extinction, transplanted in France it is flourishing. Along with other North African refugees, the Algerian Jews have had a major impact upon French Jewry which tripled in size between 1955 and 1970. Algerian Jewish intellectuals, such as the philosopher Shmuel Trigano, are in the forefront of the current Jewish revival, commonly referred to as the 'retour du judaïsme'. A further mark of the importance of Algerian Jewry was the election of Algerian-born René Sirat as Chief Rabbi of France in 1980, the first Sephardi to hold that office.

Tunisia

As in the case of Morocco, the government of Tunisia has consistently shown a benign attitude towards its Jewish population over the years. Both governments had a Jew in their first cabinets after achieving independence in 1956. Both countries have allowed Jews freedom of movement in and out of the country, and both have had leaders who have advocated moderation and compromise in the Arab-Israeli conflict. Unlike Morocco, however, the Tunisian authorities have not always been able to protect the Jewish population during periods of tension. The national press from time to time over the years has printed blatantly antisemitic articles in addition to the usual anti-Zionist coverage. At the height of the crisis with France in 1961 over the continued presence of the French naval base at Bizerte, Tunisian Jewry was accused by the press of being sympathetic to France and a potentially disloyal element. During the Six Day War, widespread anti-Jewish rioting erupted in Tunis, the capital, where the vast majority of Jews lived, resulting in the looting of most Jewish shops and businesses and the desecration and burning of the Great Synagogue. On 9 May 1979, the venerable Ghriba synagogue on the island of Jerba was set ablaze only a week before the Lag B'Omer pilgrimage, destroying the ark, several Torah scrolls and prayerbooks. The incident was dismissed by the government as an accident, although this was not accepted by the Jewish community.

Anti-Jewish agitation in Tunisia, though not propagated by the government, was exacerbated over the past decade by a number of factors. These include: the transfer of the Arab League Secretariat from Cairo to Tunis following Egypt's signing of the Camp David accords, the transfer of the Palestine Liberation Organization's headquarters also to Tunis after the Israeli invasion of Lebanon, continual barrages of anti-Jewish radio broadcasts beamed from neighbouring Libya and the growth of Islamic fundamentalism which made inroads in Tunisia as elsewhere in the Arab world during the 1980s, despite the staunchly secularist policies of then President Habib Bourguiba.

One incident that was indicative of the rising force of religious fundamentalism and its ominous implications for Tunisian Jewry was the case of Gabriel Haddad, a 14-year-old Jewish boy from Jerba. In October 1980, he was sentenced, after much public agitation and despite repeated official reluctance to prosecute the case, to a five-year prison term for allegedly tearing an Islamic religious textbook during a fight between Jewish and Muslim schoolboys two years earlier. The boy was finally released from custody two months after sentence and allowed to leave the country.

On Yom Kippur, 27 September 1982, despite government efforts to maintain calm following the Sabra and Shatila massacre, Jewish homes and businesses were vandalized and a number of Jews injured in demonstrations that occurred in several towns in southern Tunisia not far from the Libyan border. President Bourguiba appealed for tolerance and inter-faith co-operation, and government officials blamed the incidents upon the Islamic extremist opposition. More than a dozen people were arrested. However, only a year later, the synagogue in Zarzis, one of the towns affected the previous year, was burned in late October 1983. As in the case of the Ghriba synagogue fire on the island of Jerba in 1979, the Tunisian authorities declared it an accident, although the Jewish community believed it to be arson.

The most tragic anti-Jewish incident took place on 8 October 1985, when a Tunisian security guard assigned to protect Jewish worshippers at the Ghriba synagogue on Jerba during the Simhat Torah festival went berserk, killing three people and injuring at least 15 others (one of the dead and three of the wounded were Muslim bystanders). The shooting took place only a few days after a similar incident involving an Egyptian soldier and Israeli tourists on a Sinai beach and only a week after the Israeli air force had bombed PLO headquarters in Tunis. Tunisian Prime Minister Mohamed Mzali personally visited the wounded. In an interview with Reuters, he blamed Libya for the tragedy, stating that Libyan radio had for months been broadcasting exhortations to Tunisians to rise up and massacre the Jews in their midst.

Ever since the 1985 shooting, there appears to have been an improvement in the security of Tunisian Jewry. Neither the *intifada*, nor the recent assassination of PLO official Abu Jihad by an Israeli hit team, at his villa in Tunis, elicited any serious anti-Jewish incidents.

There was considerable concern when the increasingly senile President-for-Life Habib Bourguiba was deposed in November 1987 by Zine El Abidine Ben Ali. The new president is a devout Muslim and has made some concessions to the fundamentalist elements by publicly acknowledging the close connection between Islam and the Tunisian state and by releasing numerous political detainees, including members of the Islamic Tendency Movement. He also re-established diplomatic relations with Libya which had been severed in 1985. Ben Ali, however, moved quickly to reassure the Tunisian Jewish community that he was committed to the government's policy of religious tolerance. Meeting with local Jewish leaders only a few days after the coup, President Ben Ali promised that Tunisian Jewry would continue to enjoy the government's protection. During 1988, there was every indication that the new regime had been making good upon its commitment. Jewish institutions continue to operate normally, and there are no restrictions upon Jews leaving the country. Former Tunisian Jews now living in France and Italy still come to Tunisia to visit. In May 1987, some 2,000 visitors came for the Lag B'Omer pilgrimage to Jerba, and the Tunisian Office of Tourism advertises the island's Jewish heritage.

Nevertheless, the future does not seem very promising, and Tunisian Jewry continues to decline. As in Morocco, there is a disproportionate number of very young and very old. Even if there are no more anti-Jewish incidents, there is no possibility of the demographic trend being reversed.

Egypt

The tiny remnant of Egyptian Jewry is slowly but inexorably slipping out of existence as its predominantly aged membership dies off. When Lois Gottesman reported on the community in her survey of Middle Eastern Jewry in the *American Jewish Yearbook 1985*, there were about 250–300 Jews left in the country. Today that number has dropped below 200. The latest American Jewish Committee figures in a report by George Gruen count only 83 Jews in Cairo and 95 in Alexandria. Cairo's Karaite community, which numbered about 40 souls in 1984, is now reduced to a mere handful of individuals according to Professor William Brinner of the University of California at Berkeley, a specialist on Karaism and a frequent visitor to Cairo. These individuals have stayed on primarily to oversee Karaite communal property and in particular the treasured collection of manuscripts and codices. The Karaite community is now so small that it can no longer hold regular services. In the past year or so, Cairo's principal Rabbanite synagogue Sha'ar Ha-Shamayim, which underwent major renovations in 1981 with funds collected by the World Sephardi Federation, has had difficulties mustering a daily minyan. A large and important collection of Hebrew books removed from Egypt's many abandoned synagogues has been brought to Sha'ar Ha-Shamayim and is now being organized into a library which will stand as a memorial to the once flourishing community.

Iraq

As in Egypt, Iraqi Jewry is merely a shadow of its former self. There are still about 300 Jews in Iraq, most of whom reside in Baghdad. There is only one synagogue left in daily use, the Meir Tweg synagogue, in al-Rusafa on the east bank of the Tigris, which was once home to about 80,000 Jews. The community is predominantly elderly, although there are some young people. A number of the latter were drafted into the army during the protracted war with Iran.

There is still a functioning Jewish Communal Council, known as it has been since Ottoman times as al-Majlis al-Jismani. Among the council's responsibilities is the administration of communal properties and endowments from whose revenues about half of the community receive assistance. (Prior to the mass exodus in 1950–51, Iraqi Jewry was the wealthiest Jewish community in the Muslim world.)

Iraqi Jews have not been subject to the kind of harassment and at times terror that they endured intermittently from the 1930s through the 1970s. In 1983, some of the more discriminatory financial restrictions that had applied to Jews, such as the freezing of assets, were lifted. The ban on taking any large sums of money out of the country, however, remained in effect. Travel abroad is not officially forbidden, but is difficult in practice. Most of the Jews who have stayed in Iraq are believed by most observers to be there by choice. They are able to maintain contacts with friends and relatives abroad, although their mail is subject to censorship. There is, of course, no direct line of communication with Israel, where most Iraqi Jews now live. The community officially supports the government's strongly anti-Zionist stance.

Syria

The Jews of Syria continue to be virtual prisoners living in a state of constant fear under the surveillance of Hafez al-Asad's dreaded secret police, the Mukhabarat. It is estimated that approximately 3–3,500 Jews live in Damascus, 7–800 in Aleppo, once the great spiritual and intellectual centre of Syrian Jewry, and only 1–200 in the isolated town of Qamishli in the north-eastern Kurdish region not far from the Turkish border.

There is considerable poverty in all three Syrian Jewish communities. Qamishli is by all accounts the worst off. Furthermore, it no longer has either a rabbi or a Jewish school. It is also under the strictest security because of the nearby frontier. Over the past few years, many of its families have moved to Aleppo which still has a functioning community. Nevertheless, Aleppo's Jewish population has been declining as its Jews leave for Damascus which is the principal centre of present-day Syrian Jewish life. In Damascus, there are a score of synagogues in regular use, as well as Jewish elementary and secondary schools, including an Ittihad (Alliance) school and the Ben Maimun religious school funded by the Ozar Hatorah organization. Damascene Jewry has a governing Communal Council which has been presided over for nearly two decades by Selim Totah, who acts as the community's official spokesman and representative to the authorities.

Syria has long been one of the most repressive states in the Arab world with little respect for the rights of individuals. Its Jewish community has been singled out for especially harsh treatment over the past forty years. Jews' identity cards had *Musawi* ('Mosaic faith') written across them in large red letters. They were barred from employment in government offices, banks and utilities. They were almost totally excluded from higher education, and at times were restricted in their ability to buy and sell property and were the objects of economic boycotts. At certain periods, their telephone service was cut off, bank accounts frozen and travel more than four kilometers from one's home made illegal without a written permit from the police. Emigration was —and remains—strictly forbidden to the Jews as a group. As President Asad has explained to American Congressman Stephen J. Solarz, who represents a district of Brooklyn that has about 25,000 Jews of Syrian extraction, and to others, he fears that if allowed to emigrate, many of them would end up in Israel. As in Iraq, those few individuals who receive permission to travel abroad for business, family or medical reasons must put up a substantial financial guarantee of their return, as well as leaving behind their closest relatives as hostages. But unlike Iraq, many if not most of Syria's Jews would like to leave the country.

Despite the tremendous risks involved both for themselves and for their families, a number of Syrian Jews have escaped across the Lebanese or Turkish borders over the years. In 1974, four young women—Laura, Mazal and Farrah Sebbagh, and Eva Saad, were raped and murdered while trying to flee the country. Their mutilated corpses were dumped in sacks upon their parents' doorsteps by the authorities. Others have been killed or seriously wounded while attempting to leave illegally. Even the suspicion of planning an escape can result in prolonged imprisonment without trial. According to Amnesty International, Jews in Syrian jails have been subjected to torture and are denied access to family or legal representation. As of the end of 1988, six Jewish men were known to be held in prison in Damascus—five of them since 1987. They are: Ibrahim (Albert) Laham and his son Victor (Yehya), Zaki Mamroud, the brothers Selim and Eli Soued, and Jacques Lalo. Jewish organizations in North America and Western Europe have been lobbying with their own governments, the United Nations and the Syrian authorities on their behalf.

Great concern has also been shown for the plight of many young Syrian Jewish women who, because of the shortage of eligible Jewish men, have been unable to marry. In 1977, 14 Jewish women were allowed to leave Syria for America to accept offers of marriage there. Since that time, however, no further group permissions have been granted, although a few individuals have been allowed out after contracting marriage by proxy with husbands in the United States and Canada. Recent estimates place the number of Syrian Jewish women of marriageable age who are unable to find husbands at about 500, an increase of 20 per cent over five years ago.

Life remains grim for Syrian Jewry despite some minor relaxations of the more burdensome restrictions on their daily lives. They are still virtual prisoners—'born in shackles . . . like birds in a cage', in the words of a young Jewish woman, recently escaped from Syria, who testified at the Second International Conference for the Freedom of Syrian Jewry which was held in Paris in May 1988.

Lebanon

Life is also grim for the handful of Jews who remain in Lebanon by choice. As late as the mid-1960s, Lebanon had a prosperous Jewish community number-ing 5–6,000 souls. Jewish life thrived in the free, laissez-faire atmosphere of the Maronite-dominated republic. Following the Six Day War and the establishment of the PLO's powerbase in Lebanon, Jews began to emigrate in ever-increasing numbers. This process was further accelerated by the civil war which began in 1975, the Israeli invasion of 1982 and withdrawal the following year, and by the continued instability and violence that has plagued the country. Today, less than 100 Jews remain. Most of them reside in the relative safety of Christian-held East Beirut.

Until 1984, Lebanese Jews were rarely singled out as targets of violence during the years of civil strife. They maintained a strict neutrality in the country's political life. Beginning in July 1984, however, prominent Lebanese Jews, most of whom lived in Muslim West Beirut, were kidnapped and in most instances murdered. The first victim was Raoul Sobhi Mizrahi, an electrical engineer and manager of an electrical supply company, who was abducted and later found beaten to death. One month later, Salim Jammous, the Secretary General of the Jewish Community was also kidnapped and has not been seen since. In 1985, there was a veritable wave of kidnappings. The victims included Elie Srour, a member of the burial society; Isaac Sasson, the president of the Jewish community; Dr Elie Hallak, a well-known physician and vice-president of the community; Henri Mann; Haim Cohen, who was in charge of kosher meat distributions; Professor Isaac Tarrab, a retired mathematician; Clement Dana, an elderly man who lived alone; and Youssef Benesti, a businessman and son of the former director of the Safra Bank. All of the victims were abducted by a group calling itself The Organization of the Oppressed of the Earth which is believed to be part of the Iranian-backed Shiite Hizballah faction. In early 1986, Yehuda and Ibrahim Benesti, the father and brother of Youssef who had been kidnapped earlier, were abducted. Only the bodies of Haim Cohen, Isaac Tarrab and Ibrahim Benesti have been found, although the kidnappers have issued statements that others of the prisoners had been executed. The only prisoners who are thought to be perhaps still alive are Salim Jammous and Isaac Sasson. The latter would be past seventy by now and is a diabetic.

For all practical purposes, Jewish communal life has ceased to exist, nor is there any likelihood that it will be revived in the foreseeable future.

Yemen

It is difficult to know with any certainty how many Jews are living in the Yemen Arab Republic (North Yemen). Figures ranging from as low as 500 to as high as 7,000 have been quoted, with 2,000 being the most plausible. (It has been suggested that the higher numbers might include converts to Islam, some of whom are still said to be practising Judaism in secret.) Most of the Yemenite Jews reside in more than 50 towns and villages in the mountainous region along the Saudi border to the north and north-east of San'a, the capital. A small number may still be in the Najran region which is within Saudi territory. Some communities consist of only one or two families. Others count in excess of 100 persons. Only about two dozen people remain in San'a, which once boasted a Jewish population of 6,000. Most of the Jews now in San'a are members of the family of Mori (Rabbi) Ya'ish b. Yihya Levi, the spiritual head of Yemenite Jewry who maintains a residence in the capital which he occupies only part of the year. According to all accounts, most of the Jews earn their livelihoods, as they always have, as Yemen's skilled craftsmen and artisans.

There are sharply conflicting reports on the general condition of Yemenite Jews. Some Yemenite Jewish groups and individuals in the United States, Canada and Israel have alleged that their brethren in Yemen are denied basic human rights such as freedom to practise their religion and freedom to travel outside their own towns. They also charge that their co-religionists are persecuted by members of the PLO who took refuge in Yemen after being expelled from Lebanon by the Israelis. American State Department sources, some European anthropologists and ethnographers, and members of the ultra-orthodox Satmar Hasidim and the Neturei Karta who have been able to visit Yemenite Jewish communities because of their strong anti-Zionist credentials, have contended that although Yemenite Jews are not allowed to travel abroad, they are on the whole relatively well off in Yemen. They are permitted to practise their religion, and indeed are devoutly observant of their traditions. Some towns have several synagogues. All agree, however, that there is a shortage of Hebrew books and religious articles. These are no restrictions on travel within the country. They also deny reports that Jews are harassed by the Palestinians, noting that the latter are situated far to the south of the region in which the Jews are concentrated. Yoram Kapeliuk, an Israeli journalist with ties in the Arab world, reports that during his visit to Yemen in 1984, he found that some Jews living in Sa'ada had permission to carry guns (although not the curved dagger, or *jambiyya*, carried by all Arab males). According to Rabbi Yosef Brecher, a Neturei Karta official, who visited Yemen for the seventh time in 1988, the Jews were living peacefully alongside their Muslim neighbours and were relatively well off economically. 'Most of the young people', he said in an interview with the *Jerusalem Post*, 'have four-wheel Toyotas'.

The Jewish community in Yemen appears to be growing and has a large proportion of young people. One problem, however, is a surplus of males over females. Despite some reports to the contrary (noted above), the Jews living in Yemen today do not appear to be in any imminent danger. In fact, the government of President Ali Abdallah Salih has taken steps to improve international public opinion on his country's treatment of its Jewish population. For example, during the 1987 Independence Day celebrations in San'a, Jewish craftsmen were invited to display their handiwork at an official exhibition. Also, talks have been conducted between Yemeni officials and representatives of one major American Jewish organization on the possibility of a visit by a Jewish group to the Yemenite Jewish communities.

The Non-Arab Countries

Turkey
The Jewish community of Turkey, which numbers about 20,000 persons, enjoys what are arguably the most favourable circumstances of any Jewry within the Islamic orbit. This is due in no small measure to the Turkish Republic's commitment to a Western, secular and generally democratic society. Although the Turkish government supports the Palestinian cause, it maintains consular and commercial ties with Israel. When two Arab terrorists carried out a suicide attack upon sabbath worshippers in Istanbul's Neve Shalom synagogue in September 1986, killing 20 people, there was a general outpouring of public outrage within both Turkish officialdom and society at large and genuine expressions of sympathy and demonstrations of solidarity with the country's Jewish community. On the other hand, as recently as March 1988, Islamic fundamentalists have given voice to anti-Jewish slogans at large rallies. For their part, the Turkish authorities have not hesitated to clamp down upon such activities and to deal severely with any instigators of religious or ethnic hatred.

There are a variety of Jewish institutions operating in Turkey today. The Chief Rabbinate (Hahambaşiligi) in Istanbul is the central body in charge of spiritual affairs and is headed by Chief Rabbi David Asseo and his assistant, Rabbi Isaac Haleva. The Chief Rabbi still wears the traditional gold-braided robes of the Ottoman Empire. Synagogues and Jewish schools function normally, and kosher food is readily available. There has been, however, a marked decline in traditional observance. There is a chronic shortage of religious functionaries and qualified Hebrew teachers. Some future personnel is being trained abroad. (For example, Rabbi Haleva's son is currently studying at New York's Yeshiva University.) In addition to a Jewish hospital in Istanbul and an old-age home, there are a variety of clubs and associations. The weekly voice of Turkish Jewry is the newspaper *Şalom* which gives coverage to both political and cultural affairs. The paper is published primarily in Turkish, but has one page in Ladino in Latin characters. Ladino, or Judaeo-Spanish, is no longer the primary language of Turkish Jews.

Turkish Jewry is on the whole prosperous and well-educated. Most of the adult male population consists of businessmen and professionals. Women are also represented in the professional ranks. Many of the more affluent families send their children abroad for their higher education, and not all return by any means. The community is declining, albeit slowly.

For the time being, Turkish Jewry is comfortable and stable as it prepared to celebrate the 500th anniversary of the Ottoman Empire's opening its gates to Jews who were expelled from Spain in 1492.

Iran

Iranian Jewry has undergone a precipitous numerical decline parallelling a no less dramatic decline in its fortunes over the past decade. Prior to the fall of the Shah in January 1979, there was a large and, on the whole, flourishing community of some 80,000 Jews living in Iran—about three-quarters of them in Tehran. Many international Jewish educational and social welfare organizations such as ORT, the Joint, Alliance Israelite, Ozar Hatorah and Habad, were active in Iran. There were more than 22,000 Jewish children and young people in school. About half of them attended Jewish institutions. The percentage of Jewish students in Iranian universities was the highest for any single ethnic group. The government of Muhammad Reza Shah maintained close, albeit officially low-level, ties with the state of Israel. Iranian Jews travelled freely, including to Israel, where more than 60,000 of their brethren had settled since 1948.

All of this changed with the collapse of the Pahlavi monarchy. Despite assurances by the Ayatollah Khomeini before his return from exile on 1 February 1979, that Jews and other non-Muslim minorities would continue to have 'full rights and protection ... and need not fear for the future', Jews began leaving the country to see what would happen from abroad. Many were frightened by the Ayatollah's violent rhetoric which frequently did not distinguish between Israel and Zionism on the one hand and Jews on the other. They were also fearful of their lot in a Shiite theocracy. Although Jews as a group were not specifically singled out for retribution during the revolutionary reign of terror that followed Khomeini's return, a number of Jews, including one or two prominent individuals such as Habib Elghanian and Ibrahim Beroukhim, were executed. Elghanian, a wealthy businessman who had been well-connected with Iranian government leaders prior to the revolution, was a former president of the national Association of Iranian Jewry, the Anjoman Kalimian. Among the charges against the Jews who had been executed were such things as spying for Israel and/or the United States, drug trafficking and the more generalized sin of 'corruption on earth'. Most of the charges were believed to be trumped up. Several hundred Iranian Jews were held in jail during this period, and the community was thoroughly demoralized.

It is estimated that today only about 22,000 Jews remain in all of Iran, most of them in the capital. The Anjoman Kalimian continues to function, as do synagogues, schools and other communal institutions, all under close scrutiny by the regime. Indeed, synagogues are fuller than ever as the community tries to demonstrate its piety in the intensely theocratic official atmosphere. The state requires all Jewish children to receive religious instruction as it does for members of all recognized confessional groups. The community is also allowed a representative in the Majlis, or parliament. Although not persecuted, Iranian Jewry lives in a state of constant fear under an authoritarian, theocratic regime that is vociferously anti-Israel and anti-Western and that not infrequently indulges in anti-Jewish rhetoric. Those Jews who have remained in the country have endured along with the rest of the population economic hardships and other deprivations caused by anarchic internal policies and by the prolonged war with Iraq. More than a dozen Jews are reported to have been killed during the Iraqi bombings of Tehran and other towns, and a number of Jewish draftees are said to have been among the Iranian prisoners taken by the Iraqis. Although there is some hope that there will be some improvement in the general conditions of life in Iran now that the war has ended, the immediate prospects of the community still seem bleak under the Islamic Republic, and like everywhere else in the Muslim world, the long-term prospects seem even more clouded.

13

Marriage, Conversion, Children and Jewish Continuity: Some Demographic Aspects of 'Who is a Jew?'

SERGIO DELLAPERGOLA

The 'Who is a Jew?' question re-emerged at the head of the Jewish public agenda in the aftermath of the 1 November 1988 general elections in Israel. Prominent among the issues raised during the process of coalition formation was the request by some of the religious parties for a revision in the current text of the Law of Return (*Hok Hashvut*), which awards automatic citizenship and inherent rights to Jews immigrating to Israel and wishing to benefit from such provisions. One major request concerned the inclusion in the Law of Return of an explicit caveat that the definition 'Jewish' applies to persons born Jewish or converted to Judaism *according to Halakha* (Jewish law). An alternative request concerned the formulation in consonance with Halakha of Israel's Law of Conversion (*Hok Hahamarah*).

Technically, these legal refinements would only concern very tiny sections of the Jewish population. They would mostly apply to new immigrants to Israel, among whom converts (orthodox or otherwise) generally constituted a small fraction of the total—at a time in which *aliya* (immigration to Israel) was close to its absolute minimum levels since Israel's independence (10–15,000 new immigrants annually during most of the 1980s).[1] Religious conversion might therefore be contested on Jewish legal grounds for no more than a handful of new immigrants. Yet the issue carried far greater general significance for the role, legitimacy and power-sharing on the contemporary world Jewish scene of different Jewish ideological streams and spiritual leaders.

Sergio DellaPergola is Director, Division of Jewish Demography and Statistics, the Institute of Contemporary Jewry, the Hebrew University of Jerusalem. He has published extensively on the demography of the Jewish family, Jewish international migrations and other aspects of Jewish population in Italy, France, the United States, Latin America, South Africa and Israel.

Although the subsequent political developments in Israel made the 'Who is a Jew?' issue all but disappear as a major item on the Israeli political agenda, the topic continued to be important as a latent factor of internal tension and divisiveness within the Jewish people. Because the issue is complex and multifaceted, it is usually confronted from quite one-sided and value-oriented points of view.

The debate itself touched upon the fundamental issue of the historical continuity of the Jewish people in the context of the current confrontation with the challenges of modernity and assimilation. The implications for research are twofold. First, the methodological question arises of the criteria for ascription of a person to the Jewish group that are adopted by demographers and other social scientists in their Jewish population counts and various other assessments of social trends among the Jewish community. Second, and more substantively, do the complex socio-demographic processes—namely, the interplay of demographic and identificational variables—connected with the 'Who is a Jew?' question currently lead towards net gains, stability, or net losses to the Jewish side?

A Demographer's Definition of Who is a Jew

From a demographic perspective, the qualitative issue of 'Who is a Jew?' is obviously connected with the quantitative issue of 'How many Jews and where?'. Counting Jewish population, after all, reflects the definitions that underlie the process. Unlike some other disciplinary approaches, demography aims to address the issue in a non-normative way, more by trying to assess the structure and various steps of the relevant process, or suggesting alternative answers, than by providing single solutions to the dilemma of Jewish identity. The Jewish demographer, then, needs to operate, at least at the beginning, from a very extended definitional framework. Only this may enable us 'to throw a net' broad enough to cover the whole and complex range of persons actually or potentially pertaining to the Jewish population.[2]

Ideally, socio-demographic research should relate to as representative a sample as possible of the many kinds of religious and secular, affiliated and unaffiliated, identified and unidentified, current and past Jews, in addition to all of their household members—whether Jewish or not. Only by adopting such all-inclusive initial criteria, may we gain a truly unbiased picture of that broader human aggregate which we define as the 'enlarged' or 'extended' Jewish population, part of which may be, and part of which may not be, Jewish. It is within this 'enlarged' Jewish population, in any event, that the relevant demographic, socio-economic, and socio-cultural processes, including intermarriage and conversion, occur and that their consequences for the Jewish population should be assessed.

It should be realized that the situation of Jewish population data is far from ideal. Although there are numerous sources for the socio-demographic study of Jewish populations, the amount of data available for systematic comparisons between different places and over extended periods of time is rather limited. Geographical dispersion of the Jews throughout the world entails their past and present exposure to different political regimes and legal frameworks. This implies a great diversity of situations concerning two basic aspects of data sources on Jewish population: (a) whether or not the Jews are classified as one among other religious or ethnic groups in statistics collected and released by official state or local authorities; (b) the degree of institutional centralization of the Jewish community in a certain place, and the proportion of the Jewish population which is formally affiliated with any Jewish institutions.

Official population censuses and/or registers, where available, provide a good source of information on the characteristics of Jewish population, as well as of other religio-ethnic groups. But, besides the major exception of the state of Israel, less than 25 per cent of Diaspora Jewry live in countries where census or other official data on the Jewish population are customarily collected.

Centralized listings of Jewish households, kept by Jewish organizations, may provide a useful source of information for research purposes. But in most contemporary Jewish communities such central listings do not exist, and alternative research techniques must be adopted. The major avenue today consists of developing a sampling framework of Jewish households through one of several possible techniques, such as merging of available Jewish lists and random scanning of general directories. These efforts, unfortunately, tend to be time- and resource-consuming. Once a representative sample of Jewish households is available, however, data on many socio-demographic and attitudinal topics—beyond the limited array offered by the typical official census—can be collected through appropriate questionnaires and direct interviewing. Further Jewish population data may stem from registrations of current vital events, such as marriages, births and deaths.

Several sample studies of Jewish populations were undertaken since the mid-1960s in various countries, nationally or concerning selected urban areas. But the lack of co-ordination regarding survey techniques, questionnaire contents and publication of data detracts from the scientific and practical value of these local studies for an evaluation of global trends. Only recently new steps were taken toward greater co-ordination of research initiatives and concepts, and it can be hoped that the situation will improve substantially towards the 1990s.[3]

Jewish Continuity: a Lifecycle Approach

The remainder of this article mostly focuses on certain measurable stages of the lifecycle where the demographic fundamentals of marriage and children

**FIGURE 1 SIMPLIFIED SIMULATION PATH OF JEWISH INTER-
GENERATIONAL REPLACEMENT: BIRTH, CHILD
SOCIALIZATION, FAMILY FORMATION AND IDENTITY[a]**

(1)	(If) A child is born:
(2)	Child is initially raised as [Jewish . . . . non-Jewish]
(3)	Subsequent child socialization, including schooling, is [Jewish . . . . non-Jewish]
(4)	Person reaches adulthood, the stage of family formation is [Attained . . . . not attained]
(5)	with a partner born [Jewish . . . . non-Jewish]
(6)	Partner's identity after marriage is [Jewish . . . . non-Jewish]
(7)	Person's identity after marriage is [Jewish . . . . non-Jewish]
(8)	following which a child is [Born . . . . not born]

[a] Based on binary divisions, each iteration generates 72 different possible paths, including some very unlikely but theoretically feasible ones, and allowing for births outside marriage.

interact with Jewish identity in determining community continuity. One way to introduce the substance of this issue is to try to deduce the demographic-identificational path which links one generation of Jews to the next. Figure 1 lists in very simplified form the main steps involved in intergenerational group continuity: from the birth of a child through his or her initial definition as part of the Jewish community (no matter how defined), through the subsequent stages of child socialization, including formal schooling frameworks, reaching adulthood, attaining or not the rather crucial step of family formation, choice of partner, brand of group identity developed and maintained within the new family, and initiation of a further generation through birth of a child.

The importance of the interplay of purely demographic with identificational aspects in this cycle should be stressed from the outset: indeed, previous research points to significant lifecycle effects on a person's religious and communal identity. In particular, the presence of (Jewish) spouse and (Jewish) children have been shown to correlate with greater emphasis on family-centred Jewish rituals and associational activities. Jewish identity, in turn, can be expected to act powerfully as a determinant of the timing or frequency of demographic events, such as marriage and childbearing.

Can we, then, on the basis of available research provide systematic answers to the many challenging questions implicit in our simplified conceptual scheme? Namely, what are the chances of contemporary Jews passing from each of the steps listed in Figure 1 to the subsequent one? How do these chances vary across different subgroups of the Jewish population? Can we detect some stable patterns over time and across space? What qualitative and quantitative consequences cumulate for the Jewish population when the cycle here summarily illustrated is repeated over several generations?

Unfortunately, based on the current status of Jewish socio-demographic research, the answers to most of these queries must be quite tentative. Most of the available information is rather limited geographically, and often plagued by problems of quality and comparability. Nevertheless, while the picture that can be provided is by no means systematic, it is worth making an effort to review the available quantitative information and to seek patterns of behaviour which transcend a specific local situation. Identification of meaningful typologies is a necessary step towards a better understanding of current realities and formulating more definitive theories.

Family Formation Patterns

There appears to be a great amount of similarity in the basic trends now shaping the socio-economic profile of Jewish populations in different countries. This relates especially to intensive urbanization and suburbanization, high educational attainment and occupational specialization of the Jews. Consequently, parallel trends have gradually emerged in the direction of basic family processes among Jewish populations in the Diaspora. These demographic transformations also reflect general demographic changes among the total population in more developed societies: the postponement of marriage among younger adults, a growing share of never-married among adults in their late 30s and early 40s, more frequent divorce, low marital fertility, an increase in instances of births out-of-wedlock (albeit still rare among Jews) and a great increase in the frequency of one-parent households.

The combination of various extents of each of these features has produced deep changes in the structure of Jewish households. The once predominant model of the conventional Jewish nuclear family formed by two Jewish parents and their children is becoming increasingly substituted by a plurality of alternative types of household and living arrangements. Erosion in basic family processes, along with rapid ageing of the population, underlie the negative balance of Jewish births and deaths now prevailing in most Diaspora communities.[4]

Frequencies of Mixed Marriage

Most significant, in this context, is the trend affecting the choice of marital partner, whether from within or from outside the Jewish community. It is from the increasing incidence of intermarriage in most Jewish populations and communities, that the problem of 'Who is a Jew?' mostly—though by no means exclusively—derives.

Intermarriage levels, in spite, or precisely because of their relevance for Jewish population and community studies, have been the object of some controversy—among other things because of the confusion which often recurs in the literature between data referring to individual spouses and couple data, and between recent or current data on family formation and cumulative data relative to an entire existing population. A further cause of confusion is the often inconsistent terminology used to describe the various possible situations associated with the religious or other group identity of spouses. Here we follow an established convention by which the term *out-marriage* refers to all weddings where one of the partners was not born Jewish or was not Jewish at the time the two partners first met. In case of conversion to Judaism, we adopt the term *conversionary marriage*. Where the non-Jewish partner has not changed his/her original identification, the term *mixed marriage* applies.

What is, then, the current level of mixed marriage across the Jewish world? A tentative synopsis, given in Table 1, reveals a wide range of behaviour among Jews in different countries. Great variation in the quality of available data, and the conjectural character of some of the estimates presented should also be noted. Mixed marriages are extremely frequent in several rather small and veteran Jewish communities, mostly in Europe, where they already were quite widespread at the turn of the century. A major increase, though, occurred after World War II and especially since the early 1960s nearly everywhere, including some major Jewish communities where the levels of heterogamy had previously been very low. This refers not only to the remnants of Jewish communities nearly destroyed in the Shoah, but also and more significantly to the communities of some countries—such as France— which absorbed substantial Jewish immigration after the war.

At the opposite end, mixed marriages are most infrequent among the Jewish population in Israel, in spite of some occurrences, and in the small remnants of once important Jewish communities in North Africa and the Middle East. Of the major Western Jewish communities, South Africa probably has the lowest level of heterogamy, which may be somewhat related to the rigid system of social and ethnic stratification prevailing in that country. Interestingly, great variations in geographical region, political regime and socio-economic structure of the general society in the different countries do not seem to have equally significant effects on the rates of mixed marriage among Jews.

With regard to the aggregate of Jewish populations outside of Israel, about

**TABLE 1   PERCENTAGE OF MIXED MARRIAGES OUT OF ALL MARRIAGES
WITH AT LEAST ONE JEWISH SPOUSE
ROUGH ESTIMATES, WORLD JEWRY, 1980–6[a]**

Country	% Mixed marriages		Jewish population 1986	
	Per 100 new Jewish spouses	Per 100 new couples with at least one Jewish spouse	Number (000s)	% of World Jewry
Total world			12,964	100.0
West Germany,[b] East Europe				
(excl. USSR)[e]	65–74	79–85	135	1.0
Scandinavia[d]	55–64	71–78	24	0.2
Switzerland,[b] Austria,[b]				
Netherlands[d]	45–54	62–70	51	0.4
Italy,[c] France,[c] Belgium[e]	36–44	53–61	594	4.6
Argentina,[d] Brazil,[e] Other Latin				
America (excl. Mexico, Peru),[e]				
USSR[d]	33–35	49–52	1,921	14.8
United States[c]	28–32	44–48	5,700	44.0
Canada,[b] United Kingdom,[e]				
Other Europe,[e] Mexico,[e]				
Peru,[c] Australia,[d] New				
Zealand[e]	25–27	40–43	796	6.1
South Africa,[d] Zimbabwe[e]	15–24	26–39	116	0.9
North Africa,[e] Asia (excl. Israel)[e]	5–14	10–25	50	0.4
Other Africa[e]	1–5	2–10	14	0.1
Israel[b]	0–1	0–2	3,563	27.5

[a] Recent marriages between a Jewish spouse and a non-Jewish-born spouse not converted to
Judaism. Data quality is rated as follows:
 [b] recent and reliable statistical data;
 [c] partial or less recent data of sufficient quality;
 [d] rather out-dated or very incomplete data;
 [e] conjectural.

Source: Sergio DellaPergola, 'Recent trends in Jewish marriage', paper presented at the
Symposium on World Jewish Population: Research and Policies, Jerusalem, 1987.

95 per cent live in countries where the current frequency of mixed marriage
ranges between 25 per cent and 45 per cent of the Jewish individuals forming
a new family. It can be very roughly estimated that an average 30–33 per cent
of Jewish grooms and brides in the Diaspora currently marry a non-Jewish
spouse who does not convert to Judaism. This corresponds to about 45–50 per
cent of all new households involving a Jewish partner.

Considering the strong North American geographical focus of the 'Who is a
Jew?' debate, and the numerical weight of North American Jewry on the
world Jewish scene, a further and more detailed look should be given at the

TABLE 2   PERCENTAGES OF JEWS OUT-MARRYING AND OF NON-JEWISH BORN SPOUSES CONVERTING TO JUDAISM, SELECTED PLACES, 1970–87

Place	Year	% married with spouse:		% converted to Judaism out of all non-Jewish born spouses[a]
		born non-Jewish	currently non-Jewish	
United States				
Total	1970–1			
by year of marriage:[b]				
1900–24		2	1	18
1925–34		3	3	15
1935–44		5	5	7
1945–54		6	5	8
1955–64		9	7	19
1965–71		29	22	23
Selected cities	1972–87			
by age at survey:[c]				
30–39		23–27	18–22	19–23
18–29		35–39	28–32	16–20
Brazil				
Saõ Paulo	1981[d]	40	29	21

[a] Including passages to Judaism without a formal conversion procedure.
[b] Retrospective National Jewish Population Study (NJPS) data.
[c] Median values in the observed range of local survey results.
[d] Year of marriage.

Sources: Uziel O. Schmelz and Sergio DellaPergola, 'The demographic consequences of US Jewish population trends', *American Jewish Year Book 1983* (Philadelphia, 1983), pp. 141–87; Sergio DellaPergola and Uziel O. Schmelz, 'Demographic transformations of American Jewry: marriage and mixed marriage in the 1980s', *Studies in Contemporary Jewry*, vol. 5 (Oxford/New York, 1989); Federaçao Israelita do Estado de Saõ Paulo, *Annuario Estadistico da Comunidade Judaica de Estado de Saõ Paulo* (Saõ Paulo, 1983).

trends there. As shown in Table 1, US Jewry occupies an intermediate position in the ranking of countries by frequency of mixed marriage, followed quite closely by Canadian Jewry. Table 2 provides a synthesis from a wider compilation of data on the patterns of diffusion and variation in levels of mixed marriage in the United States.[5] Frequencies are shown separately for all marriages of Jews with non-Jewish born spouses, and for those fewer instances in which the non-Jewish spouse did not convert to Judaism.

National trends towards more frequent mixed marriages are shown from the outset of the century through 1987. Individual mixed marriage rates among American Jewry were very low until the 1950s: less than 2 per cent during the first quarter of the century, 3–5 per cent during the 1930s and 1940s, and 5 per cent during the 1950s. The percentages doubled to a still modest 10 per cent in 1960–64, and then more than doubled to over 22 per cent in 1965–71. While we lack more recent national data for US Jews, numerous local Jewish community studies conducted since 1971 basically confirm the patterns known for the earlier period, whilst also pointing to a continuing increase in the percentages of mixed marriage. This is confirmed by repeated observation of major communities (such as Boston and Los Angeles) over time. Also, the available comparisons between survey respondents and their married children in certain communities point to strong intergenerational increases in mixed marriage. Since such increases appear also after controlling for age, this amounts to an indication of the compound effect of age and generation in the choice of spouse on the part of American Jews. The trends for Canadian Jewry are very similar, though the more recent level of mixed marriage there is slightly lower than in the United States.

These findings indicate a discontinuity in mixed marriage patterns after the mid-1960s. It may be noted that at that time the third generation of American Jews—while becoming structurally more assimilated into American society— was coming of age and marrying. College studies were becoming almost universal among Jews, leading to intensified interaction between young Jews and non-Jews. These socio-demographic changes and other socio-cultural factors underlie a trend which does not yet seem to have reached its peak.

Further data, not shown here, indicate a reduction in the differential frequency of mixed marriage by gender, which means that the recent increase has been comparatively more rapid among Jewish women. This different pace of change may be mostly attributed to the evolving role of women, and of Jewish women in particular, in society. Previously noticeable gender gaps in education attainment, labour force participation and occupational opportunities have narrowed, while the range of personal choices, including spouse selection, has expanded. The further effect of structural demographic factors should also be noted. Because of the alternating low and high birthrates in the past, there have been significant imbalances in the respective numbers of Jewish men and slightly younger Jewish women reaching the age of marriage in any given year. The relative shortage of potential Jewish male marriage candidates may have been a factor in the increased proportion of out-marrying Jewish women in the 1970s. During the early 1990s the situation is expected to reverse, and Jewish males should again outnumber Jewish females among the candidates for first marriage.

Increases in mixed marriage should also be understood in the context of the markedly increased frequencies of divorce in general and, albeit at lower levels, among the Jews. Available research bears out a significant correlation between the two trends. Whereas mixed marriages appear to be less stable, on the whole, than homogamous marriages, subsequent marriages are more often religiously mixed than first marriages.[6]

The most salient finding from the more recent surveys is the enormous local variations that prevail in the United States and also appear in local Canadian data. Among the younger age groups and more recent marriage cohorts surveyed during the late 1970s and early 1980s, the proportion of Jewish spouses with a non-converted non-Jewish partner ranged between 11 per cent in New York and 61 per cent in Denver.[7] Substantial variations also existed within different parts of the same metropolitan area. While the generally greater diffusion of mixed marriage is a trend common to all places, differences of level chronologically equivalent to the span of fully one generation may separate two Jewish communities located at a few tenths of a kilometre from one another. Differences between the more veteran and established communities in the North-eastern United States, and the newer and more rapidly growing ones in the South and especially in the West are most striking. The challenging question is whether these regional differences can be interpreted as only transitional, or, as seems more likely, reflecting more permanent differences in the American social structure.

In any event, the research imperative demands that we do not overgeneralize the findings of one place in the United States for the totality of American Jewry (as has been done so often), or from one country for the whole Jewish Diaspora, since the peculiarity of each local community must be individually understood and assessed. This pertains particularly to the size and composition of Jewish 'marriage markets' (related in turn to local Jewish population size), the structure and level of activity of local employment markets (related, among other factors, to total population size and to socio-economic development), and the character and complexity of Jewish institutional systems (in turn related to historical developments and regional factors).

Conversion Patterns

Since the trends in out-marriage can be assumed to be related to the frequency of conversion to Judaism, it is interesting to compare the respective fluctuations over time (see last column in Table 2). In the United States the proportion of non-Jewish spouses who converted to Judaism seems to have declined until the 1930s, out of a pool of out-marriages which was in any event very small. Subsequently, and until the early 1970s, the propensity to convert to Judaism substantially increased, along with the gradual increase in out-marriage. The more recent survey findings point to a renewed decline in conversion frequencies, in spite of, or along with the continued increase in out-marriages. Local US survey data reveal an extremely wide range of conversion frequencies. Among non-Jewish born spouses covered in surveys between 1972 and 1987 and aged under 40 at the time of survey, between 7 per cent and 42 per cent converted to Judaism, according to locality. The median values of this range, though, declined from 19–23 per cent among spouses aged 30–39, to 16–20 per cent among those under 30. These estimates, it should be noted, include all types of conversion including some instances in which the passage to Judaism was not sanctioned through any formal procedure but reflected the current personal identification of a formerly non-Jewish spouse.

Similar levels of conversion to Judaism—about one fifth out of all non-Jewish-born spouses—obtain for Saõ Paulo, Brazil's largest Jewish community. In certain other Western countries, marriages celebrated by the reform and liberal denominations include comparatively higher percentages of converts than do orthodox marriages. In Britain the percentage of reform and liberal out of total synagogue marriages was 24 per cent in 1987 (18 per cent reform, 6 per cent liberal), against an average of 21–22 per cent in 1982–86.[8] In Greater Paris in the early 1980s, whereas the vast majority of synagogue marriages were handled through the Consistoire Israélite, about 7 per cent of Jewish marriages were celebrated by the Union Libérale.[9]

These figures say nothing about the actual rate of conversion to Judaism in Britain or France, but might be taken as extremely rough indicators of the possible maximum extent of such marriage-related conversions in the respective communities. Available data indeed indicate that the frequency of conversionary marriages out of all Jewish marriages celebrated is higher for reform and liberal congregations than for the orthodox. Based on such an assumption, conversion to Judaism would appear to be significantly less frequent in Western Europe than it is in the United States.

The basic weakness of these data is that they show only the Jewish side of the picture, while the opposite process of conversion out of Judaism is usually ignored and lost. A necessary corrective is provided for the United States by a detailed analysis of the General Social Surveys periodically conducted by the National Opinion Research Center (NORC), based on a pool of several national samples of Americans spread over the period 1972–83.[10] Compared to each of the other major religious denominations, the Jews displayed the lowest amount of access by new joiners. The percentage of current Jews raised in the same faith was 93 per cent, versus an average of 69 per cent for all religious groups together. On the other hand, American Jews displayed the lowest ratio of 'converts to disaffiliators': for every 40 persons who joined the Jewish group, 100 persons left. Highest 'conversion/disaffiliation' ratios, and consequently relative growth, appeared for the inter- and non-denominational group, and for those people who lacked any denominational preference. Another religious denomination offering great attraction to new joiners were the Christian fundamentalists, confirming the existence of a process of religious polarization in America.

It is, of course, entirely possible that some of the non-identified were Jewish, and that some of these passages from Jewish to non-identified are reversible. However, these comparative findings on American religious denominations quite clearly indicate that the Jewish conversional balance may be more precarious than can be deduced solely on the basis of Jewish community surveys. The basic possibility that the balance of passages to and from Judaism is significantly passive should be seriously taken into account.

Children and Grandchildren of Mixed Marriage

Besides its possible direct influence on Jewish population size, conversion obviously affects differences in the patterns of Jewishness of conversionary versus mixed households. In the United States, measured by a variety of attitudinal and behavioural indicators, conversionary marriages do not seem to differ much from average in-married households; mixed marriages, on the other hand, appear to be much weaker Jewishly.[11] These differences are best exemplified by the choice of religious or otherwise defined group identity for the children of such marriages.

Table 3 shows that, as might be expected, the vast majority of conversionary families define their children as Jewish. On the other hand, mixed families, who constitute the overwhelming majority of the intermarried in the United States, and virtually all the cases in some other countries, most often raise less than one half of their children as Jews. Interestingly, the reported frequencies in a variety of recent American Jewish surveys do not differ substantially from earlier survey results in other Western countries. A major difference, though, concerns the influence of either father or mother on the group socialization of children of mixed marriages. In the United States the dominant parent most often is the mother, which interestingly also conforms with Jewish Halakha. A patrilinear influence appears to be predominant in Mediterranean and Latin American societies. These differences hint, among other things, at the different role of women in society, as well as the different position of religion in the social stratification systems of the respective countries.

A further correlate of mixed marriage is the growing proportion of persons who identify themselves by a multiple denomination. In a recent pre-test for the forthcoming major survey of American Jews planned for 1990 and sponsored by the Council of Jewish Federations, about 6 per cent of those identifying as Jews reported their identification with another religion as well. For one half of this group, Judaism was the primary identification, and for the other half it was the secondary identification.[12]

Demographically, if at least 50 per cent of the relevant children were raised Jewishly, mixed marriage would have little consequence for the Jewish community. But the data available so far quite consistently point to losses on the Jewish side, ranging from moderate to very significant. And these facts are compounded by the comparatively smaller family sizes that have generally been observed among mixed marriages.[13]

A further question is whether mixed marriages, or even out-marriages in the broader sense, have any long-term influence on patterns of group identification and behavioural choices related to family formation and child-rearing. Two very tentative tests of this question are reported in Tables 4 and 5, which refer, respectively, to the frequency of out-marriage among adults who are themselves the children of out-married parents; and to the percentage

TABLE 3   PERCENTAGE JEWISH OF ALL CHILDREN OF CURRENT OUT-
MARRIAGES, BY PARENTS' MARRIAGE TYPE, SELECTED
PLACES, 1960–87

Place	Year	Jewish population	Type of out-marriage				
			Total	Conversionary	Mixed		
					Total	Father Jewish	Mother Jewish
United States[a]							
Total	1970–1	5,600,000	49	94	44	17	86
New York	1981	1,671,000			53	35	73
Chicago	1981	248,000			40		
Eight communities	1982	2,584,000	44	84	24	30	19
Philadelphia	1983–4	240,000		83	31	22	40
Baltimore	1985	92,000	54				
Kansas City	1985	22,000			38		
Rhode Island	1987	17,000	78	98	61		
Argentina[b]							
Salta	1986	1,000			23	25	21
France[b]							
Greater Paris	1972–6	270,000			44	49	18
The Netherlands[c]							
Total	1966	30,000			45		
Italy[a]							
Total	1965	31,000			36	41	30
USSR[d]							
Six cities	1960–8	60–65,000			0–28		

[a] Survey data. Percentages reflect Jewishness of children as assessed by the respondent parents.

[b] Survey data. Percentages of male children who reportedly underwent circumcision.

[c] Jewish community register data. Percentage based on Jewishness of mother, unless otherwise stated.

[d] Police Ministry register. Percentage of 16-year-olds requesting mention of Jewish nationality on internal passport.

Sources: Schmelz and DellaPergola (1983); Paul Ritterband and Steven M. Cohen, 'The social characteristics of the New York area Jewish community, 1981', *American Jewish Year Book 1984* (Philadelphia, 1984), pp. 61–117; Peter Friedman *et al.*, *Metropolitan Chicago Jewish Population 1981; Preliminary Tables* (Chicago, 1981); Egon Mayer, *Love and Tradition: Marriage Between Jews and Christians* (New York, 1987); William L. Yancey and Ira Goldstein, *The Jewish Population of Greater Philadelphia* (Philadelphia, 1984); Gary A. Tobin, *Jewish Population Study of Greater Baltimore* (Baltimore, 1986); Gary A. Tobin, *A Demographic Study of the Jewish Community of Greater Kansas City* (Kansas City, 1986); Sidney Goldstein and Calvin Goldscheider, *The Jewish Community of Rhode Island: A Social and Demographic Study 1987* (Providence, RI, 1988); Rosa N. Geldstein, *Censo de la poblacion judia de la Ciudad de Salta, 1986* (Buenos Aires, 1988); Doris Bensimon and Sergio DellaPergola, *La population juive de France: socio-démographie et identité* (Jewish Population Studies, no. 17; Jerusalem, 1984); Ph. van Praag, *Demography of the Jews in the Netherlands* (Jewish Population Studies, no. 8; Jerusalem, 1976); Sergio DellaPergola, *Jewish and Mixed Marriages in Milan 1901–1968* (Jewish Population Studies, no. 3; Jerusalem, 1972); Mordechai Altshuler, *Soviet Jewry since the Second World War: Population and Social Structure* (Westport, CT, 1987).

TABLE 4   PERCENTAGE OF JEWS CURRENTLY OUT-MARRIED, BY PARENTS' MARRIAGE TYPE, SELECTED PLACES, 1965–86

Place	Year	Parents Jewish	Parents out-married
United States			
Eight communities	1982	36	92
Philadelphia	1983–4	12	65
Argentina			
Salta	1986	21	70
Italy			
Total (males)	1965	21	43

Sources: Mayer (1983), Yancey and Goldstein (1984); Geldstein (1988); DellaPergola (1972).

TABLE 5   PERCENTAGE JEWISH OUT OF ALL CHILDREN OF CURRENT OUT-MARRIAGE, BY GRANDPARENTS' MARRIAGE TYPE SELECTED PLACES, 1983–6

Place	Year	Grandparents Jewish	Grandparents out-married
United States			
Philadelphia	1983–4	37	0
Argentina			
Salta	1986	30	10

Sources: Yancey and Goldstein (1984); Geldstein (1988).

of children raised as Jews by out-married parents who are themselves the children of out-marriage. Even though the geographical coverage of available data is clearly inadequate to allow more extended generalizations, the similarity of findings is quite intriguing. The hypothesis of a chain effect is in fact supported by these data. Jewish children of out-marriages are much more likely to out-marry themselves than children of homogamous marriages, and they also are much less likely to raise their children as Jews.

These findings reflect a development which spreads over three generations, and whose initial stage occurred at a time when out-marriage was far less frequent and also far less legitimized among Jews in America—and perhaps elsewhere—than is the case today. Therefore it may be premature to infer future patterns from past trends. On the other hand, the case contradicting the relevance of these findings rests more on theoretical assumptions than on firm empirical evidence.[14]

Based on what we know, in any event, it seems legitimate to assume that the process set into motion by mixed marriage, if not entirely unidirectional, is strongly erosive, and its conclusion may even be the complete loss of the original sense of Jewishness among the families involved within the span of a few generations. Moreover, it can be quite reasonably expected that greater legitimation of current out-marriages goes hand in hand with future increases in out-marriage, and with diminished pressure on the non-Jewish spouses to convert to Judaism. It should be realized, at the same time, that under contemporary conditions of high longevity, populations are characterized by a great deal of demographic continuity. Cultural disappearance at the periphery of a community should not be confused with physical disappearance.

The real problem, on the face of the available evidence, seems to be that of the ability to transmit a viable Jewish identity to the children of out-marriage. A discussion of this problem entails addressing, on the one hand, the nature of extended family and other social networks which are formed and developed following out-marriage in general and mixed marriage in particular; and on the other hand, the nature of the cultural contents transmitted from generation to generation, and the ways in which these contents are absorbed by the young recipients.

One significant and perhaps surprising implication of the trends here reviewed for the 'Who is a Jew?' debate is that many of the cases whose Jewish identity may be contested on Jewish or other legal grounds are not bound to long term permanence in the Jewish community context. They rather belong to a transitional stage in the intergenerational process, after which the nature of personal and family Jewish identity and continuity is precarious, to say the least.

Jewish Continuity: a Wider Agenda

The above conclusions, though derived from the somewhat narrowly defined focus of the present analysis, may stimulate the formulation of a wider agenda regarding central socio-demographic issues of Jewish continuity, in the context of the 'Who is a Jew?' debate and beyond. Intergenerational group continuity, for the Jews and for any other community defined by religious, ethnic or cultural terms of reference, involves the simultaneous unfolding of at least three distinct processes of reproduction: (a) biologic-demographic; (b) social-structural; and (c) cultural-symbolic. Of these three major types of process, probably the one most clearly pointing to continuity among current Diaspora Jewries is the persisting uniqueness of the Jews' socio-economic composition. Despite the intensive geographical mobility and intergenerational occupational change of the last decades, most survey data still point to the existence of robust educational attainment differences between Jews and non-Jews and to the peculiar concentration of Jews in certain residential areas in cities, and in specialized sub-sectors of economic activity. These structural features do provide a measure of cohesiveness and continuity to the Jewish community.

On the other hand, analysis of current demographic trends—of which we have here examined only one important facet—rather clearly points to attrition and recession. Observed marriage and fertility levels—as distinct from marriage and fertility aspirations—have been low or very low for the past 20 years, which in turn has generated a marked process of ageing among the Jewish populations in the Diaspora. Mixed-marriage appears to be a factor contributing to the futher lowering of a Jewish fertility which is already low *per se*. The most recent survey data indicate that what was predicted years ago, namely that at current fertility levels cohorts of Jewish women born during or after World War II would end their reproductive years with less than the minimum number of Jewish children needed to ensure generational replacement, is now seen to be true as is indeed the case for the general population of some of the more developed countries.[15] No, or very little, substantiation has so far appeared of the alternative hypothesis that the low marriage and fertility rates observed during the 1960s and 1970s were merely postponements of these events to later dates.

As already noted above, low birth rates, ageing and assimilatory trends currently converge in most communities in the Diaspora to determine a diminution in Jewish population. Paradoxically, this decline in Jewish populations sometimes goes hand-in-hand with an actual increase in the number of households composing the 'enlarged' or 'extended' Jewish population, which also include persons who were once Jewish, or are of Jewish origin, but no longer identify as Jews. Occasionally, potential Jewish population decline is being masked by Jewish immigration. But even in such cases, short of a substantial redirection of the demographic process, migration may prove to be no more than a palliative.

The most problematic issue, though, is that of the definition and transmission of Jewish content. To be preserved in the longer term, this content needs to be both sufficiently attractive and recognizably Jewish. It is not only a matter of a sense of community being generated locally. This may be and still is achieved, in spite of the possible weakening of the original cultural content. It is rather the global sense of peoplehood and the universal meaning of Jewish solidarity that are at stake. So is the ability to transmit the principle of boundary maintenance, that has been crucial in Jewish continuity in the past, and seems problematic in the new social context in which group boundaries have become so flexible and porous.

This is, in any event, the demographic, socio-economic and socio-cultural context out of which the current 'Who is a Jew?' debate has been generated. It is the trends now unfolding from this context that will determine the future size and composition of the Jewish population, the patterns of Jewish continuity and change, and the nature of the continuing debate about 'Who is a Jew?'.

Notes

1. Sergio DellaPergola, 'Mass "aliya"—a thing of the past?', *Jerusalem Quarterly* (forthcoming, 1989).

2. Sidney Goldstein, 'A 1990 national population study: why and how', paper presented at the Symposium on World Jewish Population: Research and Policies, Jerusalem 1987 (hereafter cited as 'Symposium 1987').

3. See the proceedings of the *First Meeting of the International Scientific Advisory Committee (ISAC) for the 1990 World Jewish Population Surveys, December 1988*, Jerusalem (the Hebrew University, Institute of Contemporary Jewry, 1989).

4. Uziel O. Schmelz, 'World Jewish population in the 1980s: a short outline', Symposium 1987.

5. Sergio DellaPergola and Uziel O. Schmelz, 'Demographic transformations of American Jewry: marriage and mixed marriage in the 1980s', *Studies in Contemporary Jewry*, vol. 5 (Oxford/New York, 1989).

6. Ibid.; Yisrael Ellman, 'Intermarriage in the United States: a comparative study of Jews and other ethnic groups', *Jewish Social Studies*, vol. 49, no. 1, winter 1987, pp. 1–26.

7. Paul Ritterband and Steven M. Cohen, 'The social characteristics of the New York area Jewish community, 1981', *American Jewish Year Book 1984* (Philadelphia, 1984), pp. 61–117; Bruce A. Phillips, 'Factors associated with intermarriage in the Western United States', paper presented at the 9th World Congress of Jewish Studies, Jerusalem, 1985.

8. Marlena Schmool, 'The demographic situation of the Jews in Great Britain: the known and the unknown', Symposium 1987; Stanley Waterman and Barry Kosmin, *British Jewry in the Eighties: A Statistical and Geographical Guide* (London, 1986).

9. Doris Bensimon and Sergio DellaPergola, *La population juive de France: socio-démographie et identité* (Jewish Population Studies, no. 17; Jerusalem, 1984).

10. Tom Smith, 'America's religious mosaic', *American Demographics*, June 1984, pp. 19–23.

11. Egon Mayer, *Love and Tradition: Marriage Between Jews and Christians* (New York, 1987).

12. Frank L. Mott and Susan H. Mott, 'Using a market survey for characterizing the American Jewish population: the utility of the National Family Opinion (NFO) Panel for surveying American Jews', *Towards a National Survey 1990* (New York, 1988).

13. Sergio DellaPergola, 'Recent trends in Jewish marriage', Symposium 1987.

14. Calvin Goldscheider, *The American Jewish Community: Social Science Research and Policy Implications* (Atlanta, 1986).

15. Uziel O. Schmelz and Sergio DellaPergola, *Basic Trends in American Jewish Demography* (New York Jewish Sociology Papers, no. 3; New York, 1988).

14

Soviet 'Reconstruction' and Soviet Jewry

ZVI GITELMAN

Mikhail Sergeevich Gorbachev has set in motion the most profound and comprehensive changes in the Soviet system in 30 years. Yet, in the third year of his tenure it was still unclear how deeply his reform had affected the system and society, and whether they were being institutionalized. In 1988 *glasnost*, or openness, went quite far. *Perestroika*, or restructuring, was being proposed and widely discussed, but was being implemented slowly or not at all. It is not surprising that reconstructing a huge, cumbersome, highly institutionalized system is a slow, contradictory and awkward process. One cannot alter overnight habits of mind, patterns of behaviour and vested institutional and personal interests developed over many years. Yet failure to produce visible and beneficial results, in both the economic and political spheres, could endanger the entire reform effort and provide ammunition to the foes of *glasnost* and *perestroika*, conceivably allowing them to force a change in leadership and reversal of policy.

Opposition to Gorbachev came both from those who felt the reforms had not gone far enough as well as those who felt they had gone too far. One of the most serious challenges to the leadership was from the non-Russian nationalities, whose concerns and outlooks were apparently not very well known or understood by Gorbachev, whose own political experience had been limited to the Russian republic where he was born and educated. The year saw a great political, cultural and economic debate taking place, with the ultimate resolution nowhere in sight.

The nearly two million Jews of the USSR were affected by this debate in four ways. First, as individuals, their economic, political and cultural lives

Zvi Gitelman is professor of political science at the University of Michigan in Ann Arbor. He is the author or co-author of five books and many articles on Soviet, East European and Israeli politics. His latest book is *A Century of Ambivalence: The Jews of Russia and the Soviet Union, 1881 to the Present* (Viking 1988).

were directly affected, along with everyone else. Second, as the leadership was forced to respond to challenges by the nationalities, including the Russians, Jews were affected as a nationality. Third, more than most others of the over 100 officially recognized nationalities, Soviet Jews are affected by the vicissitudes of international relations, especially the Soviet-American relationship and, to a lesser extent, the Soviet-Israeli one. Finally, as has happened previously in Russian history, Jews and 'the Jewish question' have become symbols in the debate over the nature and future of the system. Rightly or not, 'Jew' is a code word for an internationalist, liberal outlook. Sentiments toward Jews are taken as symbols of broader attitudes toward the perennial issues of whether the state should be primarily a Russian one or a genuinely multinational federation, whether free discussion of issues should be permitted, and the extent to which the country should welcome foreign cultures and friendly relations with the West. The 'Jewish question' is a substantive one but also became a surrogate for a broad range of issues. *Glasnost* brought the issue into the open to a greater extent than at any time in the recent past, but the new openness turned out to cut both ways: it allowed more public expression of antisemitism as well as criticism of this age-old evil.

Economic and Political Reforms

Several times during the year Party Secretary Gorbachev publicly expressed his anger and frustration at the slow pace of reform, though on several occasions he criticized journalists and politicians who were, in his view, too impatient and demanding of results. The party leader had the unenviable task of steering a course between radical reformers and unyielding conservatives, for neither he nor any other recent Soviet leader has had the kind of unfettered power which Joseph Stalin enjoyed and abused.

The overall thrust of Gorbachev's economic reforms was to make the economy more efficient and competitive. He had placed considerable emphasis on the 'human factor'. This means stimulating individual initiative, getting people to work harder, making more rational use of the country's immense natural and human resources, and eliminating or at least radically reducing corruption. To some extent this was a continuation of the policies of Gorbachev's political mentor and patron, Yuri Andropov. In 1988 Gorbachev began in significant ways to go beyond the 'human factor' to institutional reforms. In order to stimulate private initiative and to improve the woeful service sector, co-operatives providing consumer services had been legalized. By the beginning of the year there were over 14,000 co-operatives employing about 200,000 people. They were engaged in repair businesses, restaurants, the production of household items and a host of other functions serving the consumer. Co-operatives have the right to employ full-time labour, engage in foreign trade, own and expand capital assets, and even engage in joint ventures with foreign firms. They also have a freer hand in firing employees than do state enterprises. Some co-operatives began to make quick and handsome profits, arousing the ire of a population which had become accustomed to a high degree of egalitarianism, and which is inclined to 'levelling' of incomes. Partly to assuage popular resentment of the new entrepreneurs, frequently likened to the odious 'NEPmen' of the 1920s, the government proposed a very steep tax, in some cases reaching 90 per cent, on the co-operatives. Reflecting some of the political changes that have occurred, several deputies to the Supreme Soviet, hitherto the completely docile national legislature, protested that this was discriminatory and would kill off private initiative. The government later reduced the maximum tax to 50 per cent.

State-owned enterprises also have the right to engage in joint ventures with foreigners. However, many questions regarding the latter were only slowly being resolved, so that the number of joint ventures grew only modestly. What percentage of ownership can be held by foreigners, what will be the rules governing labour practices, and how profits can be taken out of the country were among the issues impeding the rapid development of joint ventures.

As of the beginning of 1988 the *khozraschet*, or self-financing, system was widely introduced in state-owned enterprises. This meant that they could no longer operate at a loss over long periods of time, counting on the state budget to bail them out. (Soviet officials reported that a quarter of all enterprises were operating at a loss or with marginal profits.) Instead, they were supposed to show a profit. Enterprises producing about 60 per cent of all industrial goods were supposed to switch to the *khozraschet* system. By 1990 all enterprises are supposed to operate in this manner. A major flaw in the reform was that many enterprises continued to rely on fixed state orders for their business and did not have to compete on an open market where the quality of their products would determine the volume of sales and profits. One indication of the economic burden borne by a state which props up inefficient enterprises was given by the Finance Minister, Boris Gostev, who admitted in the autumn that the budget had been in deficit for many years and that in 1988 there would be a deficit of 36.3 billion rubles, amounting to 4 per cent of the value of total production.

Food production was a glaring weak spot of the economy. When Gorbachev visited the Siberian city of Krasnoyarsk in September, he heard many citizens grumble about the lack of food and common household items, a complaint echoed throughout the country and referred to by the party leader in his speeches and interviews. One economist reported that 59 per cent of families' budgets were devoted to food, compared to only 15 per cent in the United States. Yet, even many basic foods were in short supply or unavailable. Meat, butter, sugar and other items were rationed in many parts of the country.

Sugar was in especially short supply since much of it was being diverted for the production of home brew, a booming industry as a result of official curbs on the sale of alcohol.

In an attempt to improve the food supply, at least in the long run, Gorbachev called for leasing farms to peasants for periods of up to 50 years. He encouraged the organization of such farms as co-operatives, family farms or even individual ones, challenging the 60-year-old practice of limiting farms to state and collective enterprises. Thus far, there seem to have been few concrete changes in the organization of agriculture, but Gorbachev's intentions were clear, and they were consistent with the overall strategy of following Chinese and Hungarian precedents in giving individuals greater freedom of economic activity, primarily in the consumer and services sectors.

There was a major change in the political structure of the USSR approved by a special party conference, the first such since 1941, held in June, and approved by the Supreme Soviet in late November. A new body, the Congress of Peoples' Deputies, would be constituted with 2,250 delegates, 1,500 to be elected from territorial and national districts and 750 from public organizations. This congress would then elect a smaller Supreme Soviet, consisting of only 400–500 members. The congress would also elect a president who would have broad powers in legislation, foreign policy and defence. It was widely assumed that Gorbachev would be this president and would also continue as First Secretary of the Party, thus concentrating greater governmental and party powers in his hands. At the same time, the party conference recommended that the party leader at each level of the hierarchy be nominated to head the corresponding government body, replicating the concentration of power at the top on each successive level of the system.

On the other hand, it was recommended that the party's role in economic life be reduced and that a five-year maximum term of office be set for both party and government officials. Reflecting the controversial nature of the proposals and the fears of some that too much power was being concentrated in the hands of one man, 209 delegates to the Conference voted against the proposals. *Glasnost* also manifested itself in an open debate between Boris Yeltsin, the deposed head of the Moscow party organization, who had been removed from the Politburo in February because he had argued that reform was not proceeding fast enough, and Yegor Ligachev, generally considered the spokesman of more conservative politicians apprehensive about the scope and speed of reform which they believe excessive.

The new institutional arrangements were severely criticized by Andrei Sakharov, nuclear scientist and human rights activist who had been brought back to Moscow from exile in Gorky and who had generally supported Gorbachev and his reforms. Speaking both at home and abroad, where he was allowed to travel for the first time in November, Sakharov warned that the new system would concentrate too much power in one person's hands, and that this was dangerous even if that person were Gorbachev. The arrangements were also criticized openly by representatives of the Baltic nationalities, especially the Estonians. They argued that the new system would allow the central authorities to override the republics on important issues and would thus destroy any vestige of federalism. Moreover, since the 750 delegates would be chosen only by *national* public bodies, the nascent popular organizations in the Baltic and similar groups would not be able to influence the choice of delegates. These protests were carried by influential Estonian politicians to the federal government, and in November the latter agreed to adopt additional, as yet unspecified, measures to widen the political and economic independence of the republics.

In the September elections in the primary party organizations (the approximately 400,000 basic party units), about half the elections were contested and a substantial number of new leaders came into office. On the other hand, in a special election to fill three vacancies in the Armenian Supreme Soviet, a write-in candidate defeated a party candidate, the interior minister, winning 78 per cent of the vote, but the election was invalidated. In May about 100 people declared themselves members of an opposition party called the Democratic Union but no official recognition was accorded them. In July the Supreme Soviet issued a decree giving troops of the interior ministry broader authority to bear arms, suppress public demonstrations and enter private homes in pursuit of criminals. Planned demonstrations would have to be registered ten days in advance and local authorities were given broad powers to prohibit them. When the decree came up for legislative approval in October, 13 of 1,350 Supreme Soviet members voted against it, the first such vote in more than 50 years. Interior Minister Aleksandr Vlasov reported that there had been about 600 meetings and street demonstrations through August.

The limitations on the government's ability to reshape society were starkly illustrated by the announcement that wine, champagne and beer would be sold once again in groceries, the number of liquor stores would be increased and their hours lengthened, and that wine and beer bars would re-open. One of Gorbachev's first major campaigns had been the drive against alcoholism, but the population had coped with it by stepping up production of home-brew, a highly dangerous product which also soaked up huge amounts of sugar and led to widespread shortages of that commodity.

In sum, institutional reforms proposed in 1988 were controversial and did not point unambiguously in a democratizing direction. Gorbachev's purpose in proposing them seemed to be to concentrate enough power in his hands and in those of his supporters throughout the hierarchy to facilitate the passage and implementation of economic changes. A multi-party system would not be tolerated and power would not be widely dispersed throughout the system. However, people would generally have more latitude in choosing those who will exercise that power. It remained to be seen whether a political system which continued to concentrate power could coexist with an economic one which had devolved decision-making authority to a variety of bodies.

Perhaps because Gorbachev was both dissatisfied with the pace of reform, and also felt himself politically secure enough to forge ahead, he called a special meeting of the Party Central Committee in October. It resulted in the removal from the Politburo, the most powerful party organ, of its four oldest members, including Andrei Gromyko. The number of Central Committee departments was reduced from 22 to six, four of them to be headed by supporters of reform. The latter changes were in line with the aim of distancing the party from the day-to-day management of the economy.

Glasnost moved ahead faster than *perestroika*. Emigré writers such as Vladimir Nabokov and Joseph Brodsky were published for the first time, as was Boris Pasternak's novel *Dr Zhivago* and other works formerly banned. Some films made years ago but never released were shown to the public for the first time. Attacks on Stalinism continued unabated, but in the spirit of freer expression the media also carried defences of Stalin and his policies. Nearly 700 victims of the purges were 'rehabilitated' by a special commission appointed for that purpose. Politically the most significant rehabilitation was that of Nikolai Bukharin, leader of the 'Right Opposition' to Stalin, and a man whose policies in the 1920s somewhat resembled those of Gorbachev. Some of Bukharin's works were scheduled for republication. Most people interpreted Bukharin's rehabilitation as a partial legitimation of Gorbachev's reforms. Significantly, Leon Trotsky, who advocated policies almost diametrically opposed to Bukharin's and who led the 'Left Opposition' to Stalin, was not rehabilitated.

Because of uncertainty as to the correct interpretation of recent historical events, especially those connected with the Stalinist period, no final examinations were given in history in the secondary schools. Instead, teachers were told to substitute ungraded oral discussions of current events. This reflected both the uncertainty and fluidity of re-evaluations of the system which, after all, were a prerequisite to *perestroika*, for one cannot restructure a system intelligently without understanding how it evolved.

Some reconsideration of Jewish history also resulted from the policy of *glasnost*. In April the magazine *Druzhba Narodov* (Friendship of the Peoples) published 90-year-old Yakov Rapaport's memoir of the 'Doctors' Plot' of 1953 when Kremlin doctors, most of them Jews, were accused of poisoning top Soviet leaders. This led to a pogrom atmosphere in the entire country, and Jewish doctors, such as Rapaport, bore the brunt of popular rage. His daughter's memoir of the time was published simultaneously in *Yunost*, a youth magazine. In July, *Sovetskaya Kultura* published a long article on the death in 1948 of Solomon Mikhoels, Yiddish actor and director, and admitted that he was murdered, that the murder was 'sanctioned' and that the official version of his death was a fabrication.

Religion and the Nationalities

There was a pronounced relaxation of strictures on religion during the year, perhaps because the Russian Orthodox Church, the largest denomination in the country, celebrated the millenium of Christianity in Russia, Ukraine and Belorussia. Perhaps also this was part of Gorbachev's movement away from the more irrational and repressive aspects of the system. The campaign against Islam, very militant in the previous years, seemed to tone down somewhat, Jewish religious groups were no longer harrassed by and large and Christianity was treated with a respect it has not enjoyed since World War II. Konstantin Kharchev, the government official in charge of religions, claimed that in the first half of the year alone, almost 160 new religious congregations had registered with the authorities. Cathedrals in Klaipeda and Vilnius in the Baltic were returned to the Catholic Church after they had been used for other purposes during many years. The number of seminarians was increased. For example, in the Catholic seminary in Kaunas, Lithuania, 125 were enrolled, four times as many as before 1985. In April, Party Secretary Gorbachev met with the highest leaders of the Orthodox Church, condemned anti-religious represssions in the past and promised to propose a new law which would protect the rights of believers more effectively. To the viewers' great astonishment, this meeting was shown on television. In June an Orthodox Church council gave priests greater jurisdiction and called for expanded religious education. The official celebrations of the millenium of Christianity attracted worldwide attention and delegates from many religions and countries. Gorbachev met with Agostino Cardinal Casaroli, Vatican Secretary of State, and Vatican officials met with representatives of the outlawed Ukrainian Catholic (Uniate) Church. A Soviet Human Rights Commission headed by the prominent political commentator Fyodor Burlatsky recommended pardoning all prisoners jailed under laws limiting religious activities. Thus, while no fundamental, institutionalized changes were made the authorities displayed a more or less consistently more benign attitude towards the organized religions.

Nationalities problems surfaced and loomed very large during the year, the most dramatic events taking place in the southern republics of Armenia and Azarbaijan and in the Baltic republics. In the former there were violent clashes reflecting deep-seated ethnic tensions, traditionally denied by Soviet officials, and in the latter national sentiments were channelled into popular movements demanding radical reform of the relationship between centre and periphery. In the Caucasus the central authorities found it very difficult to control mass violence which they had no part in initiating, whereas in the Baltic they themselves seemed to have initiated tendencies which later seemed to get out of control.

As elsewhere in the USSR and Eastern Europe, concern for a deteriorating environment mobilized some groups in Armenia to demand governmental action. Armenian activism began with protests against plans to build a chemical plant outside the republic capital, Erevan. In February, Armenians in the Nagorno-Karabakh area of the neighbouring Azerbaijani republic held public rallies and boycotted schools to reinforce their demands that the region be transferred from Azerbaijan to Armenia, where it had been in the early 1920s, because the cultural needs of Armenians were insufficiently served in Azerbaijan. Huge demonstrations in Erevan expressed sympathy for the demands of their co-ethnics in Nagorno-Karabakh. In late February violence broke out in Sumgait, a city in Nagorno-Karabakh, and at least 32 Armenians were killed. Throughout the year there were clashes between Armenians and Azerbaijanis in both republics and mass rallies in the capitals. A two-month general strike was called in Nagorno-Karabakh and lasted until late July. In June, the Supreme Soviet of Armenia voted to incorporate Nagorno-Karabakh into the Armenian SSR, while the Azerbaijani Supreme Soviet voted not to transfer it. Such a clash between two republican legislatures was unheard of in recent Soviet history. On July 18 the Supreme Soviet of the USSR voted against the transfer, the three-hour debate being shown on national television. Gorbachev explained the decision, arguing that such a transfer would open a Pandora's box of territorial changes and lead to administrative and ethnic chaos. Further armed clashes in Nagorno-Karabakh in September left at least 49 wounded, and a state of emergency was declared in the region. Troops were deployed in Erevan as well in response to mass demonstrations, strikes and the brief takeover by Armenian nationalists of the municipal airport. As a result of the continuing unrest, thousands of Armenians from Azerbaijan took refuge in Armenia, and large numbers of Azerbaijanis fled the Armenian republic to their own. Some estimated that 300,000 refugees were created by the ethnic violence on a scale not seen since World War II. In addition to the pain caused to the nationalities involved, events in the Caucasus cast a long shadow on the myth of 'friendship of the peoples' and embarrassed the Gorbachev leadership. Conservative critics suggested that the disorders were a direct result of *perestroika* and the forces it had unleashed. The devastating earthquake in Armenia on 7 December, in which tens of thousands were killed and many more wounded or made homeless, overshadowed the nationality frictions, at least temporarily.

Events in the Baltic republics posed a more direct political challenge. In Estonia, Latvia and Lithuania popular, officially recognized movements emerged demanding greater political, economic and cultural autonomy from Moscow. The Movement for the Support of *perestroika* in Lithuania, the Latvian Popular Front, and the Estonian Peoples Front were registered among the 30,000 or so 'grassroots' organizations permitted by the reforms. Claiming about 100,000 members or so each, these movements were tolerated by the central authorities, though it was not clear why. Some suggested that the Baltic republics were the most likely venues of successful economic reform and that Gorbachev was willing to permit this spontaneous political and cultural activity in return for demonstrations of how successful economic *perestroika* could be. Mass rallies were held in each of the republics featuring the first public display since the 1940s of the pre-war flags and the singing of the pre-war anthems of the republics. From the symbolic level, Baltic activists soon moved to the practical political one. The Latvian Popular Front pressed for the declaration of Latvian as the official language of the republic, which was legislated by the Latvian Supreme Soviet in October. This meant that all official business in the republic must be transacted in Latvian. The Front also demanded economic autonomy from the centre, a separate Latvian currency, the right to establish independent relations with other countries, and an end to the teaching of atheism in the schools. Because Latvia and Estonia had received a large influx of Russians and other non-indigenous peoples, the demand that migration be regulated was made in both republics. The demand for economic autonomy also was aimed in part at slowing or halting industrialization so that there would be no reason to bring in workers and engineers from Slavic republics. Similar positions were adopted in Lithuania, where it was also demanded that Lithuanian soldiers not serve in other republics, that there be independent Lithuanian missions abroad, and that the republic nominate its own candidates for government and party posts. The militancy and brazenness of these demands were shocking not only to the Soviet population but to foreign observers as well. The movements came very close to demanding full independence from the USSR, and yet they were not repressed. Emissaries from the centre warned them against going too far, but newly appointed party secretaries in each republic cast their lots with the popular movements and embraced their causes. The Estonian legislature passed a resolution declaring that it would not be bound by decisions of the federal government, clearly negating the Soviet constitution. Rather than condemning the resolution outright, officials in Moscow agreed to discuss the matter with an Estonian delegation. How far the Baltic republics would be able to go in asserting their autonomy was of great interest to all nationalities and even to the East European states.

International Relations

Clearly, Mikhail Gorbachev's priorities are domestic. In order to revive the economy and breathe life into a political system which lost its dynamism during the 'years of stagnation', the current euphemism for the Brezhnev era, Gorbachev had to reduce Soviet commitments abroad as well as divert resources going to the military towards the domestic economy. To that end, the Soviet leadership attempted to reduce tensions in all the areas which have the potential to flare up: with the Chinese, in Western Europe and the Middle East, with Japan and the United States. In May the pullout of Soviet troops from Afghanistan began, cutting a commitment first made in 1979. By the end of 1988 there were said to be 50,000 troops left there, down from 115,000 when the withdrawal began. For the first time the Soviets admitted the magnitude of their casualties: 13,310 killed and 35,478 wounded. An internal party circular acknowledged that fundamental errors had been made in the Afghan adventure.

Political prisoners were released and prominent refuseniks were permitted to emigrate, partly in order to remove the 'human rights obstacle' from improving relations with the West. In fact, Western Europe responded favourably to Soviet invitations to help the economy. The Federal Republic of Germany granted $1.6 billion in credits to help the consumer sector, and Western businessmen eagerly sought opportunities in the huge Soviet economy. Federal Chancellor Helmut Kohl was promised that all political prisoners would be freed by the end of the year, though the definition of 'political prisoners' remained unclear.

An ideological rationale for these policies was given by Vadim Medvedev, promoted to the Politburo in October as its new ideological specialist. He said in a speech reprinted in *Pravda* that Soviet Communism was in crisis and that it should borrow ideas from capitalist countries as well as socialist ones. He argued that universal values, such as avoiding wars and ecological catastrophes, have come to outweigh the class struggle in importance, and that peaceful coexistence would be a long-term proposition. This contrasted with statements by his predecessor, Yegor Ligachev, who warned that class struggle must not be abandoned even in periods of reform.

In June another summit meeting took place between American President Ronald Reagan and Gorbachev. Reagan met with dissidents in Moscow and addressed students at Moscow State University. However, little progress was made on arms control. Meetings between Reagan, Gorbachev and President-elect George Bush at the United Nations in December were cut short when Gorbachev had to rush home to deal with the earthquake in Armenia, but in his address to the United Nations Gorbachev did declare a unilateral, deep cut in Soviet armed forces in Western Europe.

Relations with Israel improved as well. Consular delegations were exchanged, placing relations on a lower level than those between Israel, on one hand, and Poland and Hungary, on the other, but the important point was that some formal, albeit largely symbolic, relationship was restored. On several occasions Soviet spokesmen reiterated that a full restoration of relations could occur only 'in the framework of a comprehensive Middle East settlement'. Foreign Minister Eduard Shevardnadze, meeting with the Israeli Prime Minister Yitzhak Shamir, in New York, said about the restoration of relations that 'when an effective international conference goes to work, the Soviet Union will be ready to resolve the issue.'

The Soviet Union moved on several fronts to reduce any risks to itself in the international arena. Aided by Gorbachev's flair for public relations, the USSR managed to project a more favourable, dynamic image in most parts of the world.

Soviet Jewry in a Time of Change

Jews benefited from *glasnost* and *perestroika* though there were some costs as well. On one hand, improved relations with the West and Israel raised emigration levels significantly. Moreover, greater tolerance for religious and ethnic cultural expressions benefited the Jews. On the other hand, *glasnost* has permitted antisemitism to be expressed more widely and there was no evidence that educational and vocational disabilities had been removed where Jews were concerned.

When a new emigration law went into effect in 1987, providing, among other things, that only first degree relatives could invite Soviet citizens to join them abroad, many assumed that this would severely constrict Jewish emigration. In fact, Jewish emigration more than doubled the following year. If in 1986 only 914 Jews left the USSR, and in 1987 some 8,000 did so, in 1988 more than 16,000 were permitted to leave, among them several hundred long-term refuseniks, including Yosef Begun and Pavel Abramovich, leading Hebrew teachers in Moscow. Still, some prominent refuseniks were waiting for exit visas, among them Yuli Kosharovsky, in refusal for 17 years.

Alarmed by the fact that about 90 per cent of those leaving were not headed for Israel, in June the Israeli cabinet resolved that Soviet Jews could get Israeli visas only in Bucharest and from there they would have to fly directly to Israel, thus eliminating the 'drop-out' option. Many Jews in the United States and in the Soviet Union reacted negatively, the US State Department was divided on the issue, and the plan did not seem to have been implemented. Other difficulties arose in mid-year when the United States declared that the unexpectedly large emigration, mostly Armenians, had exhausted the budgetary allocations for Soviet immigrants. In the next few months the backlog of immigrants began to grow, and many Jews found themselves stuck in Rome, awaiting transit to the United States, or being challenged as to their refugee status on the grounds that they could not prove that they were likely to be persecuted in the USSR. In December the US Attorney General agreed to exercise his 'parole power' and admit more Soviet immigrants, but those admitted under such status did not enjoy the assistance offered to refugees. American Jewish organizations promised to press the matter with the new administration and congress.

Religious study and prayer groups were harrassed less in 1988. In November 1987, the magazine *Nauka i Religiia* (Science and Religion) reported that there were 109 registered Jewish congregations in 1986, compared with 259 in 1961 and 181 in 1976. On the other hand, significant numbers of young people had become religious and organized religious groups in the larger cities. While this had been going on for some time, the year saw the emergence of several 'grass-roots' Jewish cultural groups which were not necessarily religious or oriented toward emigration. They were inspired, perhaps, by the national-cultural movements in the Baltic and elsewhere. In July a Jewish

Cultural Club was formed in Riga with B. Gaft as its coordinator. A Jewish Cultural Society was established in Estonia in March. *Literaturna Ukraina* (24 November) reported that a Jewish Cultural Society had been formed in Kiev, where a Jewish folksong ensemble, *Nigunim*, was already performing. The founding of the Society was welcomed by representatives of the Ukrainian Cultural Fund and by Aleksandr Levenbuch, director of the *Shalom* theatre in Moscow and a leader of a similar group there, one which, he said, was open to all and included Russians and Ukrainians. He was quoted as saying, 'Our aim is to develop Jewish culture, strengthen internationalism on the basis of the exchange of spiritual values with representatives of other nationalities.' A Union of Lovers of Jewish Culture was founded in Minsk and was chaired by the artist M. Dantsig. They planned to feature local actors and dance groups, offer courses in Yiddish and publish a yearbook in Yiddish and Belorussian. They also expressed the desire to link up with similar groups inside and outside the USSR.

The May issue of *Kommunistas* (Lithuania) reported an order to party committees, trade unions and the republic's Ministry of Culture to 'devote constant attention to the development of the national cultures of the Polish and Jewish populations' and to provide for art exhibits, literary evenings, the expansion of Yiddish library holdings, commemoration of Nazi victims, and to provide wider local coverage of Jewish history, culture and traditions. Jews and other national minorities were to be 'guaranteed fair representation in party, government, komsomol, trade union and economic organs, and in the ranks of the CPSU.' Such a directive was unknown anywhere else or, indeed, at any time in recent Soviet history. Indeed, a Group to Promote Jewish Culture was formed under the aegis of the Lithuanian Cultural Fund and its representatives participated in the 45th anniversary commemoration of the Warsaw Ghetto uprising. The authorities were asked to re-open the State Jewish Museum of Culture in Vilnius which had been closed in 1949, but by the year's end this had not happened. On the other hand, an exhibit of Lithuanian Jewish graphic art from the seventeenth through the twentieth centuries opened in Kaunas in June and was then shown in Vilnius. The exhibit was organized by Emenuelis Zingeris, who was active in the promotion of Yiddish culture in Lithuania.

Some claimed that in Moscow alone 25 Jewish cultural groups were active. World War II veteran Yuri Sokol opened a Jewish library in his apartment in Moscow and reported that 30–40 readers a week patronized it. He applied to the city Soviet for official recognition of the library and for the establishment of a museum highlighting the role of Soviet Jews in World War II. Mikhail Chlenov, an anthropologist, had founded a group for the historical and anthropological study of Jewry as far back as 1981. In March, along with two others, he began publishing a journal of general Jewish interest, *Shalom*. A second issue appeared in September. About six typed journals of Jewish interest were appearing in the USSR in 1988.

In May, Israeli Rabbi Adin Steinsaltz announced that a Jewish religious training institute would open in Moscow as part of a broader agreement to include Soviet-Western co-operation in surveying, preserving and studying Judaica books and manuscripts in Soviet libraries and archives. The agreement was negotiated with Evgeny Velikhov, vice-president of the Soviet Academy of Sciences. Edgar Bronfman, president of the World Jewish Congress, announced in the fall that the WJC and the Jewish Agency had agreed with the Soviet Ministry of Culture to establish a Jewish cultural centre at the site of the Jewish Musical Theatre in Moscow. The Solomon Mikhoels Cultural Centre was scheduled to open in February 1989. It was to include a Judaica library, a museum, art gallery and teaching areas. Bronfman further announced that Soviet authorities had agreed to allow the distribution of Jewish cultural and religious material. The building adjacent to the main Moscow synagogue was also to be turned into a museum of Jewish culture. The Main Archival Administration of the USSR and the United States Holocaust Memorial Council signed an agreement in the summer to permit American researchers to copy documents in Soviet archives which related to the Holocaust. The copies would be deposited in the Holocaust Museum scheduled to open in Washington, DC in 1991.

Arbit Blatas, a Lithuanian-born sculptor living in the United States, was given permission to erect a monument to the Holocaust victims in Vilnius. It was to have a specifically Jewish character and include the Hebrew word *zachor* (remember). A commemoration of the 45th anniversary of the liquidation of the Lvov ghetto was held in that city on 24 June. The officially sanctioned meeting was conducted in Yiddish, Russian and Ukrainian. Calls were heard for the preservation of Jewish cultural monuments, popularization of Yiddish language and literature, and the opening of Jewish schools and synagogues in Lvov. Luiza and Iosif Shternshtam, Lvov sculptors, presented a proposal for a monument to ghetto victims to the local soviet.

In other signs of relaxations in the cultural area, Rabbi Adolph Shaevich and Cantor Vladimir Pliss of the Moscow Choral synagogue came to study at New York's Yeshiva University for three months. Vassily Grossman's monumental novel about World War II, wherein the Jewish element is prominent, was finally published in the magazine *Oktiabr*, long after it had become an underground classic. About 100 Hebrew teachers from Moscow, Kiev and elsewhere formed a Hebrew Teachers Association headed by Lev (Aryeh) Gorodetsky of Moscow and held a national meeting in Moscow in October, attended by 55 teachers.

At this juncture it is impossible to assess the significance and viability of what seems to be a revival of Jewish culture in the USSR. Religious groups will presumably maintain themselves and grow, especially if they continue to be tolerated and if they are aided from abroad with teachers and materials, though they are likely to lose many adherents to emigration, especially to Israel. The groups forming around secular culture raise intriguing questions.

To what extent will they link to the 'establishment' Yiddish culture centred around the monthly *Sovetish Heymland*? Some of them publish in that journal, but it is generally regarded as an ideologically orthodox organ. Will the journal change with *glasnost* and *perestroika*? How viable is secular Jewish culture in any case? Perhaps we shall see the development in the USSR of a not very intensive or demanding, and yet meaningful, Jewish culture centred around the arts, literature and the study of past history and culture, a kind of culture which engages many Jews in the West without becoming an all-consuming enterprise. Obviously, prospects for this depend both on the Jews themselves as well as on the future course of the system.

Anti-Semitism and the Great Debate over the Soviet Future

Antisemitism was more widely discussed than in recent decades. The Russian nationalist organization Pamyat (Memory) organized meetings and disseminated materials in which antisemitic messages were explicit. On 1 February *Pravda* criticized Pamyat for its antisemitism and for having become an 'extremist, chauvinist organization'. *Izvestiia* of 27 February also criticized the organization and mocked its claims of a Zionist-Masonic conspiracy which was trying to establish worldwide dominance. The well known 'anti-Zionist' writers, Yevseev, Begun and Romanenko were criticized for publishing works which 'abound in a large number of various propositions and inaccuracies that make it possible to assess their works as unscientific and essentially disorienting to readers . . .' Experts from the Institute of the USA and Canada had been asked to study the works of these propagandists and concluded that they were distortions, exaggerations and 'juggling of facts'. They accused Begun of employing a 'simple device: he replaces the word "Jew" with the word "Zionist" and then he follows the original [of *Mein Kampf*] verbatim, occasionally interspersing the text with pseudo-Marxist phraseology.' This is one of the strongest criticisms seen in a Soviet publication of works which had long been viewed as antisemitic in the West but which the Soviets had insisted were merely anti-Zionist.

This did not mean that antisemitic motifs had disappeared from the press. Writing about Michael Dukakis, for example, V. Linnik said that 'The Jewish bourgeoisie's money carries colossal weight in the Democratic Party, and Dukakis' distinctly pro-Israeli stand is no accident' (*Pravda*, 22 July). In an article that became a political *cause célèbre*, Ninas Andreevna, a chemistry teacher in Leningrad, attacked *perestroika*. Like others, she made the association between Jews, lack of patriotism, and political liberalism. 'Another special feature of the views of the "left-liberals" ', she wrote, 'is an obvious or camouflaged cosmopolitan tendency, a sort of de-nationalized "internationalism" ', citing Trotsky as the epitome of this tendency. Trotsky, she asserted, slighted Russian culture and the Russian proletariat. If the

Jewish connection were not clear enough she suggested that 'Militant cosmopolitanism is now linked with the practice of "refusenikism", of refusing socialism.' Refuseniks commit 'outrages' by demonstrating publicly. 'Moreover, we are somehow gradually being trained to see this phenomenon as an almost inoffensive change of "place of residence", not as class and nationality betrayal by persons most of whom have been graduated from higher schools and graduate schools at public expense.' She mocks 'refusenik-ism' as 'some kind of manifestation of "democracy" and "human rights".' (*Sovetskaia Rossiya*, 13 March). So the connection was made between Trotsky, the cosmopolitan Jewish intellectual who had no regard for Russians, refuseniks, and democracy. Little wonder that rumours of anti-semitic pogroms connected to the church millenium spread among Jewish activist circles, especially after leaflets appeared in Leningrad calling for 'Death to the Jews'. The rumours proved unfounded.

Reformist magazines also took up the issue of antisemitism but as might be expected they condemned it. Two authors writing in *Ogonyok* in June 1988, noted that

Unfortunately, in the recent past the criticism of Zionism was not always conducted from a class position in the works of certain Soviet authors. Scientific analysis was replaced by ambiguous hints, and the concepts 'Jew' and 'Zionist' were often confused. Antisemitism and its social roots were passed over in silence ... or received an incorrect evaluation [and the influence of Zionism in capitalist countries was exaggerated].

Thus, *glasnost* permitted both freer public expression of antisemitism as well as greater criticism of it than had been seen in the USSR in the 1960s and 1970s. The Jewish issue became, if not quite a touchstone of the ongoing debate between reformers and anti-reformers, at least part of that discussion, one whose outcome would determine the future of the third largest Jewish community in the world, not to speak of the future course of the USSR itself. The conservative opposition can be expected to ally itself with Russian nationalists who would repress the autonomist stirrings in the Baltic and elsewhere and who would have no compunction in using antisemitism for their ends, and perhaps seeing it as an end in itself. Who will win the debate now going on and what the exact consequences will be is far from clear during this most exciting period of Soviet history, one promising great potential gains as well as disasters.

15

The Austrian National Socialists and the Anschluss

F. L. CARSTEN

On 13 March 1938 a triumphant Hitler entered Linz—the city where he was educated—and on the following day Vienna, among the jubilation of vast crowds and the ringing of the church bells. On the latter day *The Times* reported:

> Few conquerors in history have had such a reception. No adjective suffices to describe the jubilation which greeted him in Linz . . . or which awaited him in Vienna . . . This triumphant welcome was shared by the army he had sent into Austria; flowers were strewn in the path of the rumbling tractors and armoured cars. If any Austrians were against him on Friday [11 March], they either hid their faces or were completely converted yesterday and to-day. Austria has not known such since Imperial days, and few Austrian Emperors ever roused the people to such rejoicing.

According to the paper's description of Hitler's entry into Vienna, the city 'resembled a town which has just received news of a great victory and is preparing to welcome the returning troops . . . There are no signs of a people bowing unwillingly to the foreign yoke; on the contrary, every Viennese seemed to wear a swastika brassard or to carry a swastika flag.' Ominously *The Times* added that Jewish shops had been looted in the 10th and 13th districts of Vienna.[1] The British minister, Michael Palairet, telephoned from Vienna on 14 March: 'It is impossible to deny the enthusiasm with which both the new regime and last night's announcement of incorporation in the Reich have been received here. Herr Hitler is certainly justified in claiming that his action has been welcomed by Austrian population.'[2]

F. L. Carsten was the Masaryk Professor of Central European History in the University of London until 1978 and is now Emeritus Professor of Central European History. Among his books relevant to this subject are: *The Rise of Fascism* (rev. edition 1980), and *The First Austrian Republic* (1986).

Three weeks before, huge Nazi demonstrations had taken place in Graz and other towns of Styria. On 20 February the correspondent of the *Manchester Guardian* reported from Graz: 'Nazi Storm Troops in full uniform marched through the streets and drove in lorries with huge swastika flags. They gave the salute and shouted Nazi slogans. "Whom have we to thank for our freedom?" asked the crowd. "Adolf Hitler" was the answer, given by thousands of people demonstrating in front of Graz cathedral, the town hall and the palace of the Styrian bishop.' A week later the correspondent wrote that a visitor to Graz 'would imagine he has entered a German Nazi city. The majority of the people in the streets this afternoon wore the swastika emblem, some of them just small swastika badges, others the official German party sign.'[3] Enthusiastic demonstrations also took place in other Styrian towns as well as in Klagenfurt and Villach in Carinthia. In Linz the demonstrations at first occurred at the reception of local National Socialists who were released from prison under a government amnesty. They were given 'an uproarious welcome. The free men arrived at Linz in flower-decked motor-cars and were greeted with the Storm Troopers' song and cries of "Heil Hitler". Afterwards they were given a reception at the former Brown House in Linz', as *The Times* noted on 22 February 1938.

These and many similar reports confirm that Austrian National Socialism was a strong popular movement, a movement of opposition to the 'authoritarian regime' established by chancellor Engelbert Dollfuss in 1933—at the same time as the Hitler dictatorship in Germany—and in favour of the Anschluss to Hitler's Germany. As there had been no general election since 1930, the voting strength of the movement is impossible to establish; it varied considerably from one province to the other, with Carinthia and Styria in the forefront; and the movement was by no means confined to the towns but it strongly penetrated to many of the Austrian villages.

It would be oversimplified to consider Austrian National Socialism as just an offshoot of the German party although it was controlled by its Munich headquarters and was strongly influenced by developments in Germany. Indeed, the Austrian party was considerably older than the German one. It originated in the German-speaking districts of Bohemia in the early years of the twentieth century. There, German trade unions were established in opposition to the socialist unions, and this was followed by the foundation of a Deutsche Arbeiterpartei (German Workers' Party) in 1904; delegates from Linz, Graz and Klagenfurt participated in its foundation. The original party programme included national, political and social demands and declared its strong opposition to 'any influence of alien *völkisch* groups', principally to the immigration of Czech workers into German-speaking areas. A new programme, adopted in 1913, condemned Marxism and internationalism, 'the duplicity of Social Democracy, led by Jews and interlinked with the mobile big capital', and proclaimed adherence to the *völkisch* ideology. Before the end of the First World War the party changed its name to 'German National Socialist

Workers' Party'; it demanded the 'combination of the whole area settled by Germans in Europe in a democratic and social German Empire', and attacked the predominance of Jewish banks in the economic life.[4] The end of the First World War brought the partition of the Habsburg Empire and with it the division of the party among several new states, Czechoslovakia, Poland and Austria.

The branch of the party in the Austrian Republic was led by Dr Walter Riehl, who had been one of the leaders in Bohemia before the war and later established himself as a prominent lawyer in Vienna. But the Austrian party was very small, and its influence limited to white-collar workers, academics and students. Much more important was the Grossdeutsche Volkspartei (Pan-German People's party), which was represented in the government and polled over half a million votes in 1919 and in 1920. It had inherited the Pan-German tendencies of the party founded in the late nineteenth century by Georg Ritter von Schönerer. He not only venerated Bismarck and the German Empire founded in 1871, but he was also a violent antisemite and anti-Catholic who considered the Bible 'Jewish'. In a strongly Catholic country, there existed ancient antisemitic tendencies, locally fostered by a belief in the ritual murder of Christian children. But Schönerer was truly the father of racial antisemitism; to him, 'the founder of Christianity' was 'the son of a racial Jewess'.[5] Schönerer found many enthusiastic followers among the *Burschenschaften* (student corporations); but his conversion to Protestantism, his violent attacks on the 'Jew Bible' and on the Catholic Church, his promotion of Germanic cults and a Germanic calendar, meant that his movement remained small. The number of its parliamentary deputies shrank after the introduction of universal male suffrage in 1907 which enfranchised the lower classes. In addition, Schönerer's autocratic ways and his never-ending quarrels with other Pan-Germans led to frequent splits of the party. There was constant in-fighting between the several Pan-German and German right-wing groups—a tendency which was to remain characteristic of the *völkisch* camp in Austria.

Yet the Schönerer movement left an important legacy in Austria. It influenced large numbers of students and other nationalists with the ideas of Pan-Germanism and racial antisemitism. When these young men became middle-aged doctors and lawyers and teachers they found their old ideas revived in Hitler's Germany. In the 1930s countless Austrian *Burschenschaftler* and other students became enthusiastic National Socialists, and they found their elders ready to return to the ideas of their youth; the older and the younger generation could combine in a shared belief. The leaders and members of the Grossdeutsche Volkspartei then went over almost to a man to the Austrian National Socialists. The seed sown by Schönerer blossomed after almost half a century. In Austria as well as in Germany, the National Socialists drew many of their earlier and most ardent followers from the pre-war racialist and *völkisch* groups and parties.

At the Austrian universities, antisemitic riots had already become a regular feature in the 1920s. The meeting of a Zionist congress in Vienna in August 1925 provided the occasion for violent antisemitic scenes which were orchestrated by the National Socialists, the Pan-German and antisemitic leagues and the *völkisch* unions and sports associations, which formed an 'action committee' for the purpose. Cars were attacked, the trams were stopped and searched for Jewish passengers, and the non-Jewish correspondent of *The Times* had to use force to avoid being dragged from his taxi by youngsters armed with heavy sticks. In the same year the National Socialist group succeeded in gaining 14 out of 30 seats on the student representative body at the Technical University of Vienna. And 1925 was a year of relative prosperity and stability in Austria after the end of rampant inflation.

Meanwhile the Austrian National Socialist party remained very small and beset by internal differences. These came to a head at the party conference held at Salzburg in August 1923, over the question whether the party should participate in the forthcoming general election. The Grossdeutsche offered a combination of the two lists and the reservation of several safe places on the list to the National Socialists. Riehl and other leaders were in favour of accepting, but opposition was very strong and was stirred up by leaders of the Munich National Socialists who were present at the conference. When Hitler appeared somewhat later he came out for abstention because the party rejected all forms of parliamentarianism. This was accepted by the majority who believed—three months before the Hitler Putsch in Munich—that the national revolution was just round the corner. But Riehl and many members did not, and in 1924 he seceded and founded a new party, the Deutsch-sozialer Verein für Österreich (German Social Association for Austria), the first split in the ranks of the Austrian party. But the association from the outset was a political sect, without any influence.

Riehl's secession did not eliminate the quarrels and personal conflicts from the Austrian party, which suffered severely from lack of funds and suitable leaders. The conflicts once more erupted at the party conference held at Passau in Germany in August 1926. There Hitler, who after his release from 'honourable' imprisonment in Bavaria, had regained control of the German party, succeeded in imposing his will on the Austrian party, which he accused of being 'democratic'. Henceforth the Austrian party became a mere branch of the German NSDAP and was controlled from Munich. But again, some of the Austrian leaders declined to accept the verdict and to become the 'Austrian Gau' of the German party. Karl Schulz and others refused to bow to Hitler's will and left the meeting, to form their own National Socialist party, while the majority now added the words 'Hitler Movement' to their name in brackets. But the secession, as in the case of Dr Riehl, was not a success, although Schulz and his friends had a sizeable following among the *völkisch* tade unions and combined for elections with the Grossdeutsche and other right-wing groups. The 'Hitler Movement' too continued to suffer from financial difficulties and rivalries between various party leaders. In 1928 it had only 4,466 members in the whole of Austria—compared with 108,000 for the German party; while the party led by Schulz had 6,274 paying members. In 1929 efforts promoted by a Sudeten German National Socialist, Hans Krebs, to bring about a reconciliation of the two Austrian National Socialist parties came to nought, largely on account of fierce opposition by local Austrian leaders loyal to Hitler, and the internal quarrels continued unabated.

Yet, within a few years the Austrian National Socialists became a major party, able to win, in certain parts of the country, 20 per cent of the vote or even more. In May 1932 a worried British minister, Sir Eric Phipps, wrote from Vienna:

Last year the Nazi movement was, comparatively speaking, unheeded in the country; its leaders almost unknown to the public and its representation on public bodies virtually non-existent. But a noticeable change came over the fortunes of this party early in the present year . . . Its meetings even in Vienna—the stronghold of Socialism—are today well attended; its placards numerous; its speakers vehement and liberal in their promises to the dicontented, disappointed and bitter elements of the electorate; it offers an opportunity for parades and a promise of excitement; and it panders, as in Germany, to strong anti-Jewish feelings.

According to another dispatch, it was expected that in the general election of 1933 the party would win 25 to 40 seats at the expense of all other parties. In the municipal elections in Vienna in 1932 the National Socialists obtained more than 200,000 votes and gained 15 seats; the party was growing strong, 'particularly among government servants and in the middle and salaried classes'. As the annual report of the legation put it, '1932 was a bumper year for the Nazis in Austria . . . They had a fine field for recruitment in the large army of middle-class unemployed; they appeared to have sufficient funds for propaganda and a good organisation.'[6]

How can this sudden change in the fortunes of the party be explained? In the first instance there was, of course, the world economic crisis which hit Austria, always dependent on exports and foreign help, particularly hard. Exactly as in Germany, the unemployed, not only of the lower middle class, provided the National Socialists with many new recruits. In January 1930 the figure of unemployed receiving relief stood at 273,000; to their number another 90,000 or so had to be added who were not entitled to relief or received old age pensions on account of their unemployment. This amounted to about 6 per cent of the population. By January 1933 the figure had risen to 478,000, of whom 45 per cent were in Vienna. To that figure perhaps another 300,000 had to be added who no longer received any unemployment benefit: a total of about 12 per cent of the Austrian population. And among the victims of the crisis also were many shopkeepers, craftsmen and other small independent people.

There can be no doubt that the rise of the German NSDAP exercised a strong influence on Austria; and the German party was led by an Austrian who in January 1933 became the German chancellor. Ever since 1918 the idea of the Anschluss had exercised a powerful influence on Austrian political life. Austria was a small and poor country which hoped for help from the 'big brother' to the north. The Austrians felt that they were Germans and that only the peace treaty of St Germain prevented them from joining Germany. This conviction was held by all political parties, including the Socialists, and especially by the Grossdeutsche who never ceased to preach union with Germany. The Austrian Socialists only renounced it after Hitler seized power in Germany, but they still adhered to it for the future. With the rise of the German NSDAP, the members and voters of the Grossdeutsche, attracted by the promises and the radicalism of the National Socialists, went over to them in large numbers. The same applied to the *völkisch* sports associations and to a prominent peasant party, the Landbund.

There existed yet another large right-wing organization, which for some years had been a power in the land, the Heimwehren, founded on a local basis soon after the revolution of 1918 to defend Austria against 'Bolshevism' and the threat of 'red Vienna'. Supported with funds and weapons by fascist Italy and reactionary Hungary, they formed large, well armed paramilitary units and aimed at a seizure of power. But a local attempt in Styria in September 1931 was not supported by the other units and failed miserably. Jealousies and personal conflicts between the different provincial leaders prevented the establishment of a unified command structure and any more forceful action, and the official leader, Prince Rüdiger von Starhemberg, wavered uneasily between loyalty to Italian fascism and German National Socialism. In the election of November 1930 the Heimwehren still polled twice as many votes as the National Socialists, but soon after disintegration set in. This was particularly marked in Styria and Carinthia. There the local Heimwehr chiefs established close links with Hitler and the NSDAP, and in October 1931 a mass meeting of their uniformed members in Graz was addressed by the National Socialist Austrian leader appointed by Hitler as well as the Styrian Heimwehr chiefs. The two organizations declared unconditionally in favour of the Anschluss: they would fight 'shoulder to shoulder against this system and for the great Third German Reich' and march together 'against Bolshevism, Marxism and parliamentary democracy'. After the meeting the members of Heimwehr and SA fraternized enthusiastically in the local inns. The Styrian Heimwehren adopted the swastika as their emblem and a programme which strongly emphasized *völkisch* ideology and a 'Germanic racial consciousness'. Only 'Aryan' Germans who accepted this programme could become members.[7] In 1932 the Styrian leaders went to Munich to put themselves under the command of Captain Röhm, the German SA leader; and in 1933 the two paramilitary organizations were officially amalgamated.

In other Austrian provinces too there were mass desertions from the Heimwehren to the National Socialists. In April 1933, at a dinner with the

British military attaché, Starhemberg and other Heimwehr leaders openly admitted 'that they had under-estimated the strength of the wave of National Socialism . . . They referred to the widespread defections from the Heimwehr in Tirol', and the then minister of commerce mentioned 'that in his own village in Tirol the whole population including his own men servants who had hitherto been Heimwehr to a man had all gone across to the Nazis.' They left the attaché 'in no doubt as to the gravity of the situation from their point of view'.[8] The Heimwehren supported the authoritarian regime of chancellor Dollfuss and thereby lost much of their strength, and the Austrian SA gained many new members. As Erich Zöllner, one of the leading Austrian historians, has put it: 'The "national camp" of Austria stood predominantly under the sign of the swastika.'[9] And from 1933 onwards 'national' referred to the partisans of union with Hitler's Germany.

The Tyrol was strongly Catholic and conservative, and yet the National Socialists made rapid progress there, not only in Innsbruck but also in the villages of the Inn valley and elsewhere. Styria and Carinthia had quite a different tradition. Both had Slav minorities in the south, and already before 1914 there had been a fierce struggle between the nationalities, fostered on the German side by the Deutscher Schulverein which promoted German 'national' teaching in the schools. After the war, southern Styria was annexed by Yugoslavia, and in Carinthia bitter fighting broke out between volunteer units of Austrians and Yugoslavs which were supported by the respective governments and armies. In October 1920 a plebiscite was held under Allied supervision in the disputed part of Carinthia which ended in an Austrian victory, so that the south remained Austrian, but with a sizeable Slovene minority. In both provinces the tradition was strongly 'national', not only among the urban intelligentsia; at first, this led to the rise of the Heimwehren and later it benefited above all the National Socialists. In June 1933 the German consul reported from Klagenfurt that the progress of the National Socialist movement was simply 'astonishing'; it had gained a firm footing in the most remote valleys of Upper Carinthia and even in areas which were reputedly 'black' (Catholic). Whole Heimwehr units transferred their loyalty to National Socialism, and they took with them their stores of weapons.

In the west of Austria, in Vorarlberg—close to Germany and Switzerland—the leading manufacturers of Dornbirn, who had previously financed the local Heimwehren, joined the National Socialists. A large percentage of the people depended on work in the cotton factories and followed the example of their employers. In the opinion of the British consul at Innsbruck, the majority of the population of Vorarlberg sympathized with the National Socialists, and this was true in particular of the younger generation. In Upper Austria, National Socialism was especially strong in the Protestant villages (which had not been converted by the Counter-Reformation), and there the leading role was often played by the local clergyman.

If the strength of National Socialism varied considerably from district to district the same was true of its social distribution. After the party's success in the local elections of April 1932 its former leader Dr Riehl provided an analysis of the social background. He stated clearly that 'the entire Aryan intelligentsia and a majority of the academically trained and the higher civil servants' voted National Socialist, as did many 'people in enterprise and trade', such as architects and master-builders, and many 'who were well situated, and not at all the small men and the Christian workers, who strangely enough remained faithful to the Christian Social party.' As to the working class, especially of Vienna, they to a large extent remained loyal to the Socialists, but the National Socialists had made progress among 'small white-collar workers, chauffeurs, railwaymen and tram workers.'[10]

From other reports too we know that it was these peripheral groups of the working class which provided recruits for the National Socialists. In Austria, there existed from pre-war days several *völkisch* trade unions which were to a certain extent successful precisely among these peripheral groups. Elsewhere it was open pressure by the employers, above all by the Alpine Montangesell-schaft in Upper Styria, which forced its workers to leave the 'free' trade unions and to join, first the Heimwehren and later the National Socialists. According to the British legation in Vienna, active National Socialists were to be found especially among 'small traders, factory owners and hotel keepers', whose enterprises suffered because of the German hostility to the Dollfuss regime, and equally among 'established doctors, dentists and lawyers, whose livelihood becomes each year more precarious and who attribute their difficulties largely to Jewish competition, ... as well as not a few of the government servants and teachers.' The same report stated that antisemitism found 'a fertile field in the inherently antisemitic and impoverished youth of Austria.'[11] Indeed, as in Germany, the universities became strongholds of National Socialism years before the rise of the National Socialist party.

As we have seen, antisemitism had a long tradition in Austria, and in its non-racial form it was strongly present in the largest party, the Christian Socials. Its founder, Dr Karl Lueger, had declared: 'I decide who is a Jew'. It was strong in Vienna, and equally in parts of the country where the Jewish population was very small, such as the Tyrol. It was fanned by vicious National Socialist propaganda. 'Christians' were told to shop only in 'Christian' enterprises and to buy only from 'Aryan' tradesmen. The allegedly 'Jewish' department stores were singled out for attacks with stink bombs. Although the National Socialist party was dissolved by Dollfuss in 1933, the attacks continued unabated and the windows of Jewish shops were frequently smashed. In 1937 a deputy mayor of Vienna addressed a meeting of small traders and craftsmen and declared 'that the Viennese would defend them-selves with all their force against the dubious competition of post-war immigrants, leaving no doubt as to whom he meant.' But he carefully dis-tinguished 'between what he called Viennese antisemitism and the National Socialist brand.'[12]

In the same year the British consul at Innsbruck wrote about the position of Jews in the town (which had a very small Jewish community). He thought it was better there than it was at Linz or Graz, and 'in theory there is no discrimination against Jews on the ground of race or religion.' But the practice was very different:

> The one or two Jewish lawyers that practised in Innsbruck have been boycotted out of their profession by their colleagues. One or two Jewish doctors maintain themselves by working exceedingly hard and by subsisting mostly by means of a clientele among foreign tourists . . . Jewish businessmen are suffering from a silent, but effective boycott . . . In the schools non-Jewish children are not discouraged when they indulge in petty persecution of Jewish children . . . In general it can be concluded that, while in theory Jews are treated with an undiscriminating liberalism, in practice there is great anti-semitic pressure. [13]

Unfortunately, no reports seem to have survived describing the situation in Linz or Graz where antisemitic propaganda was much fiercer. In Carinthia (where hardly any Jews lived) antisemitism became so strong that Jews no longer went there on holiday.

Professor Zöllner writes that 'in the relationship between the Jews who mainly lived in Vienna and the remainder of the population no changes had occurred since the 1920s which might have justified the growth of antisemitic tendencies', for the influx of Jews from Poland, Romania and Hungary of the immediate post-war years had long ceased and the Jewish percentage of the population steadily declined on account of the low Jewish birthrate. [14] Yet antisemitism was growing in Vienna and elsewhere. Zöllner thinks that at least one of the causes was 'the expectation of new chances in enterprise and trade through the elimination of Jewish competition', and this hope seems to have played a prominent part. Even more puzzling is the fact that anti-semitism was so strong in areas with a very small Jewish population.

National Socialist propaganda, financed from Germany, continued to flourish in spite—or because—of the dissolution of the party. Its progress was temporarily checked by the murder of chancellor Dollfuss in July 1934 by members of an Austrian SS unit and by the defeat of the subsequent uprising in Styria and Carinthia. But the advance was soon resumed. Many National Socialist leaders were arrested and detained; they were released after the agreement between Austria and Germany of July 1936, and thereafter the party enjoyed a semi-legal existence. Some representatives of the 'national opposition' became members of the Schuschnigg government, and later the party was able to open a semi-legal office in Vienna. As there were no elections, no figures are available for the voting strength of the party after its dissolution. That it would have been very considerable cannot be doubted. According to its own figures, the party had 68,500 members at the time of its dissolution, and it gained another 21,000 during the following fourteen months: a total of almost 90,000—quite a considerable figure. To this must be added the large membership of the SS, SA (with about 40,000 members), the Hitler Youth and similar organizations. It is also true that the party's progress was somewhat marred by continuing rivalries and conflicts among its leaders and between the different organizations, especially the SA and the SS, which appeared openly during the attempted uprising of July 1934. Yet, in a 'German' country, the lure of the Third Reich and its power remained a force which the weak Schuschnigg government was unable to counter.

The Schuschnigg government was threatened from the left by the Socialists and from the right by the National Socialists and it enjoyed little popular support. But the Socialists were a party of the working class and influential only in Vienna and the few industrial centres of Upper and Lower Austria and Styria, and they had no foreign backing. The National Socialists, on the other hand, became strong in all parts of the country and among all social classes—although relatively weak among the industrial workers. Their propaganda affected towns and villages alike, and they could exploit ancient fears and superstitions. The 'Viennese brand' of antisemitism was based on economic anxieties at a time of severe economic crisis, which in particular hit the small independent people, but it had much older roots. On a different plane, the ardent desire for the Anschluss was nothing new: it had existed ever since 1918, and even before 1914 many Austrians had looked longingly to the 'German brother' to secure them against the rise of the Slavs and other non-German nationalities. National Socialist propaganda fell on well ploughed soil and that made it so dangerous. The Schuschnigg government tried to stem the flood by making concessions to the right, but that only increased the danger. Any compromise solution was rejected out of hand by the German as well as the Austrian National Socialists. The rapid rapprochement between Germany and Italy was the final blow which deprived Austria of foreign support.

In the Third Reich Austrian National Socialists occupied highly prominent posts. Among them were Ernst Kaltenbrunner, the successor to Heydrich as leader of the SD (the Security Service of the SS), Arthur Seyss-Inquart and Hanns Rauter (a Styrian Heimwehr leader) in occupied Holland, Odilo Globocnik and Alfred Eduard Frauenfeld in eastern Europe. Only after the disastrous experience of the Third Reich and the defeat in the Second World War did an Austrian national consciousness begin to emerge so that most Austrians no longer consider themselves Germans. Yet even today antisemitism is alive in Austria, and a minority is still hankering after the Anschluss: old ideologies are not so easily forgotten. The Waldheim affair has shown once again how difficult the Austrians find it to come to terms with their political past.

Notes

1. *The Times*, 14–15 March 1938.
2. Michael Palairet to Foreign Office, 14 March 1938, Public Record Office (PRO), FO 371, file 22315, fo. 74.
3. *Manchester Guardian*, 21 and 28 February 1938.
4. For details see F. L. Carsten, *Fascist Movements in Austria* (London/Beverly Hills 1977), pp. 32–5; Andrew Gladding Whiteside, *Austrian National Socialism before 1918* (The Hague 1962), pp. 95–8; A. Ciller, *Vorläufer des Nationalsozialismus* (Vienna 1932), p. 43, 65, 90, 108, 135–6, 140–2.
5. Quoted in Carsten, *Fascist Movements*, p. 23.
6. Sir Eric Phipps to Sir John Simon, 30 May and 26 April 1932, and 'Austria, Annual Report, 1932', p. 14, PRO, FO 371, file 15888, fos. 118, 122, 101, file 16640, fo. 2.
7. For details see Carsten, *Fascist Movements*, pp. 183–4, 213–14.
8. Lt.-Colonel Mason MacFarlane to War Office, 28 April 1933: PRO, FO 120, file 1073.
9. Erich Zöllner, *Geschichte Österreichs* (Vienna 1961), p. 511; my translation.
10. Dr Riehl to Alfred Proksch, 26 April 1932: quoted by Carsten, *Fascist Movements*, p. 199, my translation.
11. 'Austria, Annual Report, 1933', PRO, FO 371, file 18366, fo. 48.
12. 'Annual Report on Austria for 1937', PRO, FO 371, file 22320, fos. 178–9.
13. Ian Henderson to Michael Palairet, 5 January 1938: ibid., fos. 107–9.
14. Zöllner, *Geschichte Österreichs*, p. 518, also for the following quotation, my translation.

Chronology and Necrology

1987

December

2 After a two-year legal battle, William Nakash is deported to France to face charges of murdering an Algerian Arab there in 1983.

6 The World Zionist Organization opens its thirty-first congress in Jerusalem where Simcha Dinitz, a Member of Knesset and former Israeli ambassador to the US, is elected chairman of the organization.

7 Over 10,000 people attend a rally for Soviet Jewry in Tel Aviv, timed to coincide with the Washington superpower summit.

9 Serious violence breaks out in the Gaza strip followed by similar incidents on the West Bank and in East Jerusalem during the month. The Israeli Defence Minister, Yitzhak Rabin, announces a policy of 'force, might, beatings' against the rioters and warns of the possibility of expulsions. By the end of the month over 20 Palestinians have been killed and 50 Israelis injured, some 800 people have been arrested.

10 President Herzog leaves for a six-day visit to Britain.

15 Israel and the EEC sign a new trade protocol on agricultural exports.

17 The European Parliament passes a resolution urging the Israeli authorities to act with restraint in curbing the disturbances in the occupied territories.

21 Israeli Arabs hold a general strike.

23 The UN Security Council passes a resolution deploring the IDF's handling of the Palestinian uprising.

1988

January

1 Figures released by the Absorption Ministry and the Central Bureau of Statistics reveal that immigration to Israel rose by 35 per cent in 1987 to 13,658.

3 The Israeli Cabinet approves deportation orders against nine Palestinians

from the West Bank and Gaza accused of fomenting protests against Israeli rule.

5   The UN Security Council passes a resolution urging Israel not to implement the deportation orders.

6   British Foreign Office official David Mellor on a visit to the Gaza strip upsets Israelis by describing the conditions in the territories as 'an affront to civilized values'.

13   Four Palestinians are deported to Lebanon.

14   The UN Security Council votes to condemn these expulsions.

18   The Central Bureau of Statistics announces that Israel's inflation figure for 1987 was 16.1 per cent, the lowest rate for 16 years.

20   Despite growing international criticism Yitzhak Rabin says in the Knesset that the use of 'might, power and beatings' against the Palestinian uprising will continue. This policy is backed by President Herzog on 26 January in the face of criticism from American Jewish leaders.

23–24   An Arab League meeting in Tunis demands the end of the Israeli occupation of the territories and pledges support for the Palestinian uprising.

February

1   The Israeli Supreme Court orders the Interior Ministry to register the American non-Orthodox convert Shoshana Miller as Jewish.

9   EC foreign ministers meeting in Bonn issue a statement deploring Israel's handling of the Palestinian unrest demanding an end to the use of repressive measures.

11   An IDF soldier is found guilty of dereliction of duty in the November hang-glider terrorist attack and is dismissed from the army.

14   The arrest of two IDF soldiers charged with burying four Palestinians alive near Nablus in February is announced. The Druze community on the Golan heights hold violent demonstrations for the first time since the beginning of the uprising.

16   A bomb explodes outside the Israeli Embassy in Manila. There are no casualties.

22   The UN Human Rights Commission adopts a resolution accusing Israel of 'genocide' against the Palestinian people.

23   Acting on instructions from the Defence Ministry, the IDF chief of staff orders the banning of force as a punitive measure against Palestinians. President Herzog is re-elected in a Knesset secret ballot to serve a second five-year term.

25–26   A US television crew films four IDF soldiers using rocks to beat two Palestinian youths. The following day the soldiers are arrested.

March

7   Three Israeli civilians are killed when terrorists hijack a bus in the

Negev. The three terrorists, thought to belong to the Popular Front for the Liberation of Palestine, are shot dead when IDF troops storm the bus.

10   The European Parliament approves a resolution condemning Israel for 'torture, arbitrary arrests, reprisals and other acts of violence' in its handling of the Palestinian uprising.

14   Israel and Hungary establish interest sections in Budapest and Tel Aviv marking the first diplomatic ties between the countries since Hungary severed relations in 1967.

17   Three of the IDF soldiers filmed by the US television crew are charged with aggravated assault and their commanding officer is accused of inappropriate behaviour.

20   The first Israeli fatality in the Palestinian uprising occurs when a soldier is shot dead in Bethlehem.

24   Mordechai Vanunu, charged with passing secrets about Israel's nuclear arms to the *Sunday Times*, is found guilty of treason and espionage by a Jerusalem district court and sentenced to 18 years' imprisonment on 27 March. In election year Shimon Peres is re-elected as leader of the Labour Party and becomes its candidate for prime minister in the November poll.

27   A Jaffa military court sentences Private Ron Almog to eighteen months' imprisonment for leaving his post during the November hang-gliding terrorist attack.

29–31   The IDF seal off the occupied territories and declare them military zones to contain expected unrest on Land Day on 30 March. The territories are re-opened on 1 April.

April

6   An Israeli girl is accidentally shot dead by an Israeli settler guard escorting her hiking group after a violent encounter with Arabs in the West Bank village of Beita.

11   Eight Palestinians are deported to Lebanon.

18   John Demjanjuk is found guilty of war crimes, including the murder of 800,000 Jews at Treblinka, by a district court in Jerusalem. He is sentenced to death on 25 April.

19   Two of the filmed IDF soldiers are found guilty of assaulting Palestinian prisoners and are given suspended jail sentences. A further eight Palestinians including six villagers from Beita involved in the incident above are deported.

20   Official figures put Israel's population at 4.43 million of whom 3.63 million are Jewish.

21   Israel celebrates the 40th anniversay of its independence. Prime Minister Yitzhak Shamir and President Reagan sign a memorandum of understanding ensuring that the 'unique dialogue' between the countries will continue for the next five years.

May

3   The Likud Bloc backs Prime Minister Yitzhak Shamir as its leader in the coming general election.

8   In an important diplomatic breakthrough Foreign Minister Shimon Peres visits Hungary for talks with Premier Karoly Grosz. It is the first visit on such a level for twenty years.

11   In Cyprus, three people are killed when a car bomb explodes near the Israeli Embassy in Nicosia.

19   Despite orthodox objections the Israeli Supreme Court sets a significant precedent by ruling that a woman (Lea Shakdiel) may sit on a local religious council. On 23 May the Supreme Court orders the Tel Aviv City Council to allow a woman to sit on the committee that chooses the city's chief rabbis.

June

7–9   An emergency Arab League summit in Algiers promises 'to support the Palestinian uprising and to ensure its escalation'.

9   Prime Minister Shamir meets Eduard Shevardnadze, the Soviet foreign minister, at the UN for talks.

13   Palestinian activist Mubarak Awad is deported from Israel to the US despite the intervention of the US State Department on his behalf.

14   The Knesset rejects two amendments to the Law of Return proposed by the ultra-orthodox Agudat Israel and Poale Aguda parties designed to make conversion to Judaism and the acquiring of Israeli citizenship by converts more difficult.

15   The IDF issues figures showing that 156 Palestinians have been killed and 8,326 others arrested in the six months since the uprising began. One Israeli soldier and one civilian have been killed in the same period.

17   An Israeli diplomat, believed to be an intelligence agent, is expelled from the UK for activities incompatible with his status. This follows complaints from British police that Israeli agents had failed to share intelligence about PLO activity in the UK.

21   The Yugoslavian Parliament decides not to restore diplomatic ties with Israel.

30   John Demjanjuk appeals to the Supreme Court against his conviction for war crimes. The appeal is scheduled to be heard in December.

July

17   Premier Ruud Lubbers arrives in Israel, becoming the first Dutch prime minister to pay an official visit to the country.

24   The British government expels five Israelis believed to be Mossad agents.

26   The first four Israelis to become conservative rabbis are ordained in Jerusalem marking the highlight of the first World Movement of Conservative Judaism convention to be held in Israel.

28   An Israeli consular delegation arrives in Moscow—the first Israeli officials to be stationed in the USSR since diplomatic ties were broken off in 1967.

August
1   Eight Palestinian activists are deported to Lebanon bringing to 30 the number of Palestinians expelled since the beginning of the uprising. A further four are deported on 17 August.
8   Israel and the Soviet Union agree to set up bi-national chambers of commerce in Tel Aviv and Moscow.
18   The Israeli government makes membership of popular committees in the occupied territories illegal, claiming that these committees are active in maintaining the uprising.
22   Twenty-seven people are injured in a bomb explosion in a Haifa shopping mall.
30   Simcha Dinitz, chairman of the WZO, becomes the first Israeli official to visit Yugoslavia since 1967. He is accompanied by Israel Singer, Secretary General of the World Jewish Congress, and Mendel Kaplan, chairman of the Jewish Agency Board of Governors.
31   Two IDF soldiers are wounded by a Jewish settler on the West Bank who had mistaken them for Arab attackers.

September
5–6   Canvassing for the Israeli general election begins with the launch of the Labour and Likud campaigns.
15   After his two-day visit to Hungary, during which he meets Premier Grosz, Prime Minister Shamir says he expected imminent normalization of diplomatic relations.
19   Israel becomes the first Middle East space power when it launches an experimental satellite.
27   Responding to UN claims that Israeli troops are using plastic bullets indiscriminately Defence Minister Yitzhak Rabin announces that the IDF are deliberately shooting and wounding Palestinians in an effort to end the uprising. The Palestinian death toll reaches 287.

October
9   China grants Israel permission to open an academic liaison in Beijing. On October 19 a Chinese trade delegation arrives in Israel for the first time.
12   The European Parliament ratifies three trade agreements with Israel which had been signed in 1987. Ratification had been delayed because of the parliament's objections to Israel's handling of the uprising.
13   Official statistics show that tourism to Israel is down by 13 per cent in the first nine months of 1988 compared to the same period in 1987.

17 President Herzog begins the first visit by an Israeli head of state to France.
18 The Supreme Court rules that Rabbi Meir Kahane's Kach party is racist and bans it from participation in the general election.
19 Israel's polio outbreak claims its first victim.
30 An Israeli woman and her three children are killed and five others are injured in a fire bomb attack on a bus outside Jericho—the most civilian casualties in a single incident since the beginning of the uprising.

November
1 The Knesset election results in a deadlock with neither Likud nor Labour winning enough seats to form a government (Likud 40, Labour 39). The smaller right-wing and religious parties hold the balance of power.
3 The UN General Assembly overwhelmingly votes to condemn Israel's policies in the occupied territories and the measures taken to suppress the uprising.
14 President Herzog asks outgoing Prime Minister Yitzhak Shamir to form a government after the two largest religious parties in the Knesset, Shas and Agudat Israel, decide to align with Likud.
29 Shamir fails to persuade Labour to form a coalition government having submitted to pressure (notably from American Jewish leaders) not to form a government with the religious parties who demanded an amendment to the Law of Return restricting conversions to Judaism as the price for their participation. By the end of the month no new government is formed.
30 John Demjanjuk's appeal hearing is postponed until May 1989 after one of his defence lawyers, Dov Eitan, commits suicide.

Middle East

1987

December
9 The US Senate votes unanimously to prohibit the sale of the F-15E aircraft to Saudi Arabia.
15 In Italy the trial begins on murder charges of Ibrahim Mohammed Khaled, the sole survivor of four alleged members of the Abu Nidal group who attacked Rome airport in 1985 killing thirteen people.
16 The French Prime Minister, Jacques Chirac meets a PLO representative for the first time.
28 Tunisia and Libya resume diplomatic relations broken off by Tunisia in 1985.

1988

January

2 The Israeli Air Force carries out air strikes against Palestinian bases around Sidon in Lebanon. Nineteen are killed in the raids which are reportedly staged in retaliation for the November hang-glider attack.

14 PLO chief Yasser Arafat is reported as stating that he is willing to accept UN resolutions recognizing Israel's right to exist. On 19 January Arafat meets the Greek Prime Minister Andreas Papandreou in Athens.

20 Three Palestinian terrorists are killed by IDF troops after crossing into northern Israel from Lebanon.

28 President Mubarak of Egypt arrives in the US for talks about his five-point plan for an international Middle East peace conference sponsored by the UN Security Council.

February

4 Vatican officials receive Farouk Kaddoumi, the PLO's foreign policy spokesman. The Pope had met King Hussein of Jordan on 1 February.

9 King Hussein addresses the foreign ministers of the European Community.

12 An Italian court finds Ibraham Mohammed Khaled guilty of murder and sentences him to 30 years' imprisonment.

14–15 Three PLO terrorists are killed in Cyprus when their car blows up. The following day a ferry chartered by the PLO is sabotaged in Limassol harbour preventing the planned voyage to Israel of 131 Palestinians recently expelled by Israel.

25 US Secretary of State George Shultz arrives in Israel at the start of a Middle East tour that will include visits to Egypt, Syria and Jordan in pursuit of a peace settlement.

March

1 In London Shultz meets King Hussein who subsequently rejects his peace proposals.

3–8 Three hostages (two Europeans and one Syrian) are released by their terrorist kidnappers in Lebanon.

16 The Israeli Prime Minister, Yitzhak Shamir, meets President Reagan in Washington who stresses that the Shultz proposals must be taken as a complete package.

22–23 Shultz meets Soviet foreign minister Eduard Shevardnadze in Washington. They disagree on the structure of an international Middle East peace conference.

28 In a speech to the Knesset Shamir criticizes Shultz for talking in the US to members of the Palestine National Council.

April

5-20   Pro-Iranian Shiite Muslims hijack a Kuwaiti airliner and hold it for fifteen days flying from Iran to Cyprus (where two hostages are killed) and then to Algeria. The Algerian government negotiates an end to the hijack whereby the hijackers are allowed to escape.

6   Having held separate talks with Shamir and Shimon Peres, Shultz leaves Israel for Cairo admitting that no tangible progress has been made in overcoming Israeli objections to his peace plan.

9   In Moscow Yasser Arafat meets Soviet leader Mikhail Gorbachev who states that broad international support should guarantee Palestinian self-determination but that recognition of Israel is a necessary part of any peace settlement.

16   Khalil al-Waziah (Abu Jihad), the PLO's second in command, is assassinated in Tunis. Israel is held responsible as Jihad was regarded as the PLO's principal co-ordinator of the uprising in the occupied territories. News of his death is marked by an intensification of the violence in Israel.

23   A car bomb explosion in Tripoli, Lebanon, kills 69 people. Meanwhile two IDF soldiers are killed when three guerillas attempt to infiltrate Israel from Lebanon. It is the eleventh such attempt in six weeks.

25-26   President Asad of Syria holds talks with Yasser Arafat for the first time in five years.

26   Saudi Arabia severs diplomatic relations with Iran after talks on restricting the number of Iranians given Saudi entry visas for the annual Haj pilgrimage to Mecca collapse.

27   The US government notifies Congress of plans to sell $825 million worth of arms to Saudi Arabia, $125 million less than previously proposed.

May

2-24   In a two-day operation against Palestinian guerillas and the pro-Iranian Hizballah, 2,000 IDF troops sweep into south Lebanon. On 24 May Israeli forces attack a Hizballah base at Lowaijeh and a Palestinian camp near Sidon.

4-5   In what is widely regarded as a move to revive his presidential campaign, Jacques Chirac announces the release of the three remaining French hostages in Beirut.

10   The Italian high court upholds the life prison sentences on the Palestinian terrorists responsible for hijacking the *Achille Lauro* cruise ship in 1985.

16   Algeria and Morocco restore diplomatic relations severed by Algeria in 1976.

28   Syrian troops are deployed for the first time in Beirut's southern suburbs following talks between Syria and Iran. Since 6 May the Syrian-backed Amal militia had been involved in fierce fighting with the Hizballah.

June

7–9   At an emergency Arab League Summit in Algiers a statement is made by the PLO advocating direct peace talks with Israel.

10   The heads of state of Libya, Tunisia, Algeria, Morocco and Mauritania hold their first-ever meeting resulting in a declaration of intent towards greater Arab Maghreb unity. Algeria and Libya announce a unification project on 28 June.

16   Iran and France resume diplomatic relations.

19–21   Leaders of the seven major industrialized nations meeting in Toronto agree on the need for a 'properly structured international conference' on Middle East peace.

27   After three months of fighting between rival Palestinian factions inside the Shatila refugee camp in Lebanon pro-Arafat forces surrender to the Syrian-backed group loyal to Abu Musa.

July

3   The UK agrees to supply $8,500 million worth of arms to Saudi Arabia. A US Navy cruiser, the *Vincennes*, accidentally shoots down an Iranian civilian airliner in the Persian Gulf.

6   Iran and the UK agree on mutual compensation payments for damage to embassies in London and Teheran. Nine years after being suspended from the Arab League Egypt is re-admitted to its Educational, Cultural and Scientific Organization.

11   Arab terrorists allegedly belonging to Abu Nidal's group kill 11 tourists and injure 90 others in an attack on a Greek ferry boat outside Athens harbour.

18   Iran announces its acceptance of UN Security Council Resolution 598 calling for an immediate ceasefire in the Iran-Iraq war.

31   King Hussein announces plans to cut Jordan's legal and administrative ties with the West Bank.

August

8   UN Secretary General Perez de Cuellar announces a ceasefire between Iraq and Iran effective from 20 August.

18   In a report to the UN, Amnesty International accuses Iraq of systematically killing a large number of Kurds.

23   Yasser Arafat announces that the PLO will assume responsibility for West Bank officials made unemployed when Jordan cut ties in July.

30   Morocco and the Polisario Front accept a UN peace plan to end the conflict in the Western Sahara.

September

6 Facing international criticism for use of chemical weapons against the Kurdish uprising Iraq grants a full amnesty to all Kurdish rebels.

13 In a speech to the socialist group of the European Parliament in Strasbourg Yasser Arafat re-states his acceptance of UN resolutions recognizing Israel.

22 Lebanese president Amin Jummayil ends his term of office with no agreement reached as to his successor. He appoints a transitional military government to rule until a new president is appointed.

26 President Reagan meets Shimon Peres and the Egyptian foreign minister in a gathering commemorating the 10th anniversary of the Camp David accords. On 28 September Peres addressed the UN General Assembly stating his support for a 'non-coercive international setting' for resolution of the Middle East conflict.

29 In Geneva an international arbitration panel rules that Israel should return the Taba beach resort to Egypt.

29 The 1988 Nobel Peace Prize is awarded to the United Nations peace-keeping forces.

October

6 A state of siege is announced in Algiers after rioting inspired by Islamic fundamentalists. It is lifted on 12 October after President Chadli Ben-jedid promises reforms.

19 Eight Israeli soldiers are killed by a car bomb as they cross the Lebanese border into Israel.

November

3 A national referendum in Algeria approves constitutional changes reducing the power of the president.

10 Iran and the UK sign a memorandum of understanding in Vienna containing an agreement to restore diplomatic relations.

12–15 At the Palestine National Council meeting in Algiers Yasser Arafat makes a unilateral declaration of Palestinian statehood. The PNC also endorses a new political programme which includes for the first time UN Security Council Resolution 242 as the basis for a Middle East peace settlement. While Israel rejects the declaration of statehood and the programme, 60 countries recognize the new Palestinian state by 25 November including all the Arab countries except Syria.

24 Egypt and Algeria restore diplomatic relations.

27 The exchange of Iranian and Iraqi prisoners of war begun on 24 November is suspended after a dispute over numbers.

United States

1987

December

2   A US District Court rules that the State Department was acting within its legal rights in ordering the closure of the PLO Information Office in Washington.

3   Two former members of a neo-Nazi group are each sentenced by a Denver court to 150 years imprisonment for murdering Jewish radio broadcaster Alan Berg in 1984.

6   At the largest rally ever held in Washington, over 200,000 people demonstrate in support of Soviet Jewry 24 hours before Mikhail Gorbachev's arrival for a summit meeting with President Reagan.

18   Wall Street broker Ivan Boesky is sentenced to three years' imprisonment for insider-trading offences on the New York stock exchange.

1988

January

20   The new US ambassador to Austria, Henry Grunwald, a Jew, presents his credentials to President Waldheim in Vienna.

21   AIPAC calls the recently-ended first session of the 100th Congress 'a benchmark in legislative activity strengthening the US-Israeli relationship'.

26   The Anti-Defamation League's (ADL) annual Audit of Antisemitic Incidents shows an increase of 17 per cent to 694 incidents in 1987.

27   The Conference of Presidents of Major American Jewish Organizations issues a statement backing Israel's handling of the unrest in the Occupied Territories.

February

11   ADL reports more than 70 antisemitic and racist groups are active in the US.

18   The State Department announces that Israel is to receive three billion dollars in US aid in 1989.

26   A district court rejects Jonathan Pollard's motion for a reduction of the life sentence he received when convicted of spying for Israel in 1987.

March

2   The UN General Assembly passes two resolutions against the US State Department's order to close the PLO observer mission to the UN in New York. In response Attorney General Edwin Meese orders the office closed by 21 March, an order the PLO ignores and the UN General Assembly rejects in a further vote on 23 March.

9   The results of the Super Tuesday primaries put George Bush for the

Republicans and Democrat Michael Dukakis ahead in the race to secure their respective parties' nominations for candidate in the presidential election. Jewish voters seem overwhelmingly to favour Dukakis.

15 Rather than face a 4.5 million dollar fine, the supermarket chain Safeway Stores Inc agrees to pay the US Commerce Dept $995,000 to settle charges that it co-operated with the Arab boycott of Israel.

17 Fourteen white supremacists on trial at Fort Smith, Arkansas, are charged with conspiring to overthrow the US government but one is acquitted through lack of evidence.

April

1 In a controversial statement Ed Koch, Mayor of New York, says that Jews would be 'crazy' to vote for Democrat candidate Jesse Jackson in the upcoming New York primaries. He later apologizes.

7 In the Fort Smith white supremacist trial the remaining thirteen defendants are acquitted of plotting to overthrow the government.

17 New York's 'Salute to Israel Parade' marking the country's 40th anniversary attracts 40,000 marchers. Meanwhile, on 13 April Nation of Islam leader, Louis Farrakhan, speaking to students at the University of Pennsylvania, accuses the Jews of doing deals with Hitler over emigration to Palestine.

19 In the New York primaries George Bush guarantees his nomination as the Republican presidential candidate and Michael Dukakis emerges as clear front runner for the Democrats securing 51 per cent of the vote. Jews vote in record numbers with more than 70 per cent opting for Dukakis.

27 The House of Representatives adopts a bill making genocide a crime in the US.

May

18 Jesse Jackson meets a delegation of Jewish leaders in Los Angeles in an effort to improve Jewish-Black relations after the New York primaries.

25 The House of Representatives adopts the foreign aid bill which includes a three billion dollar grant for Israel.

June

14 Kenneth Duberstein becomes the first Jew to be appointed White House chief of staff, replacing Howard Baker.

16 The Justice Dept. admits that ex-Nazis, including convicted war criminal Robert Jan Verbelen, worked for the US Army's Counter Intelligence Corps in Vienna from 1946 to 1956.

July

5 Attorney General Edwin Meese announces his resignation after allegations of irregular financial dealings. A special prosecutor's report finds that there is insufficient evidence to prosecute him.

8   The US Embassy in Moscow suspends issuing refugee visas to Soviet
    citizens because of lack of funds. On 18 July it announces it will resume
    processing visas for refugees on condition that those wanting to leave
    before 1 October obtain private funding.
12 At the four-day Democratic Convention which opens in Atlanta on 18
    July, Dukakis is endorsed as the Democratic nominee amid a public
    show of co-operation with his erstwhile rival Jesse Jackson.
21 Jewish groups claim that the fundamentalist Christian Moral Majority's
    campaign against the film *The Last Temptation of Christ* includes
    antisemitic implications.
28 Chicago's black and Jewish community leaders meet in a conciliatory
    effort to denounce antisemitism and racism. Earlier in the year it was
    revealed that Steve Cokely, an aide to the city's mayor, had made
    antisemitic statements in lectures to Nation of Islam followers between
    1985 and 1987.

August
2   The newly-published American Jewish Year Book estimates the US
    Jewish population in 1987 at 5.94 million, 2.5 per cent of the total
    population.
8   Faced with a possible $2.35 million fine, the Sara Lee food corporation
    agrees to pay $725,000 to settle charges that it contravened US anti-
    boycott laws.
17 At the Republican party convention in New Orleans, Vice-President
    George Bush is nominated as the party's candidate in the presidential
    elections. Earlier Bush had announced that his running mate would be
    the little-known Indiana Senator, Dan Quayle.
29 The US government decides not to appeal against the District Court's
    ruling in June that it could not order the closure of the PLO observer
    mission to the UN.

September
2   A federal appeals court in Boston rules that the Boston Symphony
    Orchestra did not violate Vanessa Redgrave's civil rights in cancelling
    her 1982 performances after threats from protestors.
8   Seven members of George Bush's ethnic coalition, one of the Republican
    party's nominee's campaign organizations, resign after allegations of
    antisemitic activity.
18 Two youths are arrested on suspicion of vandalism and arson against a
    Brooklyn synagogue.
28 The Templeton Foundation's prestigious religious prize is won by
    Pakistani Dr Inamullah Kahn, despite claims that he heads an anti-Jewish
    organization, the World Muslim Congress.

October

5   A US immigrant judge orders the deportation from the US of Josef Eckert, a former Auschwitz SS guard, who asks to be deported to Austria.

13 AIPAC denies claims made in a CBS TV report that it directs pro-Israel political action committees in their contributions to candidates running for Congress. The programme is broadcast on 24 October.

25 Anne Frank's letters are bought at auction by the Simon Wiesenthal Centre for $165,000.

November

4   President Reagan signs legislation making genocide a crime in the US, thus implementing a 40-year-old international convention banning genocide.

8   George Bush defeats Michael Dukakis in the presidential elections with 54 per cent of the vote and 426 seats in the electoral college but around 67 per cent of Jewish voters opt for Dukakis who gains 112 seats. The results mean the highest number of Jews—39—ever to sit in Congress.

15 A delegation of 3,000 gathers in New Orleans for the largest annual meeting of Jewish leaders, the General Assembly of the Council of Jewish Federations.

22 President Reagan names William Brown as the new US ambassador to Israel. He is expected to remain in the post when George Bush takes office.

26 The State Department denies Yasser Arafat, chairman of the PLO, a US visa. The UN General Assembly, which Arafat had planned to address in New York, passes a resolution on 30 November deploring the move and on 2 December decides to move the debate on Palestine to Geneva so Arafat can attend.

World Jewry

1987

December

3   It is announced that several prominent refuseniks including the longest-standing, Pavel Abramovich, have been given permission to leave the USSR. On 29 December it is reported that Soviet Jews are allowed to apply for tourist visas and the restrictions are eased on Israelis wishing to visit relatives in Moscow. On 30 December it is reported that leading Jewish cultural activist, Leonid Volovsky, and his wife Ludmila, have been given permission to emigrate.

9   In Canada, 71-year old Imre Finta is indicted for war crimes. He is the first naturalized Canadian citizen to face prosecution under the new law that permits Canadian courts to try suspected war criminals for crimes committed on foreign soil.

22 West Germany's best known TV journalist Werner Hoefer resigns after new revelations about his Nazi past.

24 The sentences of four East German neo-Nazis are lengthened by an East Berlin district court. Earlier in the month they had received light sentences for an antisemitic incident in a Protestant church. Their trial was the first public admission by East Germany that neo-Nazi groups operate in the country.

1988

January

1   The UK Chief Rabbi, Sir Immanuel Jakobovits, is elevated to the peerage as baron in the New Year Honours List.

4   The National Conference for Soviet Jewry reveals that 8,155 Jews left the Soviet Union in 1987 (899 in December), the largest number since 1981.

16 Andrija Artukovic, the war criminal convicted in 1986 for the murder of 7,000 Jews, gypsies and Serbo-croats, dies in a prison hospital in Yugoslavia.

20 Long-time refusenik Yosef Begun, arrives in Israel after receiving permission to emigrate. He is followed later in the month by other leading refuseniks including Professor Alexander Lerner and Professor Alexander Ioffe.

27 East Germany agrees in principle to pay reparations to victims of the Nazis.

February

8   Home Secretary Douglas Hurd announces the setting up of an independent inquiry into the alleged presence in the UK of Nazi war criminals.

8   The international commission of historians investigating Kurt Waldheim's alleged involvement in Nazi war crimes publishes its findings, concluding that while there is no evidence that Waldheim committed war crimes, he was aware of atrocities committed in the Balkans and had falsely portrayed his military past as 'harmless'. Waldheim rejects these findings as 'slanders'.

10 King Hussein of Jordan is the first head of state to visit Waldheim when he arrives in Vienna for a state visit.

16 It is reported that Margaret Thatcher is to order the setting up of a new inquiry to determine whether Waldheim was involved in the murder of six British commandos during World War II.

24 The last official prisoner of Zion, cellist Alexei Magarik, arrives in Israel with his family after being released from a Soviet jail.

March

9 The UN Human Rights Commission adopts a resolution calling for the prosecution and punishment of all Nazi war criminals still at large.

10–13 Austria begins the official state ceremonies commemorating the 50th anniversary of the Anschluss (union with Nazi Germany). In a televized speech Kurt Waldheim apologises for Austrian crimes in the Nazi era but claims Austria was the first of Hitler's victims.

23 The Austrian parliament decides to grant $4.2 million as a 'gift of honour' to Austrian victims of the Nazis but Jews are not happy about this.

April

18 The Polish government promises WJC officials that the Carmelite convent will be removed from Auschwitz and that there will be no permanent place of worship at the camp.

19 The 45th anniversary of the Warsaw Ghetto uprising is commemorated in Poland with thousands of Jews from abroad, including prominent Jewish leaders, attending.

20 On the 99th anniversary of Hitler's birth, vandals dressed as Nazi storm troopers desecrate a synagogue in Durban, South Africa.

24 In the first round of voting in France's presidential elections Jean-Marie Le Pen's National Front wins 14.38 per cent of the vote.

May

10 In the Danish general election the extreme right-wing Progress Party wins 16 seats in the Danish parliament as against 9 in 1987.

11 Neo-Nazi propagandist Ernst Zundel is convicted by a Toronto court of disseminating false information likely to cause racial intolerance by publishing a pamphlet denying the Holocaust. He is sentenced to 9 months imprisonment.

17 Werner Nachmann, the late president of the Jewish Central Council and a Jewish community leader in West Germany, is accused of embezzling approximately $12 million from a fund for Jewish Holocaust victims.

18 After a succession of antisemitic incidents Italian Chief Rabbi Elio Toaff claims Jews in Italy are facing the worst antisemitism for 50 years.

22 It is announced that only the Soviet Jews definitely intending to go to Israel will receive Israeli visas, a measure designed to prevent Jews obtaining Israeli visas and then going on to other countries, the USA in particular.

29–2 June Ronald Reagan and Mikhail Gorbachev hold a summit meeting in Moscow to discuss arms reduction, human rights (stressed by Reagan) and other bilateral and regional issues.

June

5–12 In the French National Assembly elections, the National Front loses all but one of its seats, including that of Le Pen, due to a change in the electoral system. The Socialist Party and its allies gain the largest number of seats, 276.

10 France issues an international arrest warrant against Nazi war criminal Alois Brunner currently living in Syria.

13 The giant German car manufacturers, Daimler-Benz AG, agree to pay $5.8 million to the Conference on Jewish Material Claims Against Germany to aid Jewish victims of the Holocaust.

19 The Israeli Cabinet decides to implement visa restrictions for Soviet Jews (see 22 May) granting Israeli visas only to those definitely intending to emigrate to Israel.

23–27 The Pope makes an official visit to Austria, meeting President Waldheim three times.

July

5 It is reported that proceedings to strip suspected war criminal Josef Schwammberger of his Argentinian citizenship have begun in Buenos Aires.

11 Manfred Poehlich is sentenced by an East German court to life imprisonment for Nazi war crimes. This is believed to be one in a series of actions designed to improve East Germany's relations with the US.

12 For the first time since the fifteenth century expulsion from Spain a Jew, Enrique Mugica Herzog, is appointed to the Spanish government. He becomes minister of justice.

14 The Conference on Jewish Material Claims Against Germany announces that over $200 million from its hardship fund has been paid to more than 71,500 Holocaust survivors since the organization's inception in 1980.

August

18 Swiss authorites rule that neo-Nazis are banned from entering the country. The decision follows the turning down of the appeal of revisionist historians Henri Roques and Pierre Guillaume who were expelled from Switzerland in 1987.

31 The International Committee of the Red Cross admits it could have saved more Jews from the Nazis.

September

2 Jean-Marie Le Pen makes an offensive reference to the crematoria at Nazi concentration camps at a meeting of his supporters.

6 It is announced that two Soviet Jews have received official permission to visit the US to study aspects of rabbinical practice for use in their own communities.

October

3   Franz Josef Strauss, the right-wing Minister President of Bavaria, and chairman of the Christian Social Union dies.

9   In Belgium the extreme right-wing Flemish bloc makes significant gains in the country's local elections. In Antwerp, a city with a large Jewish community, the party becomes the third largest on the city council.

13   Three American Jewish physicists, Leon Lederman, Melvin Schwarz and Jack Steinberger, are awarded the 1988 Nobel Prize for Physics. Gertrude Elion, a Jewish scientist, shares the prize in medicine.

16   Italian Jews commemorate the 50th anniversary of the imposition of antisemitic laws by Mussolini's fascist regime and the 45th anniversary of the deportation of Rome's Jews by the Nazis.

19   It is disclosed that earlier in the year, Maurice Papon, a cabinet minister in President Valery Giscard d'Estaing's French government, was secretly indicted for collaboration with the Nazis.

26   The West German government brings criminal proceedings against Boleslavs Maikovskis, a Soviet Nazi collaborator who had fled the US and was seeking political asylum in West Germany. In 1965 he was sentenced by a Latvian court to death in absentia.

November

2   Kurt Waldheim makes an official visit to Turkey. Nazi hunter Beate Klarsfeld is arrested by the Turkish police in Istanbul while demonstrating against the visit.

4   Prominent Jews including WJC leaders Edgar Bronfman and Israel Singer and World Zionist Organization chairman Simcha Dinitz meet Soviet Foreign Minister Eduard Shevardnadze in Moscow. Assurances are given that Hebrew teaching will be legalized in the USSR and a Jewish cultural centre will open in Moscow.

9–11   East and West Germany observe the 50th anniversary of Kristallnacht. Bundestag President Dr Philipp Jenninger resigns after accusations of insensitivity in his speech marking the occasion.

28   An Argentinian court decides that suspected war criminal Josef Schwammberger should be extradited, probably to West Germany.

Necrology

1987

Jascha Heifetz, 86, in Los Angeles, 10 December, virtuoso violinist.

Louis Littman, 62, in London, reported date 11 December, founder of the Littman Library of Jewish Civilization, chairman of the Jewish Literary Trust and promoter of Jewish scholarship.

Professor Simon Halkin, 88, in Jerusalem, reported date 11 December, head of Hebrew Literature at the Hebrew University 1949–1968.

Rabbi Leo Jung, 95, in New York, reported date 25 December, prominent Orthodox leader and scholar.

1988

Jacques Kupfermann, 61, in the United Kingdom, reported date 1 January, noted portrait painter and stage designer.

Josef Fraenkel, 84, in London, reported date 3 January, leading Zionist, journalist and biographer of Theodor Herzl.

Richard Crown, 69, in the United Kingdom, reported date 8 January, academic and B'nai B'rith leader.

Dr Isidor Isaac Rabi, 89, in New York, 11 January, Nobel prize-winning physicist.

Arkady Raikin, 76, in Moscow, reported date 15 January, comedian and satirist.

Baron Philippe de Rothschild, 85, in Paris, reported date 29 January, writer, translator and owner of the Chateau Mouton vineyards in Bordeaux.

Harry Levene, 90, in London, reported date 5 February, boxing promoter.

Dr Hugh Schonfield, 86, in the United Kingdom, reported date 5 February, biblical scholar and historian.

Marghanita Laski, 72, in the United Kingdom, reported date 12 February, writer, critic and broadcaster.

Commander Richard Jessel, 85, in the United Kingdom, reported date 19 February, twice-decorated naval hero of World War II.

Frederik Loewe, 86, in the United States, reported date 19 February, composer and noted collaborator with Alan Jay Lerner on musicals including *Gigi, Camelot* and *My Fair Lady*.

Georgy Malenkov, 86, in the Soviet Union, reported date 19 February, Soviet leader March-Autumn 1953 and Stalin's second-in-command.

Werner Nachmann, 62, in Karlsruhe, West Germany, reported date 19 February, Chairman of the Central Council of Jews in Germany.

Rabbi Seymour Siegel, 61, in New York, 24 February, architect of modern conservative Judaism and professor of ethics and humanism at the Jewish Theological Seminary.

Saul Benjamin Kagan, 109, in Leeds, reported date 26 February, Britain's second oldest man and father of Lord Kagan, textiles manufacturer.

Henryk Szeryng, 69, in Kessel, West Germany, reported date 11 March, virtuoso violinist.

Eugen Gollomb, 69, in East Germany, reported date 11 March, chairman of the Leipzig Jewish community.

Pamela Manson, 59, in the United Kingdom, 19 March, comedy actress and campaigner for Soviet Jewry.

Dr Philip Birnbaum, 83, in New York, 19 March, author and editor of works on religion.

Isaac L. Kenen, 83, in Washington, 23 March, founder of American-Israel Public Affairs Committee.

Edward Joseph, 79, in the United Kingdom, reported date 22 April, former managing director of Bank Leumi (UK) and former chairman of the Israel section of the overseas department of the Chamber of Commerce.

Henry Oscar Joseph, 87, in the United Kingdom, reported date 29 April, former chairman of the Central British Fund for World Jewish Relief.

Aron Alperin, 87, in the United States, reported date 9 May, Yiddish author, journalist and editor.

Bruno Frei, 90, in Austria, reported date 10 June, communist, journalist and author of the *Brown Book*, a celebrated exposé of Nazism.

Wellesley Aron, 86, in Jerusalem, reported date 17 June, the founder of Habonim and a father of the Jewish-Arab settlement in Israel, Neve Shalom.

Dr Ferdynand Zweig, 91, in the United Kingdom, reported date 17 June, economist, sociologist and writer of two penetrating studies of Israeli life.

Gladys Spellman, 70, in the United States, 19 June, former member of the House of Representatives.

Professor Ilya Silberstein, 84, in Moscow, reported date 8 July, Soviet Jewish scholar and founder of the *Literary Heritage* series.

George Theiner, 60, in the United Kingdom, reported date 22 July, distinguished journalist and editor of *Index on Censorship*.

Yair Hurvitz, 49, in Brussels, reported date 5 August, noted Israeli poet.

Lord Sidney Jacobson, 79, in the United Kingdom, 13 August, distinguished journalist and former editor of the *Daily Herald* and the *Sun*.

Justice (Sir John) Hazan, 61, in the United Kingdom, 19 August, High Court judge.

Dr Hans Adler, 78, in London, reported date 26 August, poet, author, historian and Holocaust survivor.

Lord Samuel Silkin of Dulwich, 70, in the United Kingdom, reported date 26 August, former Labour MP and Attorney-General 1974–1979.

Professor Akiva (Ernst) Simon, 89, in Israel, reported date 26 August, former director of Hebrew University's School of Education and winner of Israel Prize.

Jean-Paul Aron, 63, in Paris, reported date 2 September, writer and philosopher.

Max Shulman, 69, in Los Angeles, reported date 9 September, musical comedy writer, author of *The Tender Trap*.

Lord Fred Peart, in the United Kingdom, reported date 16 September, former Labour Cabinet minister and Leader of the House of Commons.

Professor Shmuel Ettinger, 69, in London, 22 September, professor of Jewish History at the Hebrew University and president of the Israel Historical Society.

Henrietta Jacobson, 82, in New York, 9 October, veteran star of Yiddish theatre.

Katriel Katz, 80, in Israel, reported date 14 October, former Israeli ambassador to the Soviet Union.

Oved Ben-Ami, 83, in Israel, reported date 21 October, founder of Natanya and father of the Israeli diamond industry.

Cynthia Freeman, 73, in the United States, reported date 4 November, best-selling American Jewish novelist.

Menachem Savidor, 70, in Israel, reported date 11 November, Speaker of the Knesset 1981–1984.

Erich Fried, 67, in the United Kingdom, reported date 2 December, leading modern German poet.

A Selected and Classified Bibliography for 1988

Israel

General

Behr, Arnold. *Israel 1948. Photographs and Recollections.* London: Gordon Fraser, 1988. 120pp.

Haim, Yehoyada. *Abandonment of Illusions: Zionist Political Attitudes toward Palestinian Arab Nationalism.* Boulder, CO/London: Westview Press, 1988. 174pp.

Huppert, Uri. *Back to the Ghetto: Zionism in Retreat.* Buffalo, NY: Prometheus, 1988. 200pp.

Reich, Bernard and Kieval, Gershon B. (eds.). *Israel Faces the Future.* New York: Praeger, 1988. 229pp.

Ullendorf, Edward. *The Two Zions: Reminiscences of Jerusalem and Ethiopia.* Oxford: Oxford University Press, 1988. 249pp., ind.

Economy/Society

Aronoff, Myron J. *Israeli Visions and Divisions.* New Brunswick, NJ: Transaction Books, 1988. 250pp.

Ben-Rafael, Eliezer. *Status, Power and Conflict in the Kibbutz.* Aldershot: Avebury, 1988. x, 166pp., notes, appends., bibl., ind., tables.

Chertok, Haim. *Stealing Home: Israel Bound and Rebound.* Bronx, NY: Fordham University Press, 1988. xii, 295pp., gloss.

Harkabi, Yehoshafat. *Israel's Fateful Decisions.* Trans. from the Hebrew by Lenn Schramm. London: I. B. Tauris, 1988. xvi, 246pp., notes, ind.

Hofman, John E. *et al. Arab Jewish Relations in Israel: A Quest in Human Understanding.* Bristol, IN: Wyndham Hall Press, 1988. vi, 335pp., bibl., tables.

Khalidi, Raja. *The Arab Economy in Israel: The Dyamics of a Region's Development.* London: Croom Helm, 1988. 248pp., notes, appends., bibl., ind., tables.

Kimmerling, Baruch. *The Israeli State and Society: Boundaries and Frontiers.* New York: State University of New York Press, 1988. 352pp.

Klieman, Aaron S. *Statecraft in the Dark: Israel's Practice of Quiet Democracy.* Boulder, CO/London: Westview Press, 1988. 140pp.

Lipman, Beata. *Embattled Ground: Women in Israel and the Left Bank*. London: Pandora Press, 1988. 232pp.

Peleg, Ilan and Seliktar, Ofira (eds.). *Emergence of Binational Israel: Second Republic in the Making*. Boulder, CO/London: Westview Press, 1988. 240pp.

Smooha, Sammy. *Arabs and Jews in Israel. Vol. 1. Conflicting and Shared Attitudes in a Divided Society*. Boulder, CO/London: Westview Press, 1988. 250pp.

Foreign Policy

Beit-Hallahmi, Benjamin. *The Israeli Connection: Who Israel Arms and Why*. London: I. B. Tauris, 1988. xiv, 289pp., bibl., ind.

Joseph, B. M. *Besieged Bedfellows: Israel and the Land of Apartheid*. London: Greenwood Press, 1988. 184pp.

Medzini, Meron (ed.). *Israel's Foreign Relations. Selected Documents, 1981–1982 (Vol. 7)*. Jerusalem: Ministry for Foreign Affairs, 1988. xvi, 365pp., ind.

Politics

Levine, Stephen (ed.). *Israeli Elections 1987*. Boulder, CO/London: Westview Press, 1988. 200pp.

Lustick, Ian S. *For the Land and the Lord: Jewish Fundamentalism in Israel*. New York: Council on Foreign Relations, 1988. 244pp.

Mezvinsky, Norton. *The Meir Kahane Phenomenon*. London: Mansell, 1988. 288pp.

Tamir, Avraham. *A Soldier in Search of Peace: An Inside Look at Israel's Strategy*. Edited by Joan Comay. London: Weidenfeld & Nicolson, 1988. x, 259pp., appends., maps, ind., illus.

Middle East

History

Cohen, Naomi W. *The Year After the Riots: American Responses to the Palestine Crisis of 1929–30*. Detroit, MI: Wayne State University Press, 1988. 210pp., notes, ind.

Dann, Uriel. *The Great Powers in the Middle East, 1919–1939: Regional Policies in their Global Context*. New York/London: Holmes & Meier, 1988. xiv, 434pp., notes, ind.

Hadawi, Sami. *Palestinian Rights and Losses in 1948: A Comprehensive Study*. London: Saqi Books, 1988. xviii, 350pp. appends., notes, tables, maps.

Mattar, Philip. *The Mufti of Jerusalem: Muhammad Amin al-Husayni and the Palestine Question*. New York: Columbia University Press, 1988. 192pp.

Morris, Benny. *The Birth of the Palestinian Refugee Problem, 1947–1949*. Cambridge: Cambridge University Press, 1988. 382pp.

Pappé, Ilan. *Britain and the Arab-Israeli Conflict, 1948–51*. London: Macmillan in assoc. with St. Anthony's College, Oxford, 1988. xii, 273pp., appends., notes, bibl., ind., maps.

Shlaim, Avi. *Collusion Across the Jordan: King Abdullah, the Zionist Movement, and the Partition of Palestine*. Oxford: Clarendon Press, 1988. 692pp.

Middle East Conflict

Cattan, Henry. *The Palestine Question*. London: Croom Helm, 1988. x, 407pp., notes, appends., map. chronology, ind.

Gresh, Alain. *The PLO: The Struggle Within. Towards an Independent Palestinian State*. New ed. London: Zed Books, 1988. xx, 270pp., chronology, notes, appends. bibl., ind.

Gresh, Alain and Vidal, Dominique. *The Middle East: War Without End?* Trans. from the French by Simon Medaney and Henrietta Bardel. London: Lawrence & Wishart, 1988. 207pp.

Lukacs, Yehuda and Battah, Abdalla (eds.). *The Arab-Israeli Conflict: Two Decades of Change*. Boulder, CO/London: Westview Press, 1988. 398pp.

Quandt, William B. (ed.). *The Middle East: Ten Years After Camp David*. Washington, D.C.: Brookings Institution, 1988. 517pp.

Rabinovich, Itamar and Shaked, Haim (eds.). *Middle East Contemporary Survey*. Vol. 10. 1986. Boulder, CO/London: Westview Press, 1988. 672pp.

Said, Edward and Hitchens, Christopher (eds.). *Blaming the Victims: Spurious Scholarship and the Palestinian Question*. London/New York: Verso, 1988. vi, 296pp., notes, tables, maps.

Stein, Georg. *Die Palästinenser: Unterdrückung und Widerstand eines Entrechteten Volkes/The Palestinians: Oppression and Resistance of a Disinherited People/Les Palestiniens/Los Palestinos*. Cologne: Pahl-Rugenstein, 1988. 154pp., maps, bibl., illus. (In German, English, French and Spanish).

Politics of Middle East Countries

Barakat, Halim (ed.). *Towards a Viable Lebanon*. London: Croom Helm/ Washington, D.C.: Center for Contemporary Arab Studies, Georgetown University, 1988. xvi, 395pp., notes, ind.

Choueiri, Youssef. *Arab History and the Nation State: A Study in Modern Arab Historiography*. London: Routledge & Kegan Paul, 1988. 272pp.

Harris, Lillian Craig (ed.). *Egypt: Internal Challenges and Regional Stability*. London: Routledge & Kegan Paul for the Royal Institute of International Affairs, 1988. vii, 116pp., bibl., map. (Chatham House Papers, 39).

Hopwood, Derek. *Syria 1945–1986: Politics and Society*. London: Unwin Hyman, 1988. 193pp.

Hussain, Asaf. *Political Terrorism and the State in the Middle East*. London/New York: Mansell, 1988. x, 203pp., notes, ind.

Luciani, Giacomo and Salame, Ghassan (eds.). *The Politics of Arab Integration*. London: Croom Helm, 1988. 334pp., bibl., inds., tables.

Salibi, Kamal. *A House of Many Mansions: The History of Lebanon Reconsidered*. London: I. B. Tauris, 1988. viii, 220pp., bibl., ind.

Policy of Countries Outside the Middle East

Beker, Avi. *The United Nations and Israel: From Recognition to Reprehension*. Lexington, MA: Lexington Books, 1988. ix, 203pp.

Green, Stephen. *Living by the Sword: America and Israel in the Middle East 1968–1987*. London: Faber & Faber, 1988. xii, 279pp., notes, ind., maps.

238   PATRICIA SCHOTTEN and CYNTHIA SHILOH

Greilsammer, Ilan and Weiler, Joseph H. H. (eds.). *Europe and Israel: Troubled Neighbours*. Berlin: De Gruyter, 1988. x, 354pp., ind. (European University Institute. Series C. Political and Social Sciences, 9).

Shavit, David. *United States in the Middle East: A Historical Dictionary*. London: Greenwood Press, 1988. 480pp.

USA

General

The American Jewish Year Book. Vol. 88. Philadelphia, PA: The Jewish Publication Society of America, 1988. 516pp.

Anti-Defamation League of the B'nai B'rith. *Hate Groups in America: A Record of Bigotry and Violence*. New rev. ed. New York, 1988. 108pp., appends., ind.

Anti-Defamation League of the B'nai B'rith. *Extremism on the Right*. New York, 1988. 200pp.

Cohen, Kitty O. *Black-Jewish Relations: The View from the State Capitol. A Survey Based on Interviews with Black State Senators*. New York/London: Cornwall Books, 1988. 108pp., appends.

Frey, Robert Seitz and Thomson-Frey, Nancy. *The Silent and the Damned: The Murder of Mary Phagan and the Lynching of Leo Frank*. Lanham, MD: Madison Books, 1988. xxii, 248pp., appends., bibl., ind., illus.

Hertzke, Allen D. *Representing God in Washington: The Role of Religious Lobbies in American Polity*. Knoxville, TX: University of Texas Press, 1988. 260pp.

House, Ernest R. *Jesse Jackson and the Politics of Charisma: The Rise and Fall of the PUSH/Excel Program*. Boulder, CO/London: Westview Press, 1988. xii, 196pp., bibl., ind.

Schwartz, Bernard. *Behind 'Bakke': Affirmative Action and the Supreme Court*. New York: New York University Press, 1988. x, 266pp., appends., ind.

Jewish Community

Ashkenazi, Elliott. *The Business of Jews in Louisiana, 1840–75*. Tuscaloosa, AL/London: University of Alabama Press, 1988. xii, 219pp., appends., notes, bibl., ind., tables, illus.

Cohen, Steven M. *American Assimilation or Jewish Revival?* Bloomington, IN: Indiana University Press, 1988. xii, 140pp., notes, bibl., ind., tables.

Gurock, Jeffrey S. *The Men and Women of Yeshiva: Higher Education, Orthodoxy and American Judaism*. New York: Columbia University Press, 1988. xvi, 362pp.

Lowenstein, Steven M. *Frankfurt on the Hudson: The German Jewish Community of Washington Heights, 1933–1983, its Structure and Culture*. Detroit, MI: Wayne State University Press, 1988. 400pp.

Shokeid, Moshe. *Children of Circumstances: Israeli Emigrants in New York*. Ithaca, NY: Cornell University Press, 1988. xvi, 248pp., bibl., ind., tables. (The Anthropology of Contemporary Issues).

Weinberg, Sydney Stahl. *The World of Our Mothers: The Lives of Jewish Immigrant Women*. Chapel Hill, NC: University of North Carolina Press, 1988. xxvi, 326pp.

Wertheimer, Jack (ed.). *The American Synagogue: A Sanctuary Transformed*. Cambridge: Cambridge University Press, 1988. 432pp.

World Jewry

General

Abramson, Glenda (ed.). *The Blackwell Companion to Jewish Culture from the Eighteenth Century to the Present*. Oxford: Blackwell, 1988. 500pp.

Bulawko, Henry (ed.). *Anthologie de l'humour juif et israelien* (Anthology of Jewish and Israeli Humour). Paris: Bibliophane, 1988. 144pp.

Calimani, Riccardo. *Storio dell 'Ebreo Erannte'* (The History of the 'Wandering Jew'). 3rd ed. Milan: Rusconi, 1988. 639pp., notes, bibl., gloss., illus.

Edelheit, Abraham J. and Edelheit, Hershel. *The Jewish World in Modern Times: A Selected Annotated Bibliography*. Boulder, CO: Westview Press/London: Mansell, 1988. xx, 569pp., gloss., inds.

Hadda, Janet. *Passionate Women, Passive Men: Suicide in Yiddish Literature*. Albany, NY: State University of New York Press, 1988. xii, 223pp., notes, ind. (SUNY Series in Modern Jewish Literature and Culture).

Herman, Simon N. *Jewish Identity: A Social Psychological Perspective*. 2nd ed. New Brunswick, NJ: Transaction Books, 1988. 285pp.

Kahler, Erich. *The Jews Among the Nations*. New Brunswick, NJ: Transaction Books, 1988. 175pp.

Knight, Robert. *Ich bin dafür, die Sache in die Lange zu ziehen: Wortprotokolle der österreichischen Bundesregierung von 1945–52 über die Entschädigung der Juden* (I am for Prolonging the Issue: Verbal Protocols of the Austrian Federal Government on Jewish Restitution). Köningstein/Ts.: Athenäum, 1988. 287pp., notes, docs.

Lehn, Walter with Davis, Uri. *The Jewish National Fund*. London: Kegan Paul International, 1988. xx, 390pp., docs., append., notes, bibl., ind., map.

Leo Baeck Institute Year Book. Vol. 33. London: Secker & Warburg for the Institute, 1988. xiv, 594pp., bibl., inds., illus.

Mendes-Flohr, Paul. *Divided Passions: Jewish Intellectuals and the Experience of Modernity*. Detroit, MI: Wayne State University Press, 1988. 374pp.

Meyer, Michael A. *Response to Modernity: A History of the Reform Movement in Judaism*. New York/Oxford: Oxford University Press, 1988. xvi, 494pp., notes, bibl., ind.

Rabinowicz, Harry M. *Hasidism: The Movement and its Masters*. New York: J. Aronson, 1988. 400pp.

Rapoport-Albert, Ada and Zipperstein, Steve (eds.). *Jewish History: Essays in Honor of Chimen Abramsky*. London: P. Halban, 1988. xii, 700pp., notes.

Ruud, Inger Marie. *Women and Judaism: A Selected Annotated Bibliography*. New York: Garland, 1988. xxiv, 232pp., inds.

Studies in Contemporary Jewry. Vol. 4.: *The Jews and the European Crisis*. New York/Oxford: Oxford University Press, 1988. 544pp.

Wolffsohn, Michael. *Ewige Schuld? 40 Jahre deutsch-jüdisch-israelische Beziehungen* (Eternal Guilt: Forty Years of German-Jewish-Israeli Relations). Munich: Piper Verlag, 1988. 187pp., bibl.

Eastern Europe

Baumann, Janina. *A Dream of Belonging: My Years in Postwar Poland.* London: Virago, 1988. 202pp.

Iancu, Carol. *Bleichroder et Cremieux: Le combat pour l'émancipation des juifs de Roumanie devant le congrès de Berlin (1878–1880)* (Bleichroder and Cremieux: The Battle for Jewish Emancipation in Romania Before the Berlin Congress). Montpellier: Centre de recherches et d'etudes juives et hëbräique, Universite Paul-Valery, 1987. 264pp.

Gitelman, Zvi. *A Century of Ambivalence: The Jews of Russia and the Soviet Union, 1881 to the Present.* London: Viking, 1988. xvi, 336pp., notes, inds., maps, illus.

Greenbaum, Avraham. *Minority Problems in Eastern Europe Between the World Wars With Emphasis on the Jewish Minorities.* Jerusalem: Institute for Advanced Studies, The Hebrew University, 1988. 162pp.

Harris, D. and Rabinovich, Itamar. *Jokes of Oppression: Soviet Jewish Humor.* New York: J. Aronson, 1988. 250pp.

Hertz, Alexander. *The Jews in Polish Culture.* Trans. by Richard Lourie. Edited by Lucjan Dobroszycki. Evanston, IL: Northwestern University Press, 1988. xvi, 200pp., notes, ind.

Kievel, Hillel J. *The Making of Czech Jewry: National Conflict and Jewish Society in Bohemia, 1870–1918.* Oxford: OUP 1988. x, 279pp, notes, bibl., ind., illus.

Levin, Nora. *The Jews in the Soviet Union Since 1917,* 2 vols. New York: New York University Press, 1988. xxxiv, 1013pp., chronology, notes, gloss., ind., maps, tables. illus.

Mendel, Hersh. *Memoirs of a Jewish Revolutionary.* Trans. from the German and Yiddish by Robert Michaels. London: Pluto Press, 1988. 384pp.

Ostow, Robin. *Jüdisches Leben in der DDR* (Jewish Life in the German Democratic Republic). Trans. from the English by Wolfgang Lotz. Frankfurt/M.: Jüdischer Verlag bei Athenäum, 1988. 224pp., bibl.

Patai, Raphael. *Apprentice in Budapest: Memories of a World That is No More.* Salt Lake City, UT: University of Utah Press, 1988. 432pp.

Pinkas Hakehilot Latvia Ve'estonia. Entsiklopedia Shel Hayeshuvim Hayehudiim Leman Hayevosdim Ve'ad Le'ahar Shaot Milhemet Ha'Olam Hasheniya (The Communities of Latvia and Estonia. Encyclopedia of Jewish Communities From Their Foundation to After the Holocaust). Jerusalem: Yad Vashem, 1988. 396pp.

Pinkus, Benjamin. *The Jews of the Soviet Union: A History of a National Minority.* Cambridge: Cambridge University Press, 1988. 468pp.

Western Europe

Andics, Hellmut. *Die Juden in Wien* (The Jews in Vienna). Munich: C. J. Bucher, 1988. 416pp., notes, ind., illus.

Assis, Yom Tov. *The Jews of Santa Colomba de Queralt: An Economic and Demographic Case Study of a Community at the End of the Thirteenth Century.* Jerusalem: Magnes, The Hebrew University, 1988. 170pp., docs., appends., bibl., inds., gloss., map, illus. (Hispana Judaica, 6).

Beinart, H. (ed.). *Yehudim Be'italia. Mihkarim Yotsim Le'or Bemeloat Meah Shana*

Lehuledeto Shel M'O Kasuto (Jews in Italy. Studies Dedicated to the Memory of U. Cassuto on the One Hundredth Anniversary of his Birth). Jerusalem: Magnes, The Hebrew University, 1988. 288, 102pp., illus. (Hebrew and English).

Benz, Wolfgang (ed.). *Die Juden in Deutschland, 1933–1945: Leben unter national-sozialistischer Herrschaft* (The Jews in Germany, 1933–1945: Life Under National Socialism). Munich: C. H. Beck, 1988. 779pp., append., notes, bibl., ind.

Collins, Kenneth. *Go and Learn: The International Story of Jews and Medicine in Scotland*. Aberdeen: Aberdeen University Press, 1988. xxii, 193pp., notes, appends., gloss., bibl., ind., illus.

Edwards, John. *The Jews in Christian Europe, 1400–1700*. London: Routledge & Kegan Paul, 1988. 200pp.

Gidal, Nachum T. *Die Juden in Deutschland: Von der Römerzeit bis zur Weimarer Republik* (The Jews in Germany: From Roman Times to the Weimar Republic). Munich: Bertelsmann Lexikon Verlag, 1988. 439pp., bibl., ind., illus.

Hertz, Deborah. *Jewish High Society in Old Regime Berlin*. New Haven, CT/London: Yale University Press, 1988. xvi, 299pp., bibl., ind., illus., figs.

Heymann, Fritz. *Tod oder Taufe: Die Vertreibung der Juden aus Spanien und Portugal im Zeitalter der Inquisition* (Death or Baptism: The Expulsion of the Jews From Spain and Portugal at the Time of the Inquisition). Edited by Julius H. Schoeps. Königstein/Ts.: Athenäum, 1988. 180pp., notes., ind.

Honigmann, Peter. *Die Austritte aus der Jüdischen Gemeinde Berlin, 1837–1941: Statistische Auswertung und historische Interpretation* (The Resignations from the Berlin Jewish Community, 1873–1941: Statistical Evaluation and Historical Interpretation). Frankfurt/M.: P. Lang, 1988. 177pp.

Josephs, Zoe. *Survivors: Jewish Refugees in Birmingham, 1933–1945*. Warley: Meridian Books, 1988. vi, 217pp., bibl., ind., illus.

Maier, Joseph B., Marcus, Judith and Tarr, Zoltan. *German Jewry: Its History and Sociology*. Selected Essays of Werner J. Cahnman. New Brunswick, NJ: Transaction Books, 1988. 250pp.

Maitek, Henry, Luthe, Franz and Willebrand, Jens. *Jüdisches LebenHeute. Eine Fotodokumentation* (Jewish Life Today: A Photographic Record). Gütersloh: Flöttman Verlag, 1988. 104pp. illus. (Jüdisches Leben—Religion und Alltag. 1. Aspekte der Gegenwart).

Mosse, W. E. *The German-Jewish Economic Elite, 1820–1935: A Socio-Cultural Profile*. Oxford: Clarendon Press, 1988. 384pp.

Perchenet, Annie. *Histoire de juifs de France* (A History of the Jews of France). Paris: Le Cerf, 1988. 239pp., chronology, bibl., ind.

Schachne, Lucio. *Education Towards Spiritual Resistance: The Jewish Landschulheim Herrlingen 1933 to 1939*. Trans. from the German by Martin M. Goldenberg. Frankfurt/M.: dipa Verlag, 1988. 247pp., notes, bibl., gloss., illus. (Examples of Education Methods: History of Individual Institutions, 3).

Schwierz, Israel. *Steinerne Zeugnisse jüdischen Lebens in Bayern. Eine Dokumentation* (Stony Evidence of Jewish Life in Bavaria: A Record [of Monuments]). Munich: Bayerische Landeszentrale für politische Bildungsarbeit, 1988. 352pp., append., bibl., illus.

Wistrich, Robert. *The Jews of Vienna in the Age of Franz Joseph*. Oxford: Oxford University Press, 1988. 704pp.

Other Communities

Abitbol, Michael. *The Jews of North Africa During the Second World War.* Trans. by Catherine Tihanyi Zentelis. Detroit, MI: Wayne State University Press, 1988. 240pp.

Friedman, Elizabeth. *An Algerian Jewish Community.* South Hadley, MA: Bergin & Garvey, 1988. xx, 170pp., append., bibl., ind. (Critical Studies in Work and Community Series).

Goiten, S. D. *A Mediterranean Society: The Jewish Communities of the Arab World as Portrayed in the Documents of the Cairo Geniza. Vol. 5.: The Individual.* Berkeley, CA: University of California Pres, 1988. 690pp.

Hillel, Shlomo. *Operation Babylon.* London: Collins, 1988. 288pp.

Lieber, Sherman. *Missionaries and Mystics: The Jews in Palestine, 1799–1840.* Detroit, MI: Wayne State University Press, 1988. 288pp.

Prawer, Joshua. *The History of the Jews in the Latin Kingdom of Jerusalem.* Oxford: Clarendon Press, 1988. xvi, 310pp., ind. maps.

Holocaust

Ben Gershom, Ezra. *David: the Testimony of a Holocaust Survivor.* London: Oswald Wolff, 1988. 292pp.

Ben-Tov, Arieh. *Facing the Holocaust in Budapest: The International Committee of the Red Cross and the Jews in Hungary, 1943–1945.* Geneva: Henri Dunant Institute/ Dordrecht: M. Nijhoff, 1988. xviii, 492pp., append., notes., bibl., ind., illus.

Crome, Len. *Unbroken: Resistance and Survival in the Concentration Camps.* London: Lawrence & Wishart, 1988. 174pp., ind., illus.

Devant l'histoire: Les documents de la controverse sur la singularité de l'extermination des Juifs par le régime nazi (Facing History: The Documents on the Controversy on the Uniqueness of the Extermination of the Jews by the Nazi Regime). Paris: Le Cerf, 1988. xxvii, 353pp.

Eisen, George. *Children and Play in the Holocaust: Games Among the Shadows.* Amherst, MA: University of Massachussetts Press, 1988. 168pp.

Gill, Anton. *The Journey Back From Hell: Conversations With Concentration Camp Survivors.* London: Grafton, 1988. 494pp.

Holocaust Studies Annual. Vol. 4.: Resistance and the Holocaust. Greenwood, FL: Penkeville Publ. Co., 1988. 200pp.

Kuperstein, Isaiah (ed.). *Directory of Holocaust Institutions.* 2nd ed. Washington, D.C.: U.S. Holocaust Memorial Council, 1988. 56pp.

Levi, Primo. *The Drowned and the Saved.* Trans. by Raymond Rosenthal. London: M. Joseph, 1988. xx, 170pp.

Lewin, Abraham. *A Cup of Tears: a Diary of the Warsaw Ghetto.* Oxford: Blackwell, 1988. 300pp.

Müller-Hill, Benno. *Murderous Science: Elimination by Scientific Selection of Jews, Gypsies and Others, Germany 1933–1945.* Trans. by George R. Fraser. Oxford: Oxford University Press, 1988. xvi, 208pp., notes, bibl.

Presser, Jacob. *Ashes in the Wind: The Destruction of Dutch Jewry.* Trans. by Arnold Pomerans. Detroit, MI: Wayne State University Press, 1988. 595pp.

Schwertfeger, Ruth. *Women of Theresienstadt: Voices From a Concentration Camp*. Oxford: Berg, 1988. 200pp.

Smolar, Hersh. *The Minsk Ghetto*. New York: Holocaust Library, 1988. 200pp.

Post-Holocaust

Braham. Randolph L. (ed.). *The Psychological Perspectives of the Holocaust and its Aftermath*. New York: Columbia University Press, 1988. 320pp.

Eckardt, Alice L. and Eckardt, A. Roy. *Long Night's Journey into Day: A Revised Retrospective on the Holocaust*. Rev. ed. Detroit, MI: Wayne State University Press/Oxford: Pergamon Press, 1988. 277pp., appends., notes, bibl., ind.

Garber, Zev, Berger, Alan L. and Lobowitz, Richard (eds.). *Methodology in the Academic Teaching of the Holocaust*. Lanham, MD/London: University Press of America, 1988. xxxvi, 327pp., ind., bibl. (Studies in Judaism).

Feinberg, Anat. *Wiedergutmachung im Programm: Jüdisches Schicksal im deutschen Nachkriegsdrama* (Atonement in Action: The Jewish Fate in German Post-War Drama). Cologne: Prometh Verlag, 1988. 176pp., append., notes, bibl., ind., illus.

Lehrke, Gisela. *Gedenkstätten für Opfer des Nationalsozialismus* (Memorials for the Victims of National Socialism). Frankfurt/M.: Campus, 1988. 250pp.

Rosenfeld, Alvin H. *A Double Dying: Reflections on Holocaust Literature*. Bloomington, IN: Indiana University Press, 1988, c1980. x, 210pp., notes, bibl.

Rosenberg, Alan and Myers, Gerald E. *Echoes From the Holocaust: Philosophical Reflections On a Dark Time*. Philadelphia, PA: Temple University Press, 1988. xii, 453pp., notes, ind.

Skloot, Robert. *The Darkness We Carry: The Drama of the Holocaust*. Madison, WI: The University of Wisconsin Press, 1988. xvi, 147pp., notes, ind.

Stehle Bernard. *Another Kind of Witness*. Philadelphia, PA: Jewish Publication Society of America, 1988. xiv, 153pp., illus.

Young, James E. *Writing and Rewriting the Holocaust: Narrative and the Consequence of Interpretation*. Bloomington, IN: Indiana University Press, 1988. xii, 243pp., notes, bibl., ind.

Kristallnacht

Döscher, Hans-Jürgen. *Reichskristallnacht: Die November-pogrome 1938* (Kristallnacht: The November Pogroms 1938). Berlin: Ullstein, 1988. 200pp.

Hoffmann, Rudolf. *Das Vorgespielgelte Revolverattentat—Vorwand zum Pogrom der 'Kristallnacht' 1938—Dargestellt an Hand der Französischen Akten des Kriminalfalls vom Rath/Grynszpan* (The Pretence of the Assassination—Pretext for the Pogrom of 'Kristallnacht' 1938—As Depicted in the French Criminal Proceedings of Von Rath/Grynszpan). Lüdenscheid: The Authors, 1988. 20pp.

Pätzold, Kurt and Runge, Irene. *Kristallnacht: Zum Pogrom 1938* (Kristallnacht: On the Pogrom of 1938). Cologne: Pahl-Rugenstein, 1988. 260pp., docs., illus.

Pehle, Walter H. (ed.). *Der Judenpogrom 1938: Von der 'Reichskristallnacht' zum Völkermord* (The Pogrom Against the Jews, 1938: From 'Kristallnacht' to Genocide). Frankfurt/M.: Fischer, 1988. 246pp., notes, ind., illus.

Biography

Aberbach, David. *Bialik*. London: P. Halban, 1988. xii, 143pp., notes, bibl., ind., map. (Jewish Thinkers).

Avineri, Shlomo. *Haprimate Haleumi: David Ben Gurion, Demuto Shel Manhig Tenuat Hapoalim* (The National Primate: David Ben-Gurion, Portrait of the Leader of the Workers' Movement). Tel-Aviv: Am Oved, 1988. 161pp.

Burt, Robert A. *Two Jewish Justices: Outcasts in the Promised Land*. Berkeley, CA: University of California Press, 1988. 165pp., notes, ind. (About Louis D. Brandeis and Felix Frankfurter).

Hansen, Phillip. *Hannah Arendt: History, Politics and Citizenship*. Oxford: Polity Press, 1988. 220pp.

Lifton, Betty Jean. *The King of Children: A Biography of Janusz Korczak*. London: Chatto & Windus, 1988. 404pp., notes, ind., illus.

Lixl-Purcell, Andreas (ed.). *Women in Exile: German-Jewish Autobiographies Since 1933*. London: Greenwood Press, 1988. 264pp.

Pearl. Chaim. *Rashi*. London: P. Halban, 1988. x, 113pp., notes, bibl., ind., map. (Jewish Thinkers).

Robertson, Ritchie. *Heine*. London: P. Halban, 1988. x, 117pp., notes, bibl., ind. (Jewish Thinkers).

Sharansky, Natan. *Fear No Evil*. Trans. by Stefani Hoffman. London: Weidenfeld & Nicolson/New York: Random House, 1988. xxiv, 437pp., ind., illus.

Sofer, Sasson. *Begin: An Anatomy of Leadership*. Oxford: Blackwell, 1988. 229pp.

Vermes, Pamela. *Buber*. London: P. Halban, 1988. xii, 116pp., notes, bibl., ind. (Jewish Thinkers).

Wasserstein, Bernard. *The Secret Lives of Trebitsch Lincoln*. New Haven, CT/ London: Yale University Press, 1988. 327pp.

Wiesenthal, Simon. *Recht, nicht Rache: Erinnerungen* (Justice, not Vengeance: Recollections). Frankfurt/M: Ullstein, 1988. 456pp., ind.

General

Bolick, Clint. *Changing Course: Civil Rights at the Crossroads*. New Brunswick, NJ: Transaction Books, 1988. 192pp.

Cashmore, E. Ellis. *Dictionary of Race and Ethnic Relations*. 2nd ed. London: Routledge & Kegan Paul, 1988. 320pp.

Charny, Israel W. (ed.). *Genocide: A Critical Bibliographic Review*. London: Mansell, 1988. xiv, 273pp., ind.

Engelmann, Bernt. *Deutschland ohne Juden: Eine Bilanz* (Germany Without Jews: A Stock-Taking). Rev. & enlarged ed. Cologne: Pahl-Rugenstein, 1988. 493pp., docs., bibl., ind., illus.

Lyotard, Jean-Francois. *Heidegger et 'les Juifs'* (Heidegger and 'the Jews'). Paris: Éds. Galilee, 1988. 164pp., bibl.

Matas, David. *Justice Delayed: Nazi War Criminals in Canada*. Toronto: Summerhill Press, 1988. 275pp.

Momigliano, Arnoldo. *On Pagans, Jews and Christians*. Middletown, CT: Wesleyan University Press, 1988. xiv, 343pp., bibls., notes, ind.

Rubenstein, Philip (ed.). *Report on the Entry of Nazi War Criminals and Collaborators into the UK, 1945–1950*. London: The All-Party Parliamentary War Group, House of Commons, 1988. iv, 92pp., appends.

Sichrovsky, Peter. *Born Guilty: Children of Nazi Families*. Trans. from the German by Jean Steinberg. London: I. B. Tauris, 1988. vi, 175pp.

Wehler, Hans-Ulrich. *Entsorgung der deutschen Vergangenheit? Ein polemischer Essay zum 'Historikerstreit'* (Skirting the German Past? A Polemic Essay on the 'Historians' Debate'). Munich: Beck, 1988. 249pp., notes.

The Waldheim Affair

Bassett, Richard. *Waldheim and Austria*. London: Viking, 1988. 236pp.

Hertzstein, Robert. *Waldheim: The Missing Years*. London: Grafton, 1988. 320pp.

Palumbo, Michael. *The Waldheim Files: Myth and Reality*. London: Faber & Faber, 1988. xviii, 205pp., bibl., ind.

Saltman, Jack. *Kurt Waldheim: A Case to Answer?* London: Robson Books, 1988. 400pp.

Antisemitism

Arkel, D. van. *The Roots of Antisemitism in Europe: From the Turn of the Era to the Middle Ages*. London: Croom Helm, 1988. 300pp.

Bergmann, Werner (ed.). *Error Without Trial: Psychological Research on Antisemitism*. Berlin: W. de Gruyter, 1988. xii, 546pp., tables. (Current Research on Antisemitism, 2).

Casillo, Robert. *The Genealogy of Demons: Anti-Semitism, Fascism and the Myths of Ezra Pound*. Evanston, IL: Northwestern University Press, 1988. xiv, 463pp., notes, bibl., ind.

Hsia, R. Po-Chia. *The Myth of Ritual Murder: Jews and Reformation Germany*. New Haven, CT/London: Yale University Press, 1988. 248pp.

Litvinoff, Barnet. *The Burning Bush: Antisemitism and World History*. London: Collins, 1988. 493pp., bibl., ind.

Pototschnig, Franz, Putzer, Peter and Rinnerthaler, Alfred. *Semitismus und Antisemitismus in Österreich* (Semitism and Anti-Semitism in Austria). Munich: Roman Kovar Verlag, 1988. 270pp.

Oppenheimer, Max, Stuckmann, Horst and Schneider, Rudi. *Als die synagogen brannten: Antisemitismus und Rassismus gestern und heute* (When the Synagogues Burned: Anti-Semitism and Racism Yesterday and Today). Cologne: Pahl-Rugenstein, 1988. 158pp., docs., chronology, bibl., illus.

Pulzer, Peter. *The Rise of Political Antisemitism in Germany and Austria*. Rev. ed. London: P. Halban, 1988. 357pp.

Vogt, Judith. *Billedet som Politisk vaben* (Cartoons as Political Weapons). Copenhagen: C. A. Reitzels/Oslo: J. W. Cappelens, 1988. 235pp., gloss., bibl., appends., ind., illus.

Christian-Jewish Relations

Brockway, Allan and Rendtorff, Rolf (eds.). *The Theology of the Churches and the Jewish People*. Statements by the World Council of Churches and its member Churches. Geneva: World Council of Churches, 1988. 144pp.

Brooks, R. (ed.). *Unanswered Questions: Theological View of Jewish-Catholic Relations*. Notre Dame, IN: University of Notre Dame Press, 1988. 208pp.

Hilton, Michael with Marshall, Gordian. *The Gospels and Rabbinic Judaism: A Study Guide*. London: SCM Press, 1988. viii, 167pp.

International Catholic-Jewish Liaison Committee. *Fifteen Years of Catholic-Jewish Dialogue, 1970–1985. Selected Papers*. Vatican: Libreria Editrice Vaticana/Rome: Libreria Editrice Laternanse, 1988. xxxii, 325pp., append.

Lux, Rüdiger (ed.). '*. . . und Friede auf Erden': Beiträge zur Friedensverantwortung von Kirche und Israel. Festschrift für Christoph Hinz zum 60. Geburtstag* ('. . . and Peace on Earth' in the Church and Israel: Contributions on Responsibility for Peace. Commemorative Publication on the Sixtieth Birthday of Christoph Hinz). Berlin: Institut Kirche und Judentum, 1988. 272pp., illus.

Petuchowski, Jakob J. (ed.). *When Jews and Christians Meet*. Albany, NY: State University of New York Press, 1988. xii, 190pp., notes, ind.

Rendtorff, Rolf and Henrix, Hans Hermann (eds.). *Die Kirche und das Judentum: Documents von 1945 bis 1985* (The Church and the Jews: Documents From 1945 to 1985). Munich: Chr. Kaiser Verlag, 1988. 746pp., ind.

Shermis, Michael. *Jewish-Christian Relations: An Annotated Bibliography and Resource Guide*. Bloomington, IN: Indiana University Pres, 1988. xvi, 291pp., inds.

Wigoder, Geoffrey. *Jewish-Christian Relations Since the Second World War*. Manchester/New York: Manchester University Press, 1988. viii, 176pp., append., bibl., ind. (Sherman Studies of Judaism in Modern Times).

Third Reich

Angress, Werner, T. *Between Fear and Hope: Jewish Youth in the Third Reich*. Trans. from the German by Werner T. Angress and Christine Granger. New York: Columbia University Press, 1988. xvi, 187pp., notes, bibl., ind., illus.

Bennhold, Martin (ed.). *Recht und Nationalsozialismus: Analysen zur historische Kontinuität* (Law and National Socialism: An Analysis of Historical Continuity). Cologne: Pahl-Rugenstein, 1988. 150pp.

Burdick, Charles B. *An American Island in Hitler's Reich: The Bad Nauheim Internment*. Menlo Park, CA: Markgraf, 1988. 120pp.

Gruchmann, Lothar. *Justiz im Dritten Reich 1933–1945: Anpassung und Unterwerfung in der Ära Gärtner* (Justice in the Third Reich, 1933–1940: Conformity and Submission in the Gaertner Era). Munich: R. Oldenbourg, 1988. xxxviii, 1297pp., append., bibl., inds. (Quellen und Darstellung zur Zeitgeschichte, 28).

Kindermann, Gottfried-Karl. *Hitler's Defeat in Austria, 1933–1934*. London: C. Hurst, 1988. 234pp.

Lichtenstein, Heiner. *Angepasst und treu ergeben: Das Rote Kreuz im Dritten Reich* (Conforming and Loyally Submissive: The Red Cross in the Third Reich). Cologne: Bund-Verlag, 1988. 160pp.

Noakes, J. and Pridham G. (eds.). *Nazism 1919–1945. Vol. 3.: Foreign Policy, War and Racial Extermination. A Documentary Reader*. Exeter: University of Exeter, 1988. pp. 608–1236, maps, notes, bibl.

World War II

Balfour, Michael. *Withstanding Hitler*. London: Routledge & Kegan Paul. 1988. 352pp.

Friedhoff, Herman R. *Requiem for the Resistance: The Civilian Struggle Against Nazism in Holland and Germany*. London: Bloomsbury, 1988. 281pp.

Hirschfeld, Gerhard. *Nazi Rule and Dutch Collaboration: The Netherlands Under German Occupation 1940–1945*. Trans. by Louise Willmot. Oxford: Berg, 1988. 360pp.

Kulka, Erich. *Jews in Svoboda's Army in the Soviet Union: Czechoslovak Jewry's Fight Against the Nazis During World War II*. Lanham, MD: University Press of America, 1988. 456pp.

Oliner, Samuel P. and Oliner, Pearl M. *The Altruistic Personality: Rescuers of Jews in Nazi Europe*. New York: Free Press/London: Collier Macmillan, 1988. xxvi, 419pp., appends., notes, bibl., ind., tables.

Stein, Andre. *Quiet Heroes: True Stories of the Rescue of Jews by Christians in Nazi-Occupied Holland*. Toronto: Lester, Orpen Dennys, 1988. vii, 311pp.

Index